Murmansk
ri
A N D
Kola
Peninsula
Kandalaksha
R. Pechora
Arctic Circle
Ust'-Tsil'ma
niemi
WHITE SEA
R. Mezen'
K
a
r
e
l
i
a
SOLOVETSKY IS.
Kem'
Archangel
R. Pinega
Onega
R. Onega
R. Northern Dvina
A N D
R. Vychegda
R. Pudozh
Krasnoborsk
Kondopoga
kyla
Sol'vychegodsk
Petrozavodsk
L. Onega
Kargopol'
Veliky Ustyug
L.
maa
Olonets
R. Kovzha
2
L. Ladoga
R. Svir'
Tot'ma
nland
Beloye Ozero
Belozersk
R. Sukhona
R. Neva
Leningrad
Vologda
R. Volkhov
R U S S I A
Novgorod
Kostroma
L. Il'men'
Yaroslavl
R. Volga
Pskov
(U. S. S. R.)
R. Lovat
Gorky
R. Volga
Suzdal'
Vladimir
Moscow

THE WOODEN CHURCHES OF EASTERN EUROPE

AN INTRODUCTORY SURVEY

THE WOODEN CHURCHES OF EASTERN EUROPE

AN INTRODUCTORY SURVEY

DAVID BUXTON

CAMBRIDGE UNIVERSITY PRESS
CAMBRIDGE
LONDON NEW YORK NEW ROCHELLE
MELBOURNE SYDNEY

Published by the Press Syndicate of the University of Cambridge
The Pitt Building, Trumpington Street, Cambridge CB2 1RP
32 East 57th Street, New York, NY 10022, USA
296 Beaconsfield Parade, Middle Park, Melbourne 3206, Australia

First published 1981

Printed in Great Britain at the University Press, Cambridge

British Library Cataloguing in Publication Data

Buxton, David
The wooden churches of Eastern Europe.
1. Church architecture - Europe, Eastern
2. Building, wooden - Europe, Eastern
I. Title
726'.5'0947 NA5450 80-41517

ISBN 0 521 23786 6

CONTENTS

PREFACE

The origins of this book go back more than fifty years, to the time when I used to travel in Russia as a young student. Among other experiences, well remembered from my first long journey there, were the weeks I spent in a typical small village in the northern forests. Since then, the wooden world of eastern Europe has always attracted me, but it was not until 1972, after a working life devoted to other pursuits, that I was able to revert to this dormant interest. Between 1972 and 1977 I travelled every year (with my Volkswagen 'Beetle' and a tent) in some part of the area concerned, collecting material for this study. The photographs are mostly my own, except that I have had to supplement them from other sources in the case of Soviet territory, owing to the prevailing restrictions on travel there.

Wooden architecture (including the wooden churches which are its finest flower) has been widely studied in most east European countries. Both the bibliography and the acknowledgements indicate the extent of my debt to relevant publications in many languages. But the great majority of these studies, besides being unavailable in our libraries, are of strictly limited scope, and I believe no general survey of the subject has yet been attempted. This book is intended to fill the gap. I hope it will stimulate the interest of many visitors from the west (whether architectural specialists or not) in one of the most attractive, but least known aspects of the rural scene in eastern Europe. I think, too, that devotees of the American log cabin will like to know what a remarkable evolution awaited its predecessor, the *European* log cabin.

I confess to a great love for countries not yet over-populated or over-mechanised, where the tempo of country life is still relatively unhurried, and where one shares the rough minor roads with horse-drawn carts, farm tractors, children on their way to school, and flocks of geese, protesting at the intrusion. Nearly always, the stranger here receives a warm welcome from ordinary people, even spontaneous hospitality that puts westerners to shame. In the majority of these countries, whatever the political complexion of their governments, I was happy to find that the foreign traveller is very free to do as he likes and seldom troubled by the authorities. But it is well to remember, in most of eastern Europe, that to be a non-native is one's greatest privilege.

Some preliminary work on this book was done while I still held a Research Fellowship at Clare Hall, Cambridge (it had been awarded on the strength of an Ethiopian project then in course of completion). Membership of the College always was, and continues to be, an agreeable and sometimes productive stimulus. I gratefully recall, also, the award of a travel grant by the British Academy for my Ukrainian journey in 1977. Many good friends in the eight countries covered by my travels, and others here in Cambridge, have helped me in various ways at various times. They must remain anonymous, except for three gentlemen whose counsel and expertise, most generously given, have greatly enhanced the value of this book. They are: Radu Creţeanu of Bucharest, Dr G. N. Logvin of Kiev, and Professor Lars Pettersson of Helsinki. I trust they will be pleased when they see the book in its final form.

Grantchester D.R.B.
July 1980

The shaded areas are keyed to chapters 2–6 and show the main distribution of the relevant church-types.

I

Introduction

Wooden architecture in Europe: the scope of this study

Eastern Europe is today the principal refuge of styles and techniques of 'solid' timber or log building which were once far more widespread. The same building methods were formerly well known in central Europe and they still survive in the Alps. At varying and uncertain periods, however, the increasing scarcity of forest resources prompted the development of timber-framing or half-timbering as a more economical alternative. That system, beautiful and successful in its own right, was itself to penetrate eastwards in the wake of Germanic expansion, besides influencing the construction of roofs and towers over wide areas of eastern Europe. Some timber-framed churches therefore find a place in Chapter 7; otherwise the book is devoted to churches built basically in solid timber – though with many refinements and embellishments.

It was Josef Strzygowski (whose revolutionary theories on wooden architecture are mentioned at the end of this chapter) who popularised the term *Blockbau* and its English rendering *blockwork* for what I shall describe as log construction. In such buildings the wall timbers lie horizontally in close contact with each other. A system of construction based on *upright* timbers in close contact (Strzygowski's *Stabbau*) also existed in Scandinavia and in Britain – witness the Saxon timbers incorporated in the church at Greenstead near Ongar, Essex. Such buildings, however, seem to have left few descendants (unless Norway's stave churches are to be so regarded) and we shall not meet them again.

In this survey I limit myself to those parts of eastern Europe where blockwork – log construction on the horizontal principle – has long been (sometimes still is) a normal method of construction and where churches built on that principle still survive. I refer only marginally to the Alpine region – an 'island' of blockwork already well documented, from which however nearly all the wooden *churches* have disappeared. Nor have I attempted to include other parts of central Europe where place names like Holzkirchen (in Bavaria) reveal their former existence. The survival of wooden churches into the present century has been the basic criterion for their inclusion here. In general, it may be said that eastern Europe alone qualifies, the well forested regions being naturally the richest in wooden buildings of every description.

Scandinavia remains, nevertheless, a problem. I must exclude the marvellous and enigmatic Norwegian stave churches which are in no sense east European nor built in blockwork. But the whole of Scandinavia, especially the far north of Norway, Sweden and Finland, forms an extension of the typically east European zone of blockwork building; there are even a few examples in the outlying Faroe Islands. It was indeed from Scandinavia that the early American log cabins – perfect examples of elementary blockwork – were apparently derived, and the lineal descendants of their European prototypes are still to be found both in northern Finland and the adjoining territory of Soviet Karelia (see Appendix 1). Another complication is introduced by the Finnish timber-built Lutheran churches of the seventeenth and eighteenth centuries, which are scarcely to be distinguished from those of northern Sweden – not unnaturally, since at the time they were evolved these countries formed but a single, uniformly Protestant State. I have therefore been obliged to draw an arbitrary line of demarcation: only Finland is included here, though Sweden must often be mentioned for purposes of comparison, or sometimes as a source of inspiration for Finnish wooden churches.

As in the case just cited, political boundaries are often irrelevant to the subject. After the upheavals of two world wars their impermanence is of course familiar to all, and it is frequently illustrated in this study. It is noteworthy, for instance, that no fewer than six of the eight countries with which we are mainly concerned had belonged, wholly or partly, to the old Austro-Hungarian empire until the great dismemberment of 1918. As an earlier example of the fluidity of frontiers one may quote those of the Ukraine, whose wooden churches figure prominently in this book. In the course of history the Ukrainians were ruthlessly and variously partitioned between Russia, Austria and Poland; the Poles themselves (as ruthlessly and variously) between Russia, Austria and Prussia. Many smaller areas have changed hands more than once even in modern times. Thus Sub-Carpathian Ruthenia (Podkarpatska Rus'), with its surprising variety of peoples and architectural styles, passed from Austria-Hungary to the new Czechoslovakia in 1918, and from Czechoslovakia to the Soviet Union in 1944. I generally refer to the area as Soviet Trans-Carpathia.

It is clear, therefore, that the accident of citizenship can have little to do with the various styles of timber building to be described in the following chapters. The all-important factor is religious affiliation, which may or may not coincide with citizenship (though it usually coincides with language). For this reason the subject matter is here divided up primarily according to religion, and many of the broad areas dealt with are intersected by the more or less arbitrary frontiers of existing States.

Orthodoxy in its various branches is the prevailing faith of eastern Europe and more than half the book is concerned mainly with the Orthodox churches of countless villages extending from northern Russia to the Ukraine and westwards through Rumania to Serbia. I say 'mainly' since some of these churches belonged, and a few still belong, to the Uniates or Greek Catholics – Catholics of the eastern rite. These Churches formerly claimed many adherents in eastern Europe, more especially in the Ukraine, but they have all suffered persecution at various periods and they were banned by several east European Governments after the Second World War. Apart from large expatriate communities I believe the only Uniates now able to practise their faith are those living in the Ukrainian enclaves of eastern Slovakia, and they too have had their troubles. Architecturally, their churches do not demand separate treatment since they are indistinguishable, except for some internal fittings, from those of the Orthodox communities.

Chapter 6 deals with the churches of Catholic Poland, whose distinctive wooden architecture extends thence into Czechoslovakia. Only in this sector of eastern Europe is the Church of Rome supreme in numbers and influence. In chapter 7 we pass to some interesting styles of Protestant church-building which, in the seventeenth and eighteenth centuries, the Lutherans made their own, while there is some reference to Calvin's Reformed Church, as represented in Hungary, in Chapter 5. Another religious community powerfully represented in eastern Europe until fate overtook them in the Second World War were the Jews. Many of their synagogues, in old Lithuania, eastern Poland and the Ukraine, were magnificent examples of timber architecture. The tragedy is that not a single one survived the war, but I shall include a brief description of these remarkable places of worship in Appendix II.

Surprisingly, few general works on the architecture of these various countries include anything more than a passing allusion to wooden buildings. Some earlier writers were apparently unaware of their existence. Others relegated them to the inferior status of folk art, or even, it seems, dismissed them altogether as unworthy of study. If so, these writers erred in their judgment. There are timber-built churches in many parts of eastern Europe whose building involved skills comparable to those of the stonemason, whose planning shows genius and whose impact on the spectator is an architectural experience. In recent years, however, vernacular art including wooden architecture has earned greater respect as a subject of study. This is particularly true in eastern Europe where many scholars have taken up the theme. Some of their writings, as detailed in the bibliography, have been of enormous value to me in compiling this survey, though too often their treatment stops short at the existing political frontier, ignoring buildings of the same group and style that lie just beyond.

Throughout eastern Europe the comparatively new trend has found expression also in the establishment of open-air museums (often called *skansens* after the pioneer venture of Skansen outside Stockholm). In these museums peasants' houses and their outbuildings, wind and watermills, farm buildings, towers and wooden churches, have been brought in from outlying areas and re-erected, thus ensuring their survival and conferring upon them the seal of respectability and official approval. Although the art lover or scholar, enamoured of traditional village life, naturally prefers to see such buildings in their native place (which he can readily do in many parts of eastern Europe, given time and patience), the *skansen* is a welcome development. In some countries it offers the only hope for the survival, albeit in artificial conditions, of an ancient culture and of some outstanding monuments of rural art and architecture.

The wooden world of eastern Europe, from prehistoric to modern times

A book devoted to wooden churches alone must give an unbalanced picture, stressing a single element in a setting where every building and almost every man-made object was also wooden. My aim here is to redress the balance by briefly reviewing the range of wooden structures which enabled man to make the most of his rural habitat in the forest belts of eastern Europe. I must first give some idea of the range in time of these wooden technologies, for there is now ample evidence of their great antiquity, and of their stability through the ages. Two east European examples, one prehistoric and one medieval, will serve to show that blockwork has been the normal building method in forested regions all through history. It is known in fact to be as old as man's earliest efforts to build in timber, in the later Stone Age.

At Lake Biskupin (north-east of Poznań in Poland) one may visit a remarkable site, excavated in the years 1934–9, which was the fortified island-village of a pre-Slav tribe in the early Iron Age (700–400 B.C.). The sodden ground has here preserved the foundations of timber ramparts and of no less than thirteen parallel rows or 'terraces', each of three to ten family houses. These were all built to the same plan (incorporating living room and entrance lobby) measuring overall about 9 × 8 m; and all faced south-east. Indeed the regularity of the layout in this very congested village is astonishing. So well preserved were these foundations that it was found possible to reconstruct some houses and parts of the rubble-filled ramparts, while the roads, consisting of logs lying transversely in contact with each other, needed no reconstruction. The jointing techniques employed are still familiar: for the ramparts, round logs intersecting at the corners; for the houses, round logs tapered at their ends and fitted into grooved uprights (usually three lengths to each wall, for the available logs were short). Both these methods are illustrated in the next section (**35** A, F).

For the Middle Ages we possess an extraordinary archaeological record from old Novgorod or Novgorod 'the Great', that ancient city which lies to the south of the upstart metropolis, now Leningrad. Novgorod grew up as a major settlement on the early trade route pioneered by the Norsemen between the Baltic and the Black Sea. Long the headquarters of an independent democratic State, it became a dependency of Kiev in the tenth century. And the excavations in question have produced a continuous record of the city's life and fortunes from that century until the middle of the fifteenth – a period of five hundred years. They threw much new light on the social conditions of the population, on their agriculture and crafts, on the city's administration and trade and historical role at various periods. The excavators even recovered some written messages exchanged by the citizens – they were scratched on the inner surface of birch bark.

The picture that emerged was, it must be said, of a somewhat insalubrious city – it seems to have resembled one great waterlogged and ever growing dung-heap. These conditions, however, proved a blessing at least to posterity, resulting as they did in the almost perfect preservation of wooden objects including the lowest courses of more than a thousand wooden buildings, half of them dwelling houses, nearly all of them datable. For the chronology, linked to known dates of construction of several masonry churches and refined by tree-ring dating, enabled the excavators to date every successive street-level (of which no less than twenty-eight were identified) not merely to the decade, but to the exact calendar year. These streets had a decking of split logs laid transversely, flat surface uppermost, and were intended for sledge traffic – no sign of wheeled vehicles was found.

One notable fact about the wooden buildings of medieval Novgorod is simply that 98% of them – all except a few sheds and stores – were of log construction. This was also true at the Iron Age site of Biskupin, it was the same at Staraya Ladoga in the seventh century A.D., and the same perennial characteristic forms the common denominator of nearly all the buildings described in this book. These old Novgorod houses opened into private yards, separated from the street by a fence of upright stakes. They measured something between 8 × 10 m and 10 × 14 m (rather larger than at Biskupin) and some are thought to have been two-storeyed. They possessed, in addition to a living room and entrance lobby, a second (unheated) room which could have been inhabited in summer. They had ceilings on which a layer of soil was spread for insulation and boarded floors with a space below as protection against damp, and a stove in one corner. These features can all be paralleled in modern peasant dwellings, which however show one positive advance: they have chimneys, while old Novgorod had none.

The great majority of Novgorod houses were built of untrimmed pine logs – always favoured for their straightness, despite the drawback that they are highly inflammable. These logs were jointed at the corners according to the simplest of the systems illustrated later (**35** A). It is interesting to note that the notches at

1 Field barn, district of Vöyri, near Vaasa, Finland.

2 Farm building from Volhynia, nineteenth century. Now in the Museum of Folk Architecture and Life, Kiev.

the points of intersection were cut from the *upper* side of each log. This is the easier system for non-experts since the notch can be hacked out with the log already positioned on the wall, and it is likely that most Novgorod citizens built their own homes. It was not, however, the ideal method since any water penetrating the hollow could lie there and initiate rot. Both systems survived, even into modern times, but from the seventeenth century onwards, in Russia at least, it became usual to cut these notches on the *under* surface of the logs.

Unfortunately, these excavations produced no conclusive evidence of the techniques of roof construction in use in the medieval city. Raftered roofs were of course already known and may have been used for the more prestigious private dwellings as well as for churches, whether their walls were of wood or masonry. It seems almost certain, however, that ordinary householders, or the carpenters they employed, having no tool but the axe, would have followed the path of least resistance and finished off their houses on the horizontal principle. This would have meant completing the two gables simply as extensions of the end walls, each successive log being cut slightly shorter than the one below. At the same time horizontal timbers (purlins) would have been laid lengthwise between the notched timbers of the gable-ends to form the foundation of the roof. This could be completed in various alternative ways, receiving a weather-proof finish of thatch or shingles.

Small buildings possessing the primitive and logical roof construction just described still exist today, though seldom in use as human habitations. I found them in plenty, in the form of small barns and stores (usually with their walls slightly inclined outwards), scattered among the fields in northern Finland, and they exist too in the adjoining territory of Soviet Karelia (**1**). No doubt similar structures were once

3 Modern farm building in Vöyri district, Finland, showing cantilevered support of overhanging roof.

4 Summer cowshed from northern Finland, now in the open-air museum at Turkansaari near Oulu.

5 Summer cowshed: internal view to show construction of the pyramidal roof.

common throughout the forested areas of eastern and central Europe. An example from Volhynia – the still largely wooded north-western sector of the Ukraine – has been re-erected in the open-air museum of Kiev (**2**). In the eastern Alps granaries and barns possessing the identical roof form (known as the *Ansdach*) still exist, and examples have been transferred to the Austrian Village Museum at Stübing. In northern Finland some bigger farm buildings exhibit a similar type of roof (but with widely spaced purlins) combined with overhanging eaves on consoles, as described later on in churches (**3**). In the same area an interesting variant can be seen: a shed with pyramidal roof, supported on a pyramidal framework of horizontal logs, and culminating at the mid-point in a ventilation shaft (**4**, **5**). In these special cowsheds the cattle can take refuge for some part of the twenty-four hours during the constant daylight of the northern summer, when mosquitoes never cease to be active.

A fascinating study of the primitive habitations of the Finno-Ugrian tribes in northern Russia and western Siberia was published in 1907–8 by Sirelius. These habitations included huts and temporary shelters built in various different techniques by the Zyrians (or Komi), the Ostyaks, the Votyaks and the Cheremisses. The majority were blockwork huts with elementary corner-jointing as in old Novgorod and roofs of the aboriginal type just described (**6**, **7**). Most of them were single-roomed and absolutely basic with earth floor, open hearth and scarcely any furniture. Only in more substantial dwellings, especially those intended for year-round occupation, were the logs channelled below to make a tighter fit and the interstices packed with moss or tow, while the amenity of a ceiling might be added, also proper windows, and sometimes a boarded floor with cellar space beneath (**8**). So these very simple buildings, many of them identical to the

7 Inside of Cheremiss summer hut (*kuda*).

6 Summer dwellings of Finno-Ugrian tribes in north-eastern Russia, early twentieth century.
A. Ostyak hut. B. Votyak hut.

8 Permanent dwellings of Finno-Ugrian tribes in the early twentieth century.
A. Cheremiss house. B. Votyak house.

9 The stockaded wooden settlement of Tsaritsyn (Stalingrad, Volgograd) on the Volga, recorded by Olearius, c. 1635. Floated timber is stacked on the shore.

surviving field barns of northern Finland, were still in use for human habitation in the early years of the century – and probably still are in remoter areas. They have the signal advantages of being easy to build, extremely solid, and well insulated against heat or cold. From such primitive but excellent buildings the 'log cabin' of America originated, introduced by Finno-Swedish immigrants in the eighteenth century. No wonder they enjoyed such a spectacular success among the pioneers. I revert to the subject in Appendix I.

From such ancient and lowly origins, represented today by Finnish barns and the log cabins cherished in North America as museum pieces, all the varied splendours of timber architecture were to develop. It is true that the crowning achievements of each style or trend must be sought among churches, and these will be described in detail in later chapters. But I cannot pass over in forgetful silence the wide variety of domestic and farm buildings which contributed so much to the setting and background of the churches themselves. Inevitably, whole wooden cities such as old Novgorod are a thing of the past, though some were recorded in the drawings of seventeenth- and eighteenth-century travellers like Olearius (**9**). Thousands of villages, on the other hand, retained their traditional wooden character, which made them a natural outgrowth of the landscape itself, well into this century, and many retain it still. Interested travellers can prove it for themselves, most easily perhaps in Rumania or in the mountain valleys of Slovakia (especially the upper reaches of the Orava and the Poprad). The very different village illustrated here is however a Russian one, where I was made welcome with my sister and parents in 1927 (**10**). A village scene of 1839 from Demidoff is not dissimilar, but shows a somewhat different design of peasant's house (*izba*) (**11**).

Throughout eastern Europe old-style peasants' houses still exist in great variety though it is often

10 Village of Sokolishchi, Nizhny Novgorod (now Gorky) district, 1927.

11 'Village of Gumnist between Kostroma and Yaroslav', from Demidoff, 1839.

12 Hutsul peasant house from Soviet Trans-Carpathia, now in Uzhgorod open-air museum.

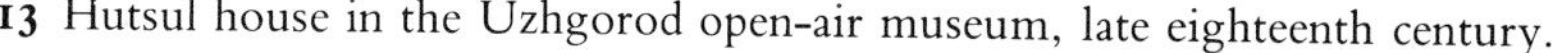

13 Hutsul house in the Uzhgorod open-air museum, late eighteenth century.

14 Enclosed farmstead (*grazhd*) of the Hutsuls, now in the museum at Uzhgorod.

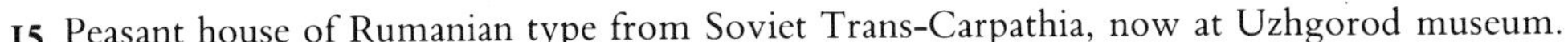

15 Peasant house of Rumanian type from Soviet Trans-Carpathia, now at Uzhgorod museum.

16 Peasants' house from the Soviet Carpathians in course of re-erection in the Museum of Folk Architecture and Life, L'vov, Ukraine.

17 Completed dwelling house, farm building and well from the Carpathians, L'vov open-air museum.

easiest to find good examples in open-air museums. On the whole they attract more interest today than churches (though 'cult' buildings too have become acceptable as an aspect of folk art and rural culture). A few random examples of these rustic dwellings are given here. First some basic Hutsul types from Trans-Carpathia: one is notable for the huge size of the split logs forming the walls (**12**), another for the rendering of the outside walls, from which only the ends of the logs are seen projecting at the corners (**13**). Another photograph shows a narrow courtyard with dwelling house to the right and farm buildings to the left (**14**). Verandahs were very widespread and usually embellished with carving as in **15**, a Carpathian example showing Rumanian influence. Some Lemk houses from the Soviet Carpathians show how the steep raftered roofs (in one case in unfinished, skeletal form) provided ample storage space (**16**, **17**). Also visible in the last-mentioned is the counter-poised draw well, resembling the Egyptian *shaduf*, which is still in almost universal use, for shallower wells, in east European villages. The neighbouring Rumanian district of Maramureş (northern Transylvania) is likewise full of steep, lofty and capacious roofs, surmounting both dwelling houses and farm buildings (**18**, **19**). Among many varieties of barn and food-stores an interesting combination is shown in **20**: it is a stone-built, vaulted and partly subterranean cold store surmounted by a wooden granary. These have a wide distribution and occur as far away as the Alps. So do the stilted store-houses (and temporary habitations) formerly built in alpine pastures, like the Swiss *mazot* (**21**).

The domestic buildings so far mentioned are all of modest size. Larger, two-storeyed houses, their verandahs, balconies and eaves often elaborately carved, are a beautiful feature of some country landscapes all over eastern Europe and have been extensively studied. In southern Poland there was a late-nineteenth-century revival and re-interpretation of older forms and techniques inspired by the architect Stanisław Witkiewicz, and the momentum of this 'Zakopane style' is not yet spent. It is not to be confused, however, with the genuine folk architecture still common in that area, as in the village of Chochołów north-west of Zakopane, where non-traditional houses are not allowed to be built. Two larger examples of traditional timber building in southern Poland are given here: an inn (*karczma*) at Zubrzyca Górna and a beautiful manor house (*dwór*) at Ożarów south of Wieluń (**22**, **23**). Both have a type of mansard roof in two ranges, the lower one accommodating the first-floor rooms.

Of the many timber-built mansions which the old Russian gentry must have possessed there are no survivors and few records. A sketch from Meyerberg (1661–2) does however show one that then stood just west of Moscow, with the Austrian embassy's tents

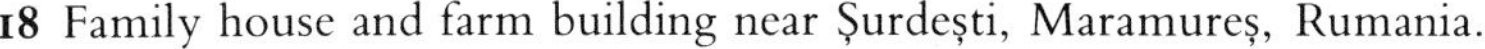

18 Family house and farm building near Şurdeşti, Maramureş, Rumania.

19 Farm building in the hills south of Aleşd, Bihor county, Rumania.

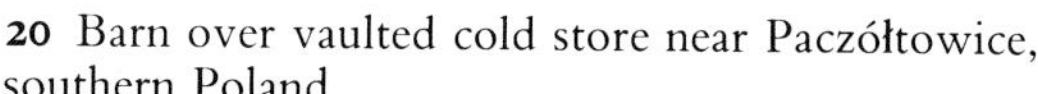

20 Barn over vaulted cold store near Paczółtowice, southern Poland.

21 Mountain barn (*mazot*) in Valais, Switzerland. The supporting posts, capped with stone slabs, are a protection against vermin.

pitched alongside and a great rain storm threatening (**24**). One sees a long covered stairway leading up to the living rooms on the upper floor and a very steep hipped roof (the so-called *palatka*) at one end. This was a modest mansion. At the other extreme, the contemporary royal palace of Kolomenskoye was perhaps one of the most entrancing architectural fantasies ever actually realised on the ground (**25**). The crazy irregularity of the plan was due to its long and complex history, but its final form was attained between 1667 and 1681 under Tsars Alexis Mikhailovich and Feodor Alexe'evich, who provided suites there for different members of the royal family. Practically every motif known to the wooden architecture of northern Russia was pressed into service here: the *palatka* again, the onion dome (*luk*), the tent tower (*shatyor*), the ogee or 'barrel' gable (*bochka*), the bulging roof of similar section (*kub*), the elaborate covered entrance-stairway (*kryltso*). This lovely, if preposterous palace was pulled down under Catherine the Great in 1768, but its likeness survived in the form of a model. The only remotely comparable edifice erected since then was probably the Russian pavilion in the Universal Exhibition at Paris in 1900.

Wooden fortifications provided much scope for the immensely solid blockwork technique. The quite plausible reconstruction of the original wooden fort at Khar'kov is photographed from a diorama in the local museum (**26**). Defensive towers and ramparts of similar design must once have existed all over the outlying regions of European Russia. In remote Siberian settlements like Bratsk and Ilimsk, founded among hostile tribes in the seventeenth and eighteenth centuries, they lasted longer, and a particularly fine gate tower is still being kept in repair at yet remoter Yakutsk (**27**). Some fortified monasteries also possessed wooden ramparts and gate towers. An excellent example from the Nikolo-Karelsky monastery, at the mouth of the Dvina near Archangel, has been moved in recent years to the open-air museum at Kolomenskoye, now in greater Moscow (**28**).

22 Inn (*karczma*) at Zubrzyca Górna, southern Poland.

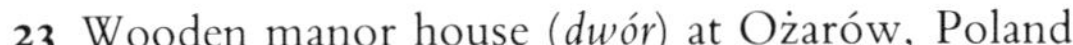

23 Wooden manor house (*dwór*) at Ożarów, Poland.

24 Boyar's house and travelling diplomats' tents at Nikolskoye, west of Moscow. From Meyerberg's journal, 1661–2.

25 Model of the wooden palace at Kolomenskoye, near Moscow, 1667–81 (dismantled 1768).

26 Reconstruction of the wooden fortifications at Khar'kov, Ukraine, from an exhibit in the city museum. Mid seventeenth century.

27 Defensive gate tower at Yakutsk, north-eastern Siberia. Seventeenth/eighteenth century.

28 Gate tower to the Nikolo-Karelsky monastery, c. 1690. Now at Kolomenskoye, Moscow.

29 Timber-built bridge over the R. Kena, south of Onega on the White Sea. The photograph shows one of four principal piers.

Other uses for the same building techniques were innumerable but must be dismissed in a few words. In north Russia some bridges still exist which are really imposing works of civil engineering: the log casing of each pier, wedge-shaped against the current, is filled with stones or rubble (**29**). In and around the villages themselves there are, or used to be, a variety of powered mills and workshops, for the old village culture of east and central Europe experienced its own industrial revolution, beginning as early as the seventeenth century. Animal power, water and wind power were all harnessed in aid of rural industry. The *suvara* of Croatia (also found in Hungary) consisted of a great horizontal, cogged wheel operating grinding and other mechanisms, and this was kept in motion by horses or oxen walking round and round all under a conical roof like a huge bell tent. Water-wheels provided the motive power not only for grinding of corn but for sawmills, smithies with mechanical hammers, ore-crushers, oil-seed presses and fulleries for the beating and felting of cloth. A few watermills, both of the under- and over-shot varieties, are still in use for some of these purposes (**30**). Functional windmills are rare, but as beautiful and ingenious adaptations of log construction they have attracted a great deal of attention and are now favourite objects for re-erection in open-air museums. Post mills appear to have been general in northern Russia (**31**, **32**), tower mills in the Ukraine and further west (**33**).

The techniques of construction

We are here concerned with wooden churches built in blockwork (and to a minor extent in timber-framing) in eastern Europe. It must not be forgotten, however, that many other important wooden styles and building methods, as well as mixed timber and masonry techniques, exist around the world. They display a great variety of constructional devices. Of all systems known to me, the most sophisticated is that originated in China and later adopted by the Japanese and other neighbouring peoples. Here the setting up of the roof is the prime consideration, walls being mere infilling. The weight of these great roofs is taken by wooden columns which break up at their apices into a complicated array of superimposed brackets or bracket-clusters, which rise and branch out like candelabra to support the horizontal beams above. The beautiful

30 Dilapidated but functional watermill in the hills south of Aleşd, Bihor county, Rumania.

31 Post mill at Shchelkovo, Vologda region.

32 Post mill at Kimzha on the R. Mezen', near the White Sea.

33 Tower mills from the Ukraine re-erected in the Museum of Folk Architecture and Life, Kiev.

curvature of the roofs themselves is made possible because the Chinese, disdaining anything so crude as the straight rafter of the west, used *horizontal* beams (purlins) as the basic elements of the structure, and these could be adjusted to any profile desired. I have shown that the germ of this system did exist in the most primitive European blockwork buildings, but (regrettably) it was superseded by the rafter and never developed further. Compared with the oriental complexities just mentioned the blockwork principle, which dominated the rural scene all the way from the Balkans to the Arctic, is simplicity itself. All the same, when disciplined by an ancient tradition and applied with subconscious artistry, it could produce whole architectural compositions of magical beauty, like the cluster of churches near the White Sea shown in **34**.

Before examining the constructional details of these log buildings I propose to describe the normal procedures traditionally used for timber buildings in general and churches in particular. Though almost every peasant could build his own house, churches required particular skills and were usually constructed by an itinerant team of carpenters employed by the village as a whole. The master carpenter and the architect were one and the same, and the church design would be discussed at length between him and the villagers, being probably drawn out – in those largely illiterate communities – on the ground rather than on paper. All this negotiation took place long before the actual building of the church, since the necessary timber had to be cut in spring before the rising of the sap. It was then left to season until the following winter, when it was moved to the site in preparation for building. Or, as sometimes happened, the main timbering of the church would actually be erected in a forest clearing not far from the village, and re-erected at a later stage on the appointed site.

Building usually began in spring a year after the timber was cut. The type of wood used depended very much on the area: in the far north pine and fir alone were available, and the same applied to the higher villages in the Carpathians. At lower levels deciduous trees were also commonly used; and oak, always noted for its durability, was sometimes selected for the massive beams of the basement framework while a softer wood followed above. In northern Russia, at least until the late eighteenth century, building proceeded with whole round logs untrimmed, except for the removal of the bark. But in the Ukraine, in Rumania and the whole Carpathian area the builders were more particular, each log being flattened off at least on its inner surface, often on all four sides. This gave a square section or, when logs were split in two (an economy measure often used in the south) an oblong one. In the earlier surviving churches – up to the seventeenth century – this great labour was apparently accomplished with the axe alone, not even saws being available.

Foundations were as a rule inadequate, which suggests that wooden churches in the villages were not

34 Three churches and a bell tower, probably no longer standing, on the R. Shuya, near the west coast of the White Sea.

35 Systems of corner-jointing. A–C from Scandinavia. D,F from Croatia. E from Slovakia.

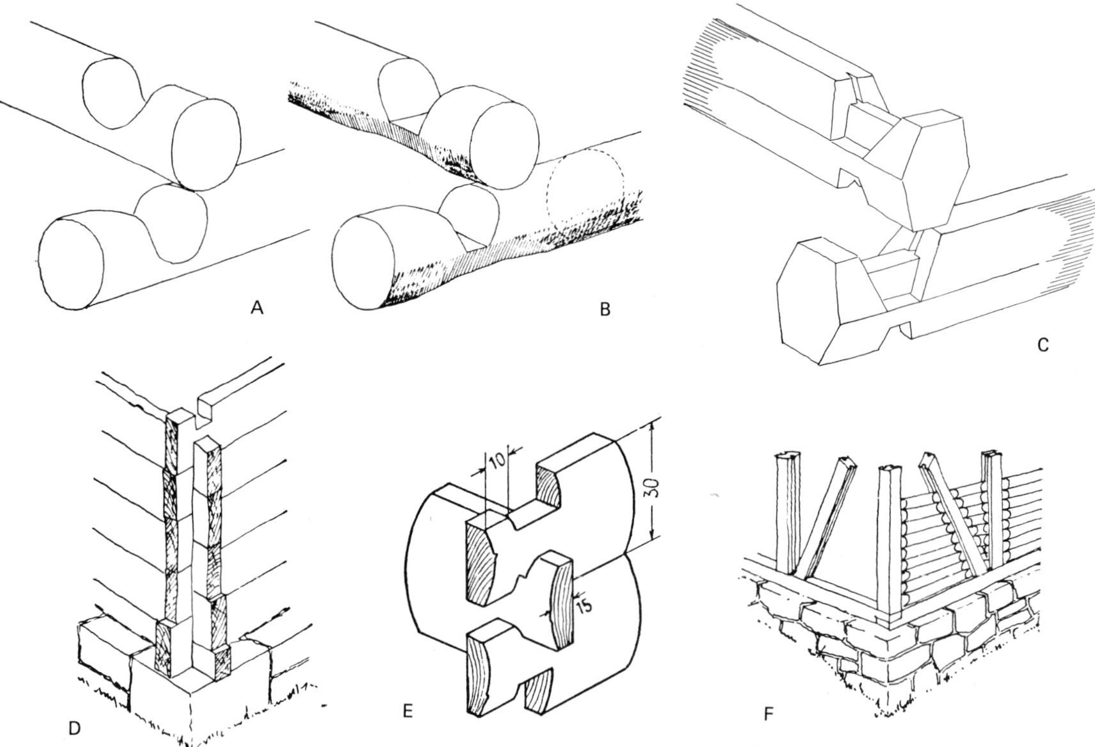

expected or intended to last indefinitely. Large stones were often used at the corners and some other strategic points, and upon them a rectangle of basement timbers was laid, at varying heights above ground level. These timbers were comparatively massive, with a section up to 45 × 35 cm and occasionally as long as 12 m (40 ft). From then on, beginning about floor-level, the normal horizontal wall timbers began to be laid. These were, of course, interrupted by doors, and higher up by windows. At these points the pared-down ends of the wall beams were made to fit into the grooved uprights of the window and door frames; the latter were also slotted into the basement timbers below.

In this method of construction one of the main problems was to devise satisfactory jointing for the horizontal wall timbers, which had to overlap and intersect at each corner of the building. Many solutions were evolved, some of the most widespread being illustrated in the accompanying figures (**35** and **41**). In **35** A–E I show the easier forms of joint, in which the wall timbers, whether left as round logs or squared, project beyond the point of intersection. In another simple system (**35** F) the horizontal pieces do not interlock at the corners. Instead, their ends are pared down to fit into grooved uprights, like the timbers impinging upon door and window frames. Apart from C, the systems shown in this figure are ancient and elementary ones and they are often reserved for outbuildings like barns, sheds and bathhouses. The corner of a roughly constructed farm building shown in **36** has its logs jointed as in **35** A except that they are notched both above and below. In American log cabin terminology this is saddle-jointing. Barns often had their timbers deliberately spaced apart to encourage circulation of air as in the

36 Corner of a farm building, Pieniny hills, southern Poland.

37 Farm building, Zalaegerszeg open-air museum, western Hungary.

38 Octagonal chapel at Belaya Sluda on the Northern Dvina, Russia (photographed 1932).

39 Detail of barn structure, Bihor county, Rumania.

41 Systems of corner-jointing. A,B from Trans-Carpathia (basement timbers in A). C,D from Rumania. E from Croatia. F from Finland.

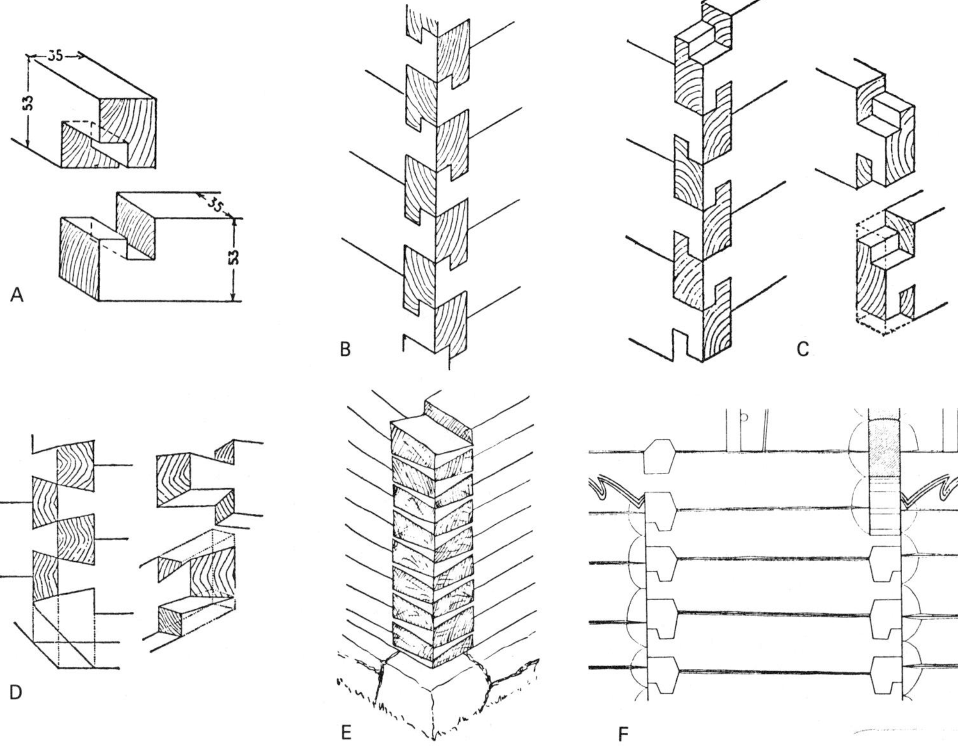

Hungarian specimen in **37**. A derelict chapel in northern Russia (where church builders had no inhibitions about round logs or elementary jointing) shows the system adapted to the angles of an octagon (**38**). In Rumania I have seen a great many farm buildings relying on the prehistoric but perfectly effective system shown in **35** F; others exhibit a mixed technique (**39**, **40**).

The second set of joints (**41**) shows methods which leave the jointed surfaces flush with the wall, and these were generally considered more elegant. The difficulty was to ensure that timbers so jointed would resist the strains of being pushed or pulled apart. To guard against this, locking systems were invented of more complex design than appears on the surface (**41** C). In the course of the eighteenth century, however, the very secure dovetail, known as the 'German' joint in areas as far apart as Croatia and Trans-Carpathia, gained widespread acceptance (**41** D, E). The corner-jointing of a Finnish church (**42**) may be compared with **41** B, and F is peculiarly Finnish (*cf.* **472**). The nice dovetails from Poland and Serbia (**43**, **44**) are the same, in principle, as **41** D, E. But these examples show the adaptation of the joint to angles of 135° or

40 Farm building in Bihor showing mixed techniques.

42 Corner of church at Petäjävesi, Finland, 1761–3.

43 Polygonal apse with dovetail jointing in a chapel of 1650. Part of church at Poniszowice, Silesia, Poland.

thereabouts, this being necessary in polygonal apses and in the octagonal cupolas of many churches, as will be seen in later chapters.

Before passing on from walls to roofs I must mention a structure common to both, which is also one of the most characteristic and attractive of the mechanical devices found in wooden buildings. This is the cantilevered bracket or console which consists of extensions of the wall timbers themselves and serves to support the eaves – which often overhang considerably to form the roof of an external gallery. In a simple form such brackets can be seen in use in the Austrian Alps as eave supports (**45**). At their most complex they adorn the Orthodox churches of the Boyks and other Orthodox peoples in the eastern Carpathians (**46** and compare Chapter 3). Curiously, this excellent system of roof support, based on the inherent resistance of wood to bending stresses, seems to have found no favour in the Catholic countries. Polish Catholic churches sometimes have another type of bracket, applied to the wall but not part of it (**47** and Chapter 6). The eaves of Serbian wooden churches are often held up by a series of struts but both systems are well known there (**275**).

This predilection for consoles among the Orthodox does not, of course, preclude the use of small auxiliary columns: in fact they are often found sharing similar tasks around the same building. Generally, it is the wide porch, which may wrap round the west end of the church, that requires such additional support. In northern Russia, floor-levels, and therefore external galleries, were commonly raised high above ground and approached through covered porches and stairways all contributing their quota to the composition. There is much to attract and charm the eye in the various details mentioned, in the texture of the wooden walls, in faceted apses, in carved door frames, balustrades and columns and brackets of various

44 Dovetailing of uncertain date in the church at Velika Mlaka, Zagreb, Croatia.

45 Eave support by cantilevered brackets in a modern house at Tobelbad near Graz, Austria.

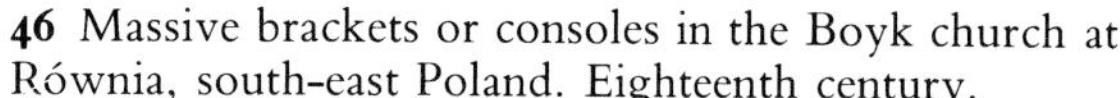

46 Massive brackets or consoles in the Boyk church at Równia, south-east Poland. Eighteenth century.

47 Attached brackets for eave support in the Catholic church at Poniszowice, Silesia. Uncertain period.

designs. These features all lead up to the towers and cupolas which crown the whole: they must be briefly explained here and more fully described in later chapters.

The most primitive roofs were touched upon, in view of their historical interest, in the last section. I now give a schematic drawing of a rather large and ornate *izba* of the Karelian type which offers points of interest in this connection, including the fact that the whole house could be constructed without the use of nails (**48**). The drawing shows a normal blockwork building which, though modern, retains a roof representing a compromise with the ancient type described earlier – that is, it retains fully timbered gables and a number of horizontal timbers (purlins) as the main roof supports, running from gable to gable. It also has a grooved gutter-like beam along the eaves (itself held in position by stout wooden hooks) to take the lower ends of the boards forming the underdecking of the roof. This is also an antique arrangement going back to primitive Finno-Ugrian houses (**8** A) but one not usually surviving. All the main features of this building, including its purlin-roof (*Pfettendach*), could be matched elsewhere, even as far west as the Austrian Alps. In the present context the main interest of the roof is that it scarcely differs from those of many wooden churches in northern Russia – in so far as they possess roofs of this simple form at all. The church in **107**, with its timbers exposed through dilapidation, shows this clearly.

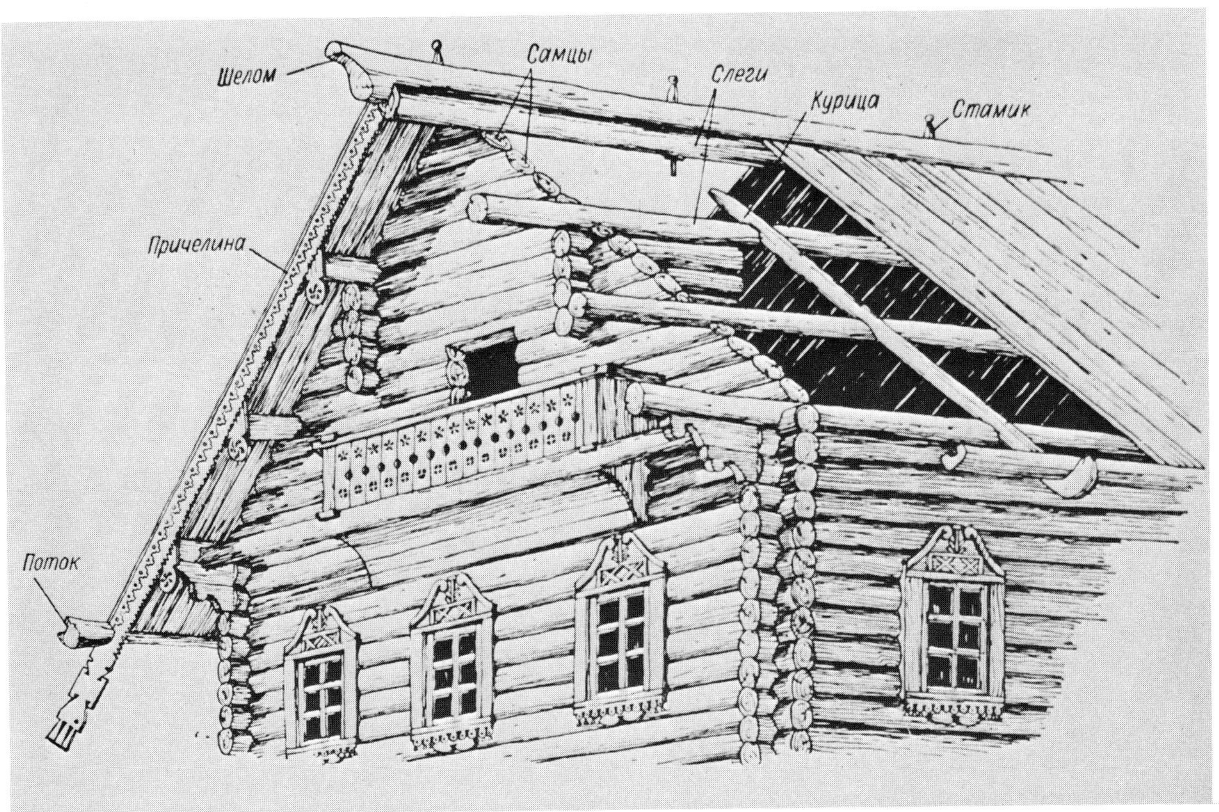

48 Roof structure of a typical large rural dwelling in Soviet Karelia.

Thus in conservative eastern areas, the concept of the purlin-roof remained influential until modern times, in domestic as in church architecture. The builders and sponsors of churches, however, were seldom content with the plain gabled roof. They gradually evolved the towers and cupolas which are the leading features of wooden churches and the mainspring of their beauty. Wherever the horizontal principle of pure blockwork reigned supreme – that is, in the eastern parts of our area – these culminating features were first built simply as an upward prolongation of the walls, and they retained, even to their summits, the same basic horizontal structure. Such were the earlier 'tent' towers of northern Russia and the stepped cupolas of the Ukrainians (**49**, **50**). To achieve these results, however, two additional techniques had to be developed. One was the conversion of the square to the octagon, the other the modification of vertical walls with their corner-jointing to form the inward-sloping surfaces of spires and cupolas.

Further west, from at least as early as the sixteenth century, blockwork began to show less stamina. Though always retained for the walls of churches (as of rural dwellings), roofs and towers ceded to the allied techniques of timber-framing and raftering

50 Typical but unidentified Boyk church with three cupolas, L'vov district, western Ukraine.

49 Church with 'tent' tower built entirely of horizontal timbers. Belaya Sluda on the Northern Dvina, 1642. Compare **71**.

51 Shingles of Orthodox church at Buzeta, Croatia.

which were advancing from western Europe and were, moreover, very well adapted to their new roles. Catholic Poland was naturally disposed to absorb such influences from the west, and they probably penetrated, for the most part, through Silesia. The Poles soon adopted the raftered roof. They also began building their church belfries on the principle of timber-framing, and in turn inspired their neighbours, the Orthodox Lemki, to do the same. Among the Rumanians, too, the influence of Gothic Transylvania, that outpost of Germanic culture, caused the appearance of raftered roofs, and of those wooden steeples for which blockwork would have been absolutely unsuitable. These towers and spires invariably have a framed skeleton. The conclusion is clear that all these types of tower, built in an alien technique, came from western sources and were attached in comparatively recent times to the churches themselves, which retain to the last their traditional log-built walls.

Many early churches were presumably finished off with thatch, as many rural dwellings still are. In all areas, however, wooden tiles or shingles came to be accepted, sooner or later, as the appropriate roof covering for wooden churches. Inevitably, they have to be renewed from time to time and since the nineteenth century decaying shingles have too often been replaced by unsightly galvanised iron or other sheet metal. But now that village architecture is enjoying an upsurge of appreciation in eastern Europe, it is a common sight to see wooden churches under restoration and their shingles being renewed – though not always in hardwood as they should be. Their traditional designs, varying from area to area, are usually respected. It will be seen from the examples which follow that roofs and cupolas owe their texture as well as their colour entirely to shingles, which in some cases stray onto walls and towers so as to clothe most of the building.

The church at Buzeta in Croatia displays shingles of varying width and very simple design – though those on the turret are given wavy ends (**51**). Those that clothe the cupolas of the Boyk church at Chotyniec (Poland) are likewise a simple, basic type (**52**). A more sophisticated system is met with, for example, among the Lemk churches of Slovakia. Shingles here are wedge-shaped in section and not only overlap the row below but slot into their neighbours on either side, by a system of tongues and grooves. These features can all be seen in **53** while the charming Baroque turret in **54**, with its frills of pointed shingles, shows their effect in the mass. Further east in Soviet Trans-Carpathia, another traditional design of shingle is

52 Shingled cupolas of Orthodox-type Boyk church, Chotyniec, south-east Poland. 1613.

53 Bundles of new shingles for restoration of a Lemk church, at Hrabová Roztoka, eastern Slovakia.

being widely used in restorations of Lemk and other churches. They are unusually thick and the resulting roughness of texture is well displayed in the beautiful church from Shelestovo, now at Uzhgorod (**56**).

Still other shapes are found in northern Russia. The domes and *bochki* at Kizhi in Lake Onega are covered in shingles of stepped outline as in **57**. In contrast, those at Kimzha on the Mezen' – one of the remoter rivers of the White Sea basin – have rounded ends (**58**). Finally, passing from north Russia to Finland, so near and yet so unlike, we find a different picture again. The Lutheran churches there likewise have shingles, which are generally tarred to lengthen their life. But there may be two or three different shapes of shingle in the same roof. This makes it possible to have a *patterned* roof, the pattern being generally one of lozenges (**59** and compare **475**).

Interactions and influences

In this book I am mainly concerned to present the

55 Shingled roof at Kolodnoye, Soviet Trans-Carpathia.

54 Baroque spirelet of Lemk church at Potoky, eastern Slovakia, 1773. (Shingles of the type shown in **53**.)

56 Newly shingled roofs of the Lemk church from Shelestovo, now at Uzhgorod. 1777.

various wooden styles as they are, rather than to engage in polemics about their role in architectural history. Nevertheless the problem of interactions between masonry and wooden buildings confronts one again and again in the different areas and will arise from time to time in the following chapters. The subject is full of interest and invites additional research, but I shall limit myself to a few generalisations.

Any research in this field must obviously involve the difficult question of dating wooden buildings, including the predecessors and early prototypes of those still standing. This is particularly true of eastern Europe where wooden buildings more than three hundred years old are extremely rare, while the vast majority considered in this book belong, in their present form, to the late seventeenth or eighteenth centuries. The fact that records may prove the existence of a wooden church on a certain site at some earlier date does not necessarily help, since decayed timbers have been replaced from time to time until the whole structure has changed its substance, and usually its style as well. While such buildings may occasionally be virtual replicas of an early original, dating possibly to the fourteenth or fifteenth century, I am personally very sceptical of any such early datings and would use the evidence they provide with caution.

In spite of these reservations, some general conclusions on the subject of interactions and influences may be stated. Among the wooden styles of eastern Europe it is the easternmost of all – those of northern Russia and, in the south, of the Ukraine – which seem to have developed with some degree of spontaneity and to be little influenced by local masonry building. Their forms were determined above all by the properties of the building material itself – the timber of the local forests. Since this was for centuries the only material generally available, wooden building retained its prestige until modern times. It was never seen as a second-rate substitute or a mere reflection of masonry architecture.

On the contrary, most Russian writers have claimed, ever since the subject was first studied in detail a century ago, that the northern wooden style had a significant influence on the development of Russian brick-built churches in the sixteenth and seven-

57 Shingles of stepped design on dome of Ust' Yandoma chapel now at Kizhi, Lake Onega.

59 Patterned shingles (recently renewed) of the church at Tornio, Finland. 1684–6.

teenth centuries. Although a few writers have contested this view and produced counter-arguments, I have always myself been convinced by the generally accepted thesis. Similarly, both Ukrainian and Russian writers have generally agreed that the Ukrainian wooden style, which reached the peak of its development as late as the seventeenth and eighteenth centuries, was a potent influence upon the Ukrainian Baroque evolving at the same time. This belief, certainly difficult to contest, will be discussed again in due course.

The converse influence – the conditioning of timber building by the prevailing international styles of the period and country – is perhaps a commoner phenomenon. Only seldom, however, does it amount to copying. The tall wooden spires of northern Rumania, manifestly inspired by Gothic steeples in the old German towns of Transylvania, are a notable re-

58 Shingled cupolas. Church of the Virgin Hodigitria at Kimzha on the R. Mezen'. 1700–63.

interpretation of the Gothic ideal as well as a triumph of village carpentry. The belfries adopted in Catholic Poland and by some Ruthenians (the Lemks) can likewise be traced to Gothic models. Here however one usually detects, superimposed upon them, the imprint of the Baroque which swept the area in the seventeenth century. A parallel case is that of Moldavia, a region long subjected to Byzantine influence: here we find, not unexpectedly, wooden versions of the dome.

Did these wooden styles of eastern Europe perform some role in the broader context of architectural history? This was certainly the view of that notorious controversialist, Josef Strzygowski. He began as the great protagonist of eastern as against classical influences in architectural history; to him 'humanism' (i.e. the cult of Rome) became a dirty word. In a long series of works beginning with *Orient oder Rom* (1901) he developed the thesis that the principal forms and techniques of medieval architecture were evolved much further east, especially in Persia and Armenia. Thence, Strzygowski maintained, they ultimately reached western Europe during the period of the great migrations, more particularly through the agency of the Goths. And it was in this process, he believed, that Ukrainian wooden architecture had played a specific role: by reproducing, in wood, the Persian dome over a square base, it had made possible the transmission of this feature to the western world. This was only the beginning of Strzygowski's involvement in a subject which was to become, for him, a life-long obsession. Alone among art historians of the last generation, he was gripped by the beauty and the fascination of wooden architecture, in which he rightly saw a monumental quality, even in many buildings of small size. Yet I can only regret some of his last writings in which he again confounded academic circles by attributing unimagined roles to the wooden architecture of northern Europe (see p. 383).

Strzygowski's theories have provoked much spirited opposition and acrimonious controversy, even if some of them have had an enduring influence. It must be admitted that, as a prophet, he could embarrass even his own devoted disciples in the First Art-Historical Institute at Vienna (not to mention members of the rival Second Institute of Art History in the same university). He recklessly alienated other workers whose approach was different from his own, giving them no credence or credit nor even admitting their works to his bibliographies. He would never admit that a compromise viewpoint in art history might come nearer to the truth than his own extremist stance. A further annoyance for the conscientious reader is the obscurity of his writings. This is aggravated by the almost unintelligible formal plan he professed to follow (yet frequently ignored) in all his later books, to the bewilderment of readers, the despair of translators.

Strzygowski's ideas on the major roles of wooden architecture will be mentioned again in their place, though I feel that for the most part they must be dismissed as extreme and unacceptable examples of his architectural diffusionism. Let us, all the same, give that great controversial and pugnacious figure his due. An admirer declared that in his chosen sphere of art history Strzygowski had 'conquered the world'. Assuredly he had stirred up and stimulated, while at the same time he exasperated, that world. And there is no doubt that in several fields of enquiry, including that of wooden architecture, his influence led for the first time to real appreciation and serious research. I too owe him a debt. My interest in wooden architecture was first sparked off by some youthful travels around the White Sea and the great Karelian lakes, but it was maintained, broadened and finally made a compelling urge by Strzygowski's writings. To my lasting regret I never met him in person.

2

Northern Russia

The architectural province we consider now differs from all the others in its vast extent and its comparative inaccessibility. Basically it is the heavily forested zone of northern Russia, where the forests of fir, pine, larch and birch are interspersed with huge areas of swamp and intersected by a number of great rivers, mostly flowing northwards to the White Sea. To the west the area extends to the complex peninsulas and islands of Lake Onega (not to be confused with the northern river of the same name) which drains through Lake Ladoga to the Gulf of Finland. However, Lake Ladoga itself with the cities of the connected waterways – modern Leningrad and ancient Novgorod – are from the point of view of this chapter marginal areas. The western shores of Ladoga will be heard of again, in another context, in Chapter 7.

As the map shows, one should include, in this province of timber architecture, the region of the upper Volga and its tributaries even including Moscow itself. In fact some modest wooden churches still exist in the countryside around the capital, besides numerous domestic buildings including the modern *dachas* of the elite. The fact remains that far more wooden buildings have disappeared from this southern area than from the lakes and forests of the far north, their last stronghold. The map must be understood, in any case, as a rough generalisation only. It marks the heart of the area in question but many scattered examples of wooden churches exist (or existed) outside it, as for instance among the settlements on the River Kama to the east.

Beyond the Urals, the whole of northern Siberia and even Alaska can be regarded as an extension of the north Russian zone of wooden architecture. The principal Siberian settlements, mostly founded in the seventeenth century by Cossack adventurers and fur traders, had massive timber fortifications, as already mentioned in Chapter 1 (**26**, **27**). Log houses were built, of course, wherever the pioneers went and churches arose even in the remotest places. But I shall concentrate on the parent zone in European Russia, and especially the northern part of it. It was here that the north Russian style really evolved, to produce in its eventual flowering some of the most impressive and beautiful wooden structures in all Europe.

In medieval times these northern forest regions, where inhabited at all, were largely occupied by Finno-Ugrian tribes. Large areas are still occupied by Finnish peoples, especially the Karelians in the west and the Komi or Zyrians in the east, both enjoying a measure of autonomy under the present regime. Russian penetration, however, began as early as the eleventh century under the aegis of the ancient State of Novgorod, centuries before the rise of Moscow. It was the Novgorodian traders who first explored and opened up all the river routes of the far north, using small boats of shallow draft which could be dragged over portages from one river system to another. Their main highway passed through Lake Ladoga and the River Svir' to Lake Onega, whence two alternative routes – by way of the Rivers Pudozh or Kovzha – led through minor streams and short portages to the River Onega and so to the White Sea. The Kovzha route, via Beloye Ozero (the White Lake), also connected with the upper reaches of the Sukhona, one of the principal head-streams of the Northern Dvina. This great river system led on the one hand downstream to the White Sea, and on the other, up a major tributary, the Vychegda, eastward towards the Urals. All these northern regions became, in time, a colony of Novgorod, and towns like Kargopol', Vologda, Tot'ma, Veliky Ustyug and Sol'vychegodsk originated as Novgorodian trading posts.

Only at the end of the fifteenth century, when Novgorod began to lose its pre-eminence to Moscow, did these great northern territories fall under Muscovite domination. It was only then that the Northern Dvina became established as the principal summer route to the White Sea. This route, together with the winter track further west, was soon to assume great importance for Muscovy's new trading link with western Europe, which led to the foundation of Archangel (Russia's only western seaport before St Petersburg). It is interesting to recall the leading part played by Britain in pioneering the White Sea trade. It was the merchant adventurer Richard Chancellor, on a voyage in search of the North-East Passage, who reached the mouth of the Dvina in 1553. Thence he travelled on by sledge to Moscow to meet Ivan the Terrible, Grand Duke of Muscovy, and relations were thus first established between Russia and Elizabethan England.

The homeland of the north Russian timber style, in Europe alone as extensive as the whole of Scandinavia, possessed but a small population and tenuous communications. Villages were confined to the banks of lakes and rivers. These far-flung settlements could mostly be reached in summer by boat, in winter by sledge, but in the two months of the spring thaw they were absolutely inaccessible. Winter was the best, sometimes the only possible travelling season, when the Russian Government operated a posting system for officials and other privileged travellers – a system still in operation throughout the nineteenth and well into the twentieth century.

The English ornithologist Henry Seebohm describes such journeys in his *Birds of Siberia*. In March 1875 he sledged the 600 miles (1000 km) from railhead at Vologda to Archangel in five days and nights, travelling continuously as the custom was, changing horses and drivers at the posting stations every 30 km. He then proceeded north-eastward to Mezen', breaking the journey there, and on to Ust'-Tsil'ma on the Pechora River – about 750 miles (1200 km) from Archangel – in eight days and seven nights of actual travel. This achievement pales, however, beside Seebohm's second journey, when he sledged 3200 miles (over 5000 km) in 229 stages from Nizhny Novgorod to the lower Yenisei, using both dogs and reindeer on the final lap. This journey, including a few short breaks, took forty-six days in March and April, 1877 – which seems a notable feat of express travel before the opening of the Trans-Siberian railway.

The facts given in the last paragraph underline the remoteness and inaccessibility of the settlements in the northern forest zone. These circumstances, unique in Europe, account for the comparative immunity of north Russian timber building to outside influences. A contributory factor was the scarcity, throughout the area, of brick or stone buildings which would otherwise have acted as the instrument of such influences. Northern towns like Veliky Ustyug did not possess a single masonry building – not even a church – until the seventeenth century. The only important exceptions to this general rule were the great fortified monasteries of St Cyril at Belozersk and its daughter foundation on the Solovetsky islands in the White Sea. Wooden architecture, therefore, was able to undergo

60 Primitive chapels in Karelia. A. Yukko-Guba (from the east). B. Akhpoila (restored view from south). C. St Lazarus from the Murom monastery, now at Kizhi (from north-west); allegedly late fourteenth century, with subsequent western porch.

its own evolution, unchallenged and untrammelled by any rival tradition.

When I travelled in northern Russia in 1932 the distances still seemed vast and the pace of life agreeably unhurried. Lake steamers, never observing the printed timetables, chugged in a leisurely manner through the great lakes and along the northern rivers; small sea-going steamers plied unpredictably between the ports of the White Sea. Conditions at that time were strained and difficult, but it was possible to go where one wished. Food was extremely scarce and beds an often unattainable luxury. But kind Russian travellers shared their black bread with me and there were plenty of bilberries in the open country. To my youthful eyes those forests and waterways, above all those fantastic wooden towers and churches, belonged to an enchanted world. I took photographs of many (on old-fashioned quarter-plate filmpacks), and a few of those pictures, nostalgic to the writer, have been admitted to this volume.

Today it is probably impossible for a foreign visitor to repeat such journeys. On the other hand there is no great difficulty in visiting the open-air museum created (largely as the result of A. V. Opolovnikov's efforts) on Kizhi island in Lake Onega. Here many wooden structures from the 'trans-Onega' region have been re-erected, including peasant dwellings, farm buildings, windmills and several churches, in addition to the two famous ones which have stood there since the eighteenth century. Wooden churches have also been transported to a number of museum sites in other places including Archangel, Kostroma, Novgorod and Suzdal'. Some of these are on tourist itineraries. One might prefer to see these fascinating buildings in their place of origin, but all is not lost.

Whether in northern Russia or in other parts of eastern Europe the basic unit for the earliest wooden structures was of course a simple rectangular 'cell' or 'cage' (*klet*). How such units were constructed and where they can still be found in use were subjects discussed in the Introduction. Undoubtedly the earliest places of worship erected by Christian communities in eastern Europe (that is, in the forested areas) would have been almost indistinguishable from their basic dwellings and farm buildings, though probably surmounted by

61 Puchuga on the Northern Dvina. Sts Peter and Paul, 1788. The narthex or *trapeza* looking east.

62 Verkhny Berezovets (north-east of Kostroma). Typical wooden interior with iconostasis. Seventeenth century?

a cross. A few primitive chapels still standing today (or until recently) in Soviet Karelia are identical in structure to the surviving Finnish barns described earlier, and the chapel of St Lazarus now at Kizhi differs from them but slightly (**60** and compare **1**).

In northern Russia a wide variety of wooden churches evolved over the centuries from these unpretentious origins, though the octagonal unit supplemented the aboriginal rectangular one from an early period. I shall describe the principal varieties in terms of their evolution from simpler to more complex forms, but it must be remembered that most of this evolution took place during the early spread of Christianity in the north – roughly between the eleventh and fourteenth centuries. It must also be borne in mind that the more sophisticated derivatives did not necessarily supersede the simpler but always existed alongside them. So more complex church-types seem to have existed as early as the fourteenth century, while very simple ones were still in use in modern times. Nevertheless, as will be seen, the eighteenth century – which here as elsewhere in eastern Europe saw the apogee of woodworking skills – did witness some remarkable developments not previously seen.

The common feature of all churches in the Orthodox countries, whether of timber or masonry, is the three-fold plan, ultimately of Byzantine origin. Following a monastic tradition the western vestibule or narthex in northern Russia can be a rather large space, often the broadest part of the church. In wooden churches, its ceiling is low and sometimes supported on posts, decoratively carved (**61**). Benches are attached to the walls. The use of the Greek word *trapeza*, also applied to a monastic refectory, suggests secular uses for the narthex: it could in fact be used for eating and drinking and on occasion worshippers from a distance might spend the night there. It could also be used for assemblies of the villagers, a function shared with the external porch and its covered stairways (*kryltso*). A door leads through from the narthex to the church proper, the nave or naos, which is devoid of pews (as the faithful stand for the liturgy)

63 St John the Evangelist on the Ishna near Rostov Veliky, 1687. Detail of Holy Door and surround, dated 1562.

and beyond this comes the sanctuary, the Byzantine *bema*. Separating these two spaces and concealing the sanctuary from view is the high icon screen or iconostasis (Russian *ikonostas*) bearing several ranges of icons in a well established pattern. In the middle is the Royal or Holy Door, itself elaborately carved, and there are side doors to left and right (**62**, **63**).

Externally, it is the middle section of these churches that attracts attention, culminating as it does in a tall roof or tower. This too is a feature shared with the modified Byzantine tradition of Russia as a whole, where prominence was invariably given to the central dome. It is true that in Russian masonry architecture the addition of a western bell tower eventually modified the Byzantine concept of the centralised church, but this did not happen until the seventeenth and, in the case of wooden churches, the eighteenth century. As far as constructional details are concerned, an almost universal characteristic of north Russian wooden architecture (in marked contrast to the Ukrainian) is the use of round, unhewn logs, which project beyond the corner-joints. Only in the latter part of the

64 The *pogost* at Yuroma on the R. Mezen' (1685 and 1729) from the east. Destroyed by fire in 1930.

eighteenth century did hewn logs and flush corners come into fashion, and then only for the more important buildings. There are few openings in these wooden walls. Generally a single western door is provided, and a minimum of small windows which are purely functional, and not intended for architectural effect.

Very often in northern Russia two wooden churches stood side by side, together with a bell tower. As a rule the larger one was the 'summer church', the smaller one being intended for winter use with provision for heating (a stove often stood in the north-west corner of the narthex). Also, there were monastic groupings including several churches and chapels along with residential buildings. But many of these clusters of churches and towers, standing in the cemetery of the region, marked the site of a *pogost*. The term, originally applied to a cemetery, implies more than this, for the *pogost*, since the days of Novgorodian rule, was the administrative centre for a whole rural area. The finest churches were built there and these served, apart from their strictly religious function, as meeting places for the populace. In these centres an array of wooden forms, matched in their material but contrasted in shape, built up a complex of singular variety and beauty – sometimes enhanced by a timber-built fortified wall with towers of its own. Little remains of most of them, though in some degree the open-air museums of today, for all their artificiality, have revived the tradition. Among long-lost *pogosts* illustrated in these pages are Yuroma on the Mezen' (**64**) and Shuya near the western White Sea coast (**34**). Podporozhie on the River Onega survives in part, and there is that wonderful sanctuary, now museum, Kizhi in Lake Onega (**95–100**).

It will already be clear that north Russian timber architecture embraces many different types of church and abounds in beautiful and original forms. I shall now attempt to follow out the evolutionary tendencies which can be traced among the once countless churches of this vast region, so as to bring some order into a fascinating but bewildering scene.

Churches of rectangular plan, lacking any octagonal elements, are derived by easy stages from the basic rectangular chapel, and they continued to be built throughout the long history of wooden architecture in the north (**65–69**). Their plans show the expected three principal divisions and often have the broadened

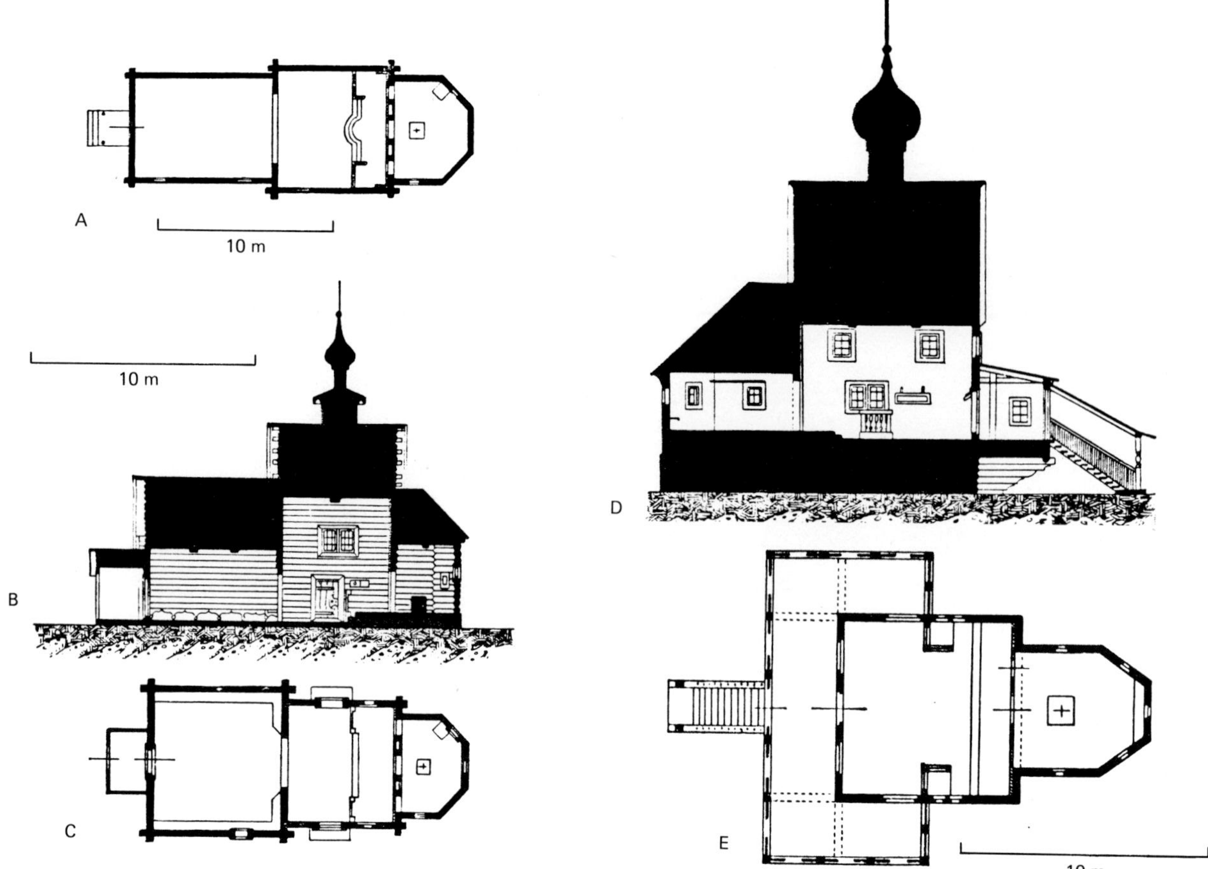

65 North Russian rectangular ('cage') plans and sections. A. Kopotna, Moscow area, seventeenth century. B,C. Lykovo, Moscow area, west–east section and plan, seventeenth century. D,E. Uyem, Archangel area, east–west section and plan. 1705.

narthex which is a rarity in eastern Europe as a whole. Externally, their leading feature is the tall wedge-shaped roof which reached extremes of height and steepness in the eighteenth century. These churches possess two decorative features which cannot have been present in their early ancestors but which came to prevail all over the north. These are the roof form known as the *bochka* (which often crowns the sanctuary as in **66** and **80**) and the bulbous dome or *luk* raised on a slender, sometimes tapering drum. They share the overhang and the ogee outline which became a favourite element in Russian architecture in general. Both would always have been clothed, in former times, in shingles, unhappily often replaced later by sheet metal. Other features to be noted in the churches illustrated are the faceted apse at the east end and the paired stairway (*kryltso*) at the west (**67–69**). An example from the open-air museum at Novgorod is enriched with reduplicated roofs, sometimes described as 'basilican', which occur also in chapels of very late date (**67** and compare **112** A).

We can pass on from the purely rectangular 'cage' type churches to those – more interesting and characteristic – which incorporate octagons. The octagon was used in its simplest possible form for small chapels, a few of which may still survive (**38**). But it was adapted at an early date – probably in the first centuries of Russian Christianity – to the purposes of full-scale church-building. It had the merit of conferring a distinctive character on churches to differentiate them from all secular buildings. It also had the important practical advantage that timbers of a given length could enclose a much larger space if used to build an octagon rather than a square. The octagon always formed the central element in the plan – the naos, where the congregation stood – the sanctuary and the narthex being added on to its eastern and western faces respectively.

The Imperial Archaeological Commission of old Russia recorded an example of such a church at the village of Led, Olonets region, which they dated to the years 1426–56 (**70**). If the dating was well founded

66 Church of the Deposition of the Robe, Borodava, seen from the south-east. 1486. Since 1958 at the monastery of St Cyril, Belozersk.

67 St Nicholas, Tukholya, seventeenth–eighteenth century, from the north-west. Now at the Yuryev monastery, Novgorod.

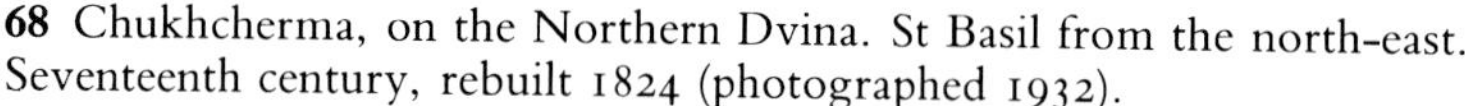

68 Chukhcherma, on the Northern Dvina. St Basil from the north-east. Seventeenth century, rebuilt 1824 (photographed 1932).

69 Church of the Saviour from Vyozha, now at Kostroma, 1628. South-east view.

this must have been by far the oldest building of its kind to survive into modern times. It exhibited every characteristic proper to the style. The sanctuary and narthex, identical in form, project from opposite sides of the central octagon, and the latter is wrapped round by a low but roomy porch. The walls of the octagon can be seen to rise vertically until, near the top, they incline outwards to form a kind of cornice (*poval*), thus providing a broadened base for the culminating feature of the building. This is the so-called *shatyor* or tent (and tent towers will henceforth be spoken of repeatedly, though they are more like spires than tents). Early examples like this one were constructed entirely, or almost entirely, of horizontal logs interlocked at the corners, becoming shorter and shorter towards the top (**71**). The tower is clothed and weatherproofed by means of shingles, and at its base, covering the junction of walls and tent, is an overhanging

70 St John the Baptist, Led, Olonets region, from an old drawing. 1426–56.

71 Verkhnaya Uftyuga. St Demetrius of Salonica, 1780s. Interior of the 'tent' tower seen from the ground.

72 Panilovo by the Northern Dvina. St Nicholas the Wonder-worker, built 1600 and burnt down early in the twentieth century. West end with *kryltso*.

roof of lesser slope (*politsa*) designed to throw rain water and snow well clear of the timbers of the octagon. The 'tent' is crowned by a bulbous dome, the sanctuary and narthex each by a *bochka*.

Although tent roofs abound among the surviving wooden churches of the north, they are generally set on the square base developed later, or form part of cruciform compositions of a newer fashion. Churches of the aboriginal, octagonal design have become very rare, though at least two have survived on the banks of the Northern Dvina. One of these, at Liavlia near Archangel, is believed to date from as early as 1589; the other was built in 1672, and transferred from the village of Vershina to Archangel open-air museum in the present decade. Two or three others, likewise among villages bordering the Dvina, did survive into the twentieth century and found their way into the earlier literature. A beautiful example at Panilovo (**72**) long continued to be cited in Russian publications as if still standing though it had been destroyed by fire in the early 1920s, as I learnt to my chagrin upon reaching the site on foot in September 1932. About a fortnight later, however, I followed the river banks from Krasnoborsk desperately hoping to find and record the similar but larger church at Belaya Sluda. Weather conditions were appalling but the church was there (**73**). This gaunt and solemn monument of old 'wooden Russia', towering 45 m above the peasants' houses which it matched, but dwarfed, made a deep and ineffaceable impression. It stood there for another thirty years. But in 1962, after a life-span of 320 years (well above average for a wooden church), the precious relic was struck by lightning and ended its days in a mighty blaze, as impressive in death as in life.

The plan and section of Belaya Sluda are typical for this old-fashioned class of church, except that the twin altars in the sanctuary were somewhat unusual (**74** A, B). The longitudinal section reveals the want of organic relationship between interior and exterior, a feature (quite usual in northern Russia) with which purists may well find fault. It was forced upon the northern church carpenters as a result of their incompatible ambitions – to build soaring churches visible from afar, and to provide cosy interiors that could be warmed in winter. The consequence is that the upper reaches of these churches are so much empty space. There may be empty space below the floor too since most church floors were raised well above ground level, probably to keep them clear of deep snow in winter and of mud or flooding in the spring thaw.

The 'tented' wooden churches whose spires are superimposed on a rectangular nave were developed later: the conversion of square to octagon involved an additional skill not generally employed, it seems, until the mid seventeenth century. Many such churches still stand in the forest zone, more especially along the Northern Dvina and its main tributaries, also in the

73 Belaya Sluda on the Northern Dvina. Church of the Virgin of Vladimir, viewed from the south. Built 1642, burnt down 1962 (photographed 1932).

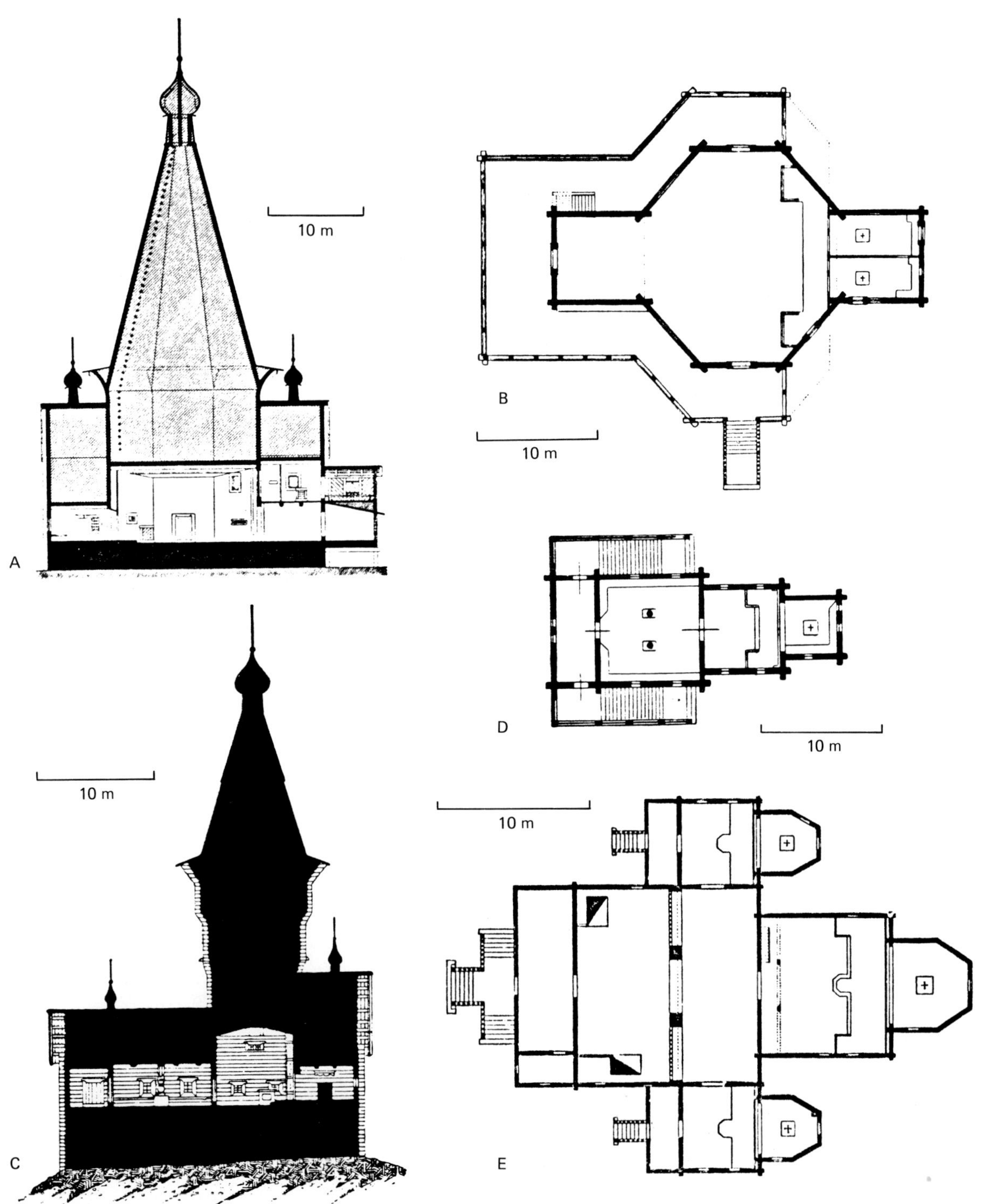

74 Sections and plans of north Russian 'tented' churches. A,B. Belaya Sluda. C,D. Kondopoga. E. Kem'.

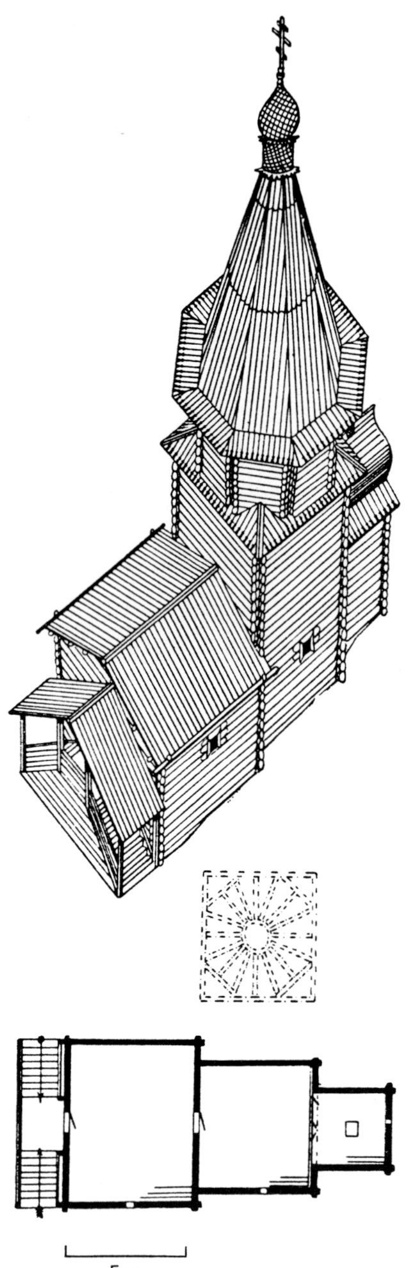

75 St Barbara, Yandomozero, Karelia. Bird's eye view, ceiling plan and ground plan to show state of the church in 1650.

architecturally rich area of Lake Onega. Yandomozero in the latter district is a typical example. Pettersson provides a history of the church beginning with the original building of 1650: this was later extended westwards and eventually joined up, late in the following century, with the newly constructed bell tower (**75**, **76**). An early sub-type with wrap-around narthex, now re-erected at Novgorod's Yuryev monastery, is shown in **77**.

During the late seventeenth and eighteenth centuries, when this church type, among others, remained popular, some interesting variants made their appearance. St Peter and Paul at Lychnoy island in Lake Sandal (north of Kondopoga) shows an octagon with two outward bulges surmounting a tall square base which terminates in triple gables on either side (**78**). At Kondopoga itself, on the western shore of Lake Onega, the church possesses an even taller central square and a tower which likewise widens at two levels, or three if one includes the 'cornice' at the top of the square base (**79**, **80** and **74** C, D). Here the octagon bears an ornamental zigzag course which is clearly a reminiscence of the small zigzagging gables as at St Peter and Paul's; it is not entirely functionless for the constituent bars serve as gutters, their channels leading down to a small waterspout in each lower angle. Kondopoga forms a nicely balanced composition, the western extension being longer and lower, the eastern, with its *bochka*, shorter and higher. As seen end-on the whole building, 42 m high, seems extraordinarily tall and narrow (**80**). It has another peculiarity: standing as it does close to the lake shore it could not be served by a *kryltso* in the usual western position. The stairways were therefore divided into two separate flights attached to the north and south sides of the church and both lead up to a closed porch or lobby built as a short westward prolongation of the narthex. As these stairways indicate, the church floor is high above ground level. The section (**74** C) shows how little of the interior is occupied by the church itself: it is mostly empty space. It is interesting to compare the closely related building at the Ryboretsky *pogost* (Olonets region) built in 1693; its *kryltso*, with single flight of stairs, stood in the normal position (**81**).

The rectangular plan of the later 'tent' churches proved advantageous when it was desired to range two or three such elements alongside each other. A fine example is the old wooden cathedral of the Assumption still standing at Kem' on the western shores of the White Sea. Here chapels of almost the same shape as the main church are attached to its narthex to north and south (**74** E). Each of the three elements has a five-sided apse surmounted by a *bochka* and each carries a tent roof. My photograph of 1932 (**82**) shows this attractive composition, but it has since been improved by the removal of the nineteenth-century external boarding. At Nyonoksa near the southern shore of the White Sea, west of Archangel, there is a church with no fewer than five tent roofs, not however built up of horizontal pieces in the traditional way. The plan is cruciform with central octa-

76 Yandomozero: present state, resulting from westward extension and bell tower of c. 1775–1800.

77 Church of the Assumption from Kuritsko, 1595. Now at the Yuryev monastery, Novgorod.

gon, the north and south arms forming side-chapels (**83** and **88** A). Decorative *bochki* once adorned alternate sides of each octagon, but some have disappeared. The exterior has carried boarding since the late nineteenth century, but one may hope that this will be removed as at Kem'.

Although cruciform wooden churches have been mentioned for the first time at this point, they were not in fact a late development. The history of the cathedral of the Assumption at Veliky Ustyug throws light on this subject. The Ustyug Chronicle records that after the third successive wooden cathedral had been burnt down in 1490 the architect appointed to rebuild it proposed a plan 'unlike the old ones' with

79 Kondopoga, on the shores of L. Onega. The church of the Assumption, 1774 (photographed 1932).

twenty walls. The implication of 'twenty walls' is clear: it means an octagon with four comparatively low rectangular arms projecting from its alternate faces (as in **88** A without the lateral sanctuaries). Although the citizenry rejected this plan, and a more traditional church was erected which stood until the seventeenth century, this invaluable record proves that the centralised, cruciform plan was already known in the fifteenth century, if not earlier.

Unfortunately no wooden churches of any cruciform plan have come down to us from such an early period. A few have been tentatively assigned to the sixteenth century, but the great majority of those surviving into modern times date, as usual, from the seventeenth and eighteenth centuries and some of these still exist. Their plans were based either on the square or the octagon and the octagon probably came first since it could more easily carry the octagonal tent roof which was invariably desired (at least until the mid seventeenth century) as the culminating feature of the whole edifice. Whichever form it took, the central element was buttressed by four arms of equal or nearly equal length, in addition to which a more or less elaborate *kryltso* would be draped around the western side of the building. Some cruciform churches which figure in seventeenth-century drawings seem to show ordinary pitched roofs on the arms (**84**, **85**). Other old drawings show arms adorned with *bochki* (**86**), and

78 St Peter and Paul on Lychnoy island, L. Sandal, 1620.

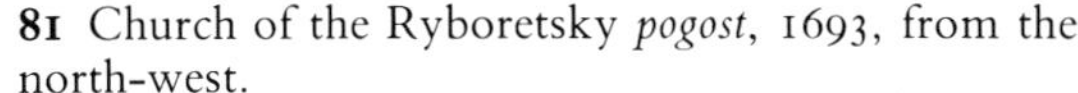

81 Church of the Ryboretsky *pogost*, 1693, from the north-west.

80 Kondopoga. Eastern view.

82 Kem', on the White Sea. Church of the Assumption, 1714 (photographed 1932).

83 Nyonoksa, west of Archangel. Church of the Trinity, 1727, from the south side.

84 A timber-built monastic(?) settlement on the River Oka recorded by Olearius, c. 1635.

85 Cruciform wooden village church between Novgorod and Tver' (now Kalinin). From Meyerberg's journal, 1661–2.

Columna ein Dorff lieget vier meilen von Kusenka, gehöret zu einem Klo.
ster in der stadt Groß Naugarten Schwetti Spaß genandt.

86 A thanksgiving service of the Siberian Christians held at Tobolsk in 1598, depicted a century later in the Remezov Chronicle. A large *Deesis* icon partly conceals a wooden cruciform church.

this is also true of most surviving specimens, like the church of the Kushta monastery (**87**). A few had miniature 'tents' instead, as at Verkhovye, Vologda region (whose basic cruciform plan is shown in **88** B). The finest existing church of this type is probably that at Vazentsi *pogost* on the River Onega (1786) where each *bochka* is surmounted by a dome. Whatever the details of these arrangements their object, whether or not consciously formulated, was to achieve, along with the central 'tent', an overall conical or pyramidal outline.

A further development of the cruciform church involved the multiplication of the *bochki*, one being placed upon another on each arm. Thus Una on the southern coast of the White Sea had two tiers of *bochki*, the upper, which were also the larger, being surmounted by small domes on drums (**88** D, E and **89**). The next stage in this evolutionary process is illustrated by the remarkable church, mercifully still surviving, at Varzuga on the Kola peninsula, between the northern shore of the White Sea and the Arctic Circle (**90**). Here, instead of domes, a third series of small

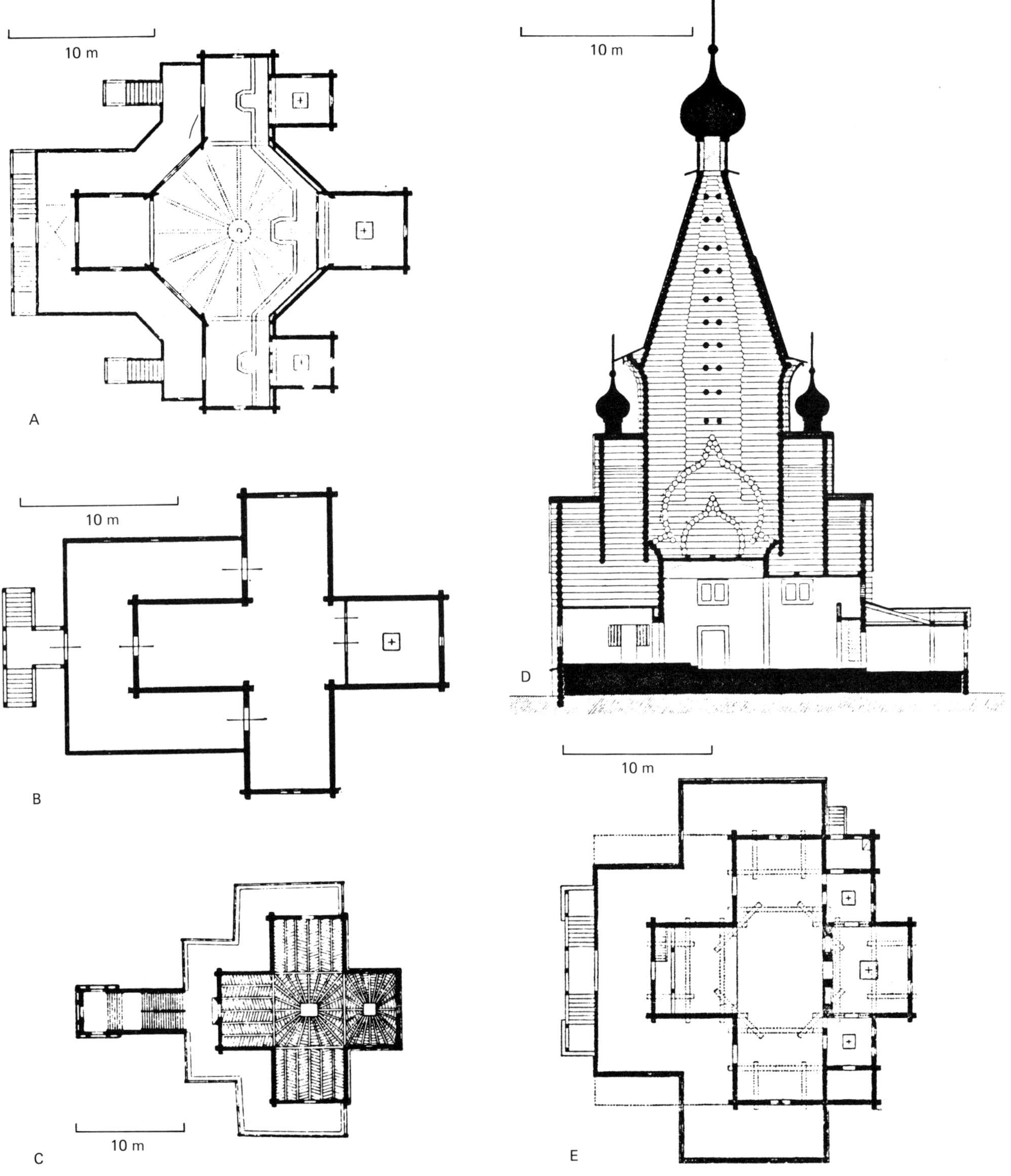

88 Plans and section of north Russian cruciform churches. A. Nyonoksa. B. Verkhovye. C. Nelazsky-Borisoglebsky. D,E. Una: east-west section and plan.

87 Church of the Assumption from the Kushta monastery of St Alexander, sixteenth century. Since 1960 at the Spaso-Prilutsky monastery ('the Saviour-on-the-Bend') on the outskirts of Vologda.

89 Una, west of Archangel. Seventeenth-century church.

ornamental *bochki* were added and these are matched by similar ones applied to the alternate faces of the octagon, where they stand on the corners of the square base. This very successful arrangement of traditional motifs, again achieving the general outline of a tall, steep pyramid, has for many years been compared with certain mid-sixteenth-century churches of the Muscovite school, which it was thought to have influenced. I shall revert to this now controversial topic later.

I must allude here to a now lost type of wooden church where the central 'tent' was apparently eliminated altogether by three tiers of superimposed *bochki*. One such was sketched by Palmquist, a visiting Swedish engineer, in 1674 in the Moscow area (**91**). The fact that such arrangements existed, at least in the mind, a century later is proved by the complex carved throne-roof (*sen*) in the church of the Georgian Virgin in Moscow (**92**). This is an architectural miniature which shows *bochki* climbing up the five 'tents' whose tips retain, however, their traditional form.

The tent was eliminated, on occasion, in another way: it could be substituted by clusters of five domes. One cannot but regard this as an anti-climax following the splendid earlier design dominated by a great central tent tower. It may well have resulted from a desire to comply with the edict of 1650 (discussed below) which required that all churches should have five domes. An extant example is the church at Nelazsky-Borisoglebsky west of Vologda (**93** and **88** c). Here the central element is square, the arms carry massive *bochki* and the domes stand on little

90 Varzuga, on the Kola peninsula. Church of the Assumption, 1674.

91 Church of the St Nicholas monastery near Moscow drawn by Palmquist in 1674.

92 Roof of a throne-canopy in the church of the Virgin of Greben', Moscow.

ones. The *kryltso* and surrounding gallery are boarded up in a claustrophobic manner, and the latter raised to the level of the church floor on tremendous consoles. A related but more attractive church once stood at Berezovets, south-east of Vologda (**94**). Its central element was octagonal instead of square and carried its domes on rectangular pedestals instead of miniature *bochki*, while a beautiful open gallery surrounded three sides of the church.

Among all these cruciform churches employing both *bochka* and dome in their adornment, it is generally agreed that the finest and most original is the great summer church of Kizhi in the Lake Onega archipelago (**95–99**). The huge lake is broken up by the complex ramifications of a peninsula jutting far out from its north-western extremity. There are many associated islands and Kizhi is one of the smaller ones, near the southern tip of the peninsula and in the very middle of the lake. Its village was a *pogost*: the rural metropolis for a considerable population living on neighbouring islands and the adjoining mainland. Its communications were and are, of necessity, only by water. I arrived there in 1932 after midnight on the third night of a slow voyage by river steamer from Leningrad. Even in the small hours of the morning rustic hospitality was not lacking on the island, where foreign visitors were then unknown. I slept briefly. Then in the early, misty daylight I stood spellbound, absorbing the impact of an architectural scenario which must be unique. Faced with such virtuosity of craftsmanship and such a marvel of ingenious fantasy, I suppose no visitor could remain unmoved.

The summer church, dedicated to the Transfiguration, was built in 1714 following the destruction by fire, in 1690, of a 'tented' church on the same site. Its designer and master-builder, whose name was Nestor, did not invent new forms but worked with traditional elements alone: the octagon-based cruciform plan, the *bochka* and the bulbous dome. Nestor's genius lay in combining these elements in a novel and marvellously successful whole. He had experimented before and the church at Vytegra (1708), near the south-eastern shore of the lake, is thought to have been the principal forerunner preparing the way for the masterpiece. There the idea of framing domes in the gable-ends of *bochki* was first tried out, and found to work well, for these elements (as seen in section) have precisely the same ogee shape.

Pettersson provides an instructive diagram which makes the basic structure of the church (shorn of its *bochki* and domes) abundantly clear (**97**). The central octagon is converted into a cross by rectangular arms projecting from alternate faces. These arms rise in two

93 Church of Nelazsky-Borisoglebsky near Cherepovets, west of Vologda. 1698.

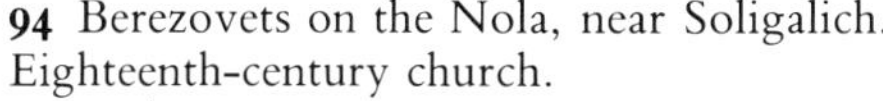

94 Berezovets on the Nola, near Soligalich. Eighteenth-century church.

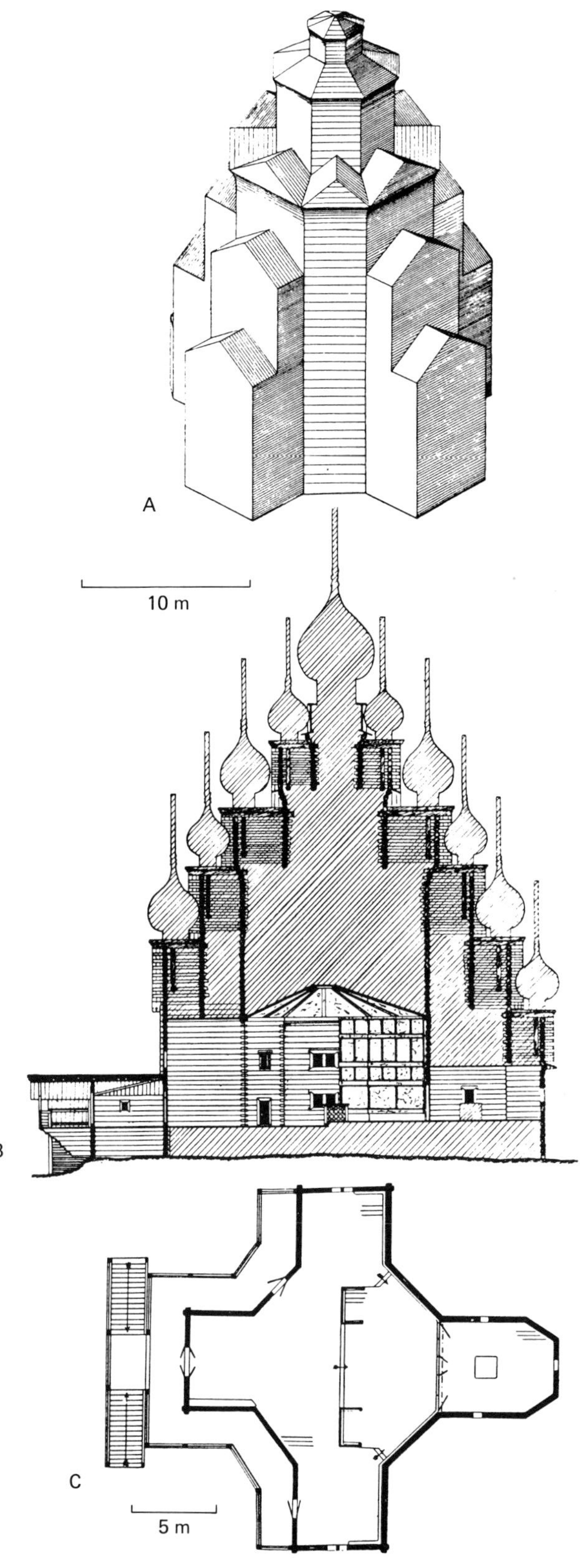

97 Kizhi. Perspective diagram, west–east section and ground plan.

95 Kizhi in Lake Onega. Church of the Transfiguration with Oshevnev House.

96 Kizhi. Church of the Transfiguration, 1714 and 1759. View from the south-east.

98 Kizhi. Interior view with iconostasis.

99 Kizhi. Paired western stairway (*kryltso*).

steps as at Una (**89**). Each step is completed by a *bochka* surmounted by a dome, and each dome fits neatly into the *bochka* of the step above. At the second level (numbering upwards from the ground) the intermediate faces of the octagon each bear a matching *bochka* in simple outline, somewhat as at Varzuga (**90**). This prepares the way for the third level, the summit of the main octagon, where domes rise in all eight available positions. Within this circle, instead of a 'tent', we find (at the fourth level) a second octagon of reduced diameter carrying four more *bochki* with their domes, and finally a third small octagon on which the larger culminating dome is poised. The effect of all this is a cataract of five domes down each aspect of the building (six to the east, since the apse carries an additional one), making twenty-two domes in all. The general outline, once again, is the much sought-after attenuated pyramid. Local legend relates that the architect, on completing the task, flung his axe into the lake exclaiming 'this church was built by the master carpenter Nestor . . . there was never one to match it nor ever shall be'. He was right, for though the church did have its influence, nothing to compare with the original was ever built thereafter.

Internally, as usual in northern Russia, the actual church occupies only a fraction of the available space, which remains largely empty (**97**, **98**). The naos possesses a very fine example of a domed 'sun roof' supported by ribs radiating from a timber ring in the centre; though such a structure should be self-supporting it is said to be partly suspended from transverse timbers in the invisible roof space above. The almost contemporary, four-tiered iconostasis is an elaborate one which not only shuts off the sanctuary but extends to all the eastern walls of the interior space, and it includes many icons of interest and beauty. As so often, the church floor lies well above ground. The *kryltso*, a nineteenth-century but perfectly traditional one with paired stairways, is supported on cantilevered brackets or consoles: these were formerly hidden behind boarding but are now exposed to view (**99**)

In recent years Kizhi has received much attention from Soviet architects and art historians, especially from A. V. Opolovnikov who has carried out important restoration work to these and many other wooden buildings. As well as the replacement of defective timber these works have included the removal of much external boarding misguidedly added in the nineteenth century. Kizhi is now one of the outstanding open-air museums in Russia. Around the nucleus of the two original churches, many other wooden buildings from Trans-Onega have been re-erected, including old peasants' houses, windmills and a number of chapels. Tourists are whirled there by hydrofoil from Petrozavodsk. For those whose interests lie in vernacular architecture Kizhi offers an experience not to be missed.

We have come to the climax but not yet to the end of this review of north Russia's wooden churches. I must now pass on to several variations on the theme, and first to the groups defined in the older literature as 'five-domed' and 'multi-domed'. Some have already been included among the churches of cruciform plan. The five-domed category, frankly inspired by masonry prototypes and therefore of lesser interest, can be dismissed rapidly. But the normal five-domed arrangements of the masonry church, when copied in wood, sometimes had extra domes added in the middle of each side producing a cluster of nine domes crowded rather tastelessly on the rectangular roof. One example, at Chukhcherma on the Dvina near Archangel, was burnt down in 1931, the year before my visit. More attractive and original is the second (winter) church at Kizhi whose middle element is a square surmounted by an octagon, the latter adorned with a zigzag course as mentioned earlier (**100**). Crowning the octagon are eight domes disposed in a ring with the ninth rising higher in their midst. A typical *bochka* with its own additional dome crowns

100 Kizhi. Church of the Intercession (Pokrov), 1764.

101 Podporozhie, near Onega on the White Sea. Church of the Trinity, 1725–7, with its bell tower (photographed 1932).

102 Yedoma on the Pinega. St Nicholas, 1700.

the apse. This is a nicely contrasted and not unworthy companion piece to the very different and far more important summer church already described.

I now turn to the '*kub*-roofed' churches which were formerly numerous along the course of the River Onega and on the White Sea shores within range of its mouth. The *kub* roof, in spite of its name, is anything but cubical. Though square in plan it has the general outline of a rather flattened bulbous dome, which takes the place of the entire main roof of the church, and normally supports its own set of five small domes. Evidently it was felt to provide an alternative

103 Ust'-Tsil'ma on the Pechora. 'Ancient church of the Old Believers' seen by Seebohm in 1875.

crowning flourish for churches deprived, by the ban of 1650 (see below), of their 'tents', for it first appears after that date. At the old *pogost* of Podporozhie, upriver from the port of Onega, there were two such churches as well as a bell tower of the type characteristic of the area. The later church is cruciform and has each arm capped by a *bochka* plus 'tent' plus dome, all devised to lead up to the topmost dome cluster and so contribute to an overall conical silhouette. Its earlier and simpler companion church (doubtfully still existing) is shown in **101**. Some other examples still stand in successive villages up the river, one of the best at Turchasovo – which narrowly escaped destruction in 1964 when the second church there was burnt down. Another good specimen from Kushereka (White Sea coast west of Onega) was transferred to the open-air museum at Archangel in 1972.

Still further north than the Onega and Northern Dvina are other big rivers – the Pinega (which eventually joins the Dvina) and the remote Mezen', which debouches directly into the Barents Sea. Their once numerous wooden churches are sadly depleted and I have already mentioned the tragic loss of the Yuroma *pogost* in 1930. But at Yedoma on the Pinega and at Kimzha on the Mezen' two interesting and very similar churches survive, the later one at Kimzha being evidently inspired by Yedoma (**58**, **102**). These churches are difficult to characterise. They each possess tall tent roofs, which are surrounded on all four sides by *bochki* carrying domes on extremely slender drums. Such flanking *bochki* with their domes are the normal attributes of a cruciform plan. But these churches are not cruciform and all their crowning elements are crowded onto the square roof of the naos, resulting in the general outline of a greatly elongated cone.

While on the subject of the northern waters I must still bring in the far-distant Pechora, that thousand-mile river which drains the northern Urals and flows finally into the Arctic Ocean. It too once had its wooden churches. In 1875 one was recorded by Seebohm, the ornithologist and Siberian traveller, at Ust'-Tsil'ma: it was a simple little 'tented' church of the Old Believers, already at that time dilapidated. His

104 The church at Zashiversk in Yakutia, north-eastern Siberia.

engraving shows, besides church, belfry and well, a Samoyed *choom* and reindeer-drawn sledge (**103**). Similar small churches existed, needless to say, in still remoter places in Asiatic Russia. I illustrate the one near Zashiversk on the Indigirka in north-eastern Siberia, over five thousand kilometres and seven time-zones east of Moscow, which has recently been recorded in Soviet publications (**104**). By now it has probably been transported piecemeal to that academic metropolis of Siberia, Novosibirsk.

One architectural category which still remains to be mentioned is the so-called storeyed church. Widely scattered but never numerous, these churches are something of an anomaly, the expected 'tent' being replaced by a stepped or storeyed naos roof. This feature is more reminiscent of the Ukraine (which might possibly have been the source of the idea) than of the Russian north, where, however, brick-built versions are also known. Upon a rectangular base we find another square of lesser diameter with superimposed octagon (**105**) or two or three successive octagons (**106**, **107**). The church at Kandalaksha, at the furthest north-western extremity of the White Sea, had an octagon on its square base, then a smaller square element with sides parallel to the base, followed by a second octagon. A beautiful and complex example, which might have been referred to under the 'cruciform' category, has been re-erected in the open-air museum at Suzdal', east of Moscow (**108**). The central square has almost disappeared behind the four arms of the cross which carry imposing *bochki*: these latter are applied to alternate faces of the lowest section of the octagonal, three-storeyed tower. The church is late enough to have hewn timbers and flush

105 Belozersk. Church of the Prophet Elijah, 1690.

106 St Peter and Paul, Ratonavolok, Kholmogory district, 1722.

corner-joints. With its sundry domes, minor *bochki*, ornamental *kryltso* and outer gallery on consoles, this building makes a delightful composition.

As a number of illustrations have shown, all these various types of church are accompanied by timber-built belfries, though when two churches stand in close proximity one belfry normally suffices. All except some very late examples are free-standing. How far back these towers go is an open question. The theory that all northern wooden belfries were descended from a fifteenth-century tower in Novgorod will be discussed below. However that may be, the mere fact that uprights are incorporated in these structures suggests a relatively late origin, since the early builders were absolutely wedded to the horizontal principle.

One of the earliest belfries known is the one dated 1658 at Tsyvozero, a village on the Northern Dvina near Krasnoborsk (**109**). Octagonal from the ground upwards, its constituent unhewn logs are attractively irregular. The eight upright columns seen exposed and decoratively carved where they traverse the bell chamber, and which have to support the roof, in reality rise from ground level, as does another in the centre of the tower. These are described as nine-post towers and are the commonest type, but others have sixteen or more uprights. Immediately below the bell chamber there is an overhang (*poval*) at the top of the octagon, as found in similar positions in churches. Here the projecting ends of the topmost logs form primitive brackets which help to support the collar-like roof or *politsa* placed here to catch any rain or melting snow thrown down by another *politsa* at the base of the tent roof above. This latter also has sup-

107 St Athanasius at Belaya Sluda near the Northern Dvina, 1753 (photographed 1932).

porting brackets built from the corresponding timber-ends; these are hewn and appear to be a replacement set of later date.

There is a great measure of uniformity among wooden bell towers, but all the later ones have a square base which is converted, at no great height, to the octagon. An imposing one of later eighteenth-century date (as can be guessed from the flush jointing at the angles) stands on the high bank of the Dvina at Chukhcherma, not far from Archangel (**110**). The Kizhi tower (**95**), though modern, is of traditional shape, except that its square base is more than usually tall. One conspicuously different form of bell tower became fashionable in the eighteenth century, especially in the chain of villages along the River Onega. The normal tent roof is here replaced by a dome surmounted by a spike or flèche (**101**). This probably resulted from Baroque influence coming in through St Petersburg after the foundation of that city in the early years of the century.

During the period of decline of wooden architecture – the late eighteenth and early nineteenth centuries – not many full-sized churches were erected. On the other hand numbers of lesser ones appeared, as well as many small chapels (which lacked a sanctuary, though the eastern wall might be adorned in the manner of an iconostasis). These little buildings are something of a paradox. Though so late in date many of them are extremely simple and no doubt look very like the earliest Christian sanctuaries of the area. Moreover, their roofs have the purlined structure proper to the most primitive surviving wooden buildings of northern Europe (pp. 5–7). An example is the Yamka chapel which sits on the highest point of Kizhi island and commands a fine view of the archipelago (**111** and compare **112** B). Others, however, built as they were

108 Church of the Transfiguration from Kozliatievo, eighteenth century. Now at Suzdal'.

at a time when western influence was penetrating through St Petersburg, have bell turrets which, instead of standing on their own, surmount the western end of the main building (**113**, **114**). Such attached or superimposed belfries were familiar in masonry architecture from the seventeenth century onwards, but (as mentioned earlier) wooden buildings did not follow suit until a century later. While their position is new, these turrets remain traditional in the details of their construction and can be beautiful examples of rural craftsmanship. An example from Kizhi is shown in **115**.

After reviewing these various church-types of northern Russia, and tracing their complex genealogy, one is left with an impression of immense variety. There is indeed no other part of eastern Europe where wooden churches exist in such diversity. This can be attributed in part to the interaction of purely wooden forms and systems with those deriving from masonry architecture, and I revert to this subject below. However, one must take account of another apparently influential factor – the abortive attempt of the Patriarch Nikon, in the middle of the seventeenth century, to impose a standard form of church upon the faithful. Among other 'reforms' he decreed that all churches should conform to the five-domed plan already widespread in the brick architecture of Muscovy, and

109 Tsyvozero, near Krasnoborsk on the Northern Dvina. Bell tower of 1658 (photographed 1932).

110 Chukhcherma, on the banks of the Northern Dvina near Archangel. Bell tower of 1783 (photographed 1932).

111 Yamka near Kizhi. Eighteenth-century chapel (photographed 1932).

112 Late chapels in Kizhi area. A. Seletskoye (1753), transverse section. B. Podgorskaya-Fominskaya (1760), longitudinal section.

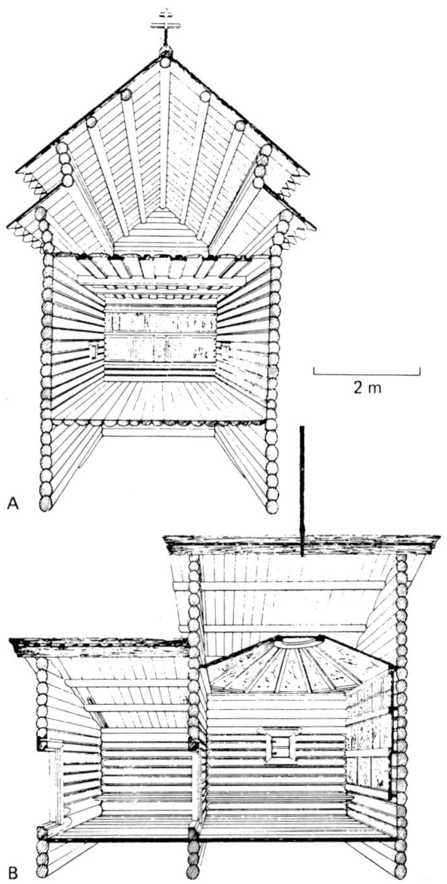

sought to relegate 'tents' to bell towers and subsidiary buildings.

The traditionalists who defied the Patriarch and ignored his architectural precepts became known as Old Believers. Threatened inevitably with persecution by Church and State, many of them took refuge in remote places in the far north. However, other villagers of the northern forest zone did not wish, or did not dare, to challenge the rulings of the Patriarch. These communities, wedded though they were to the 'tent' church, sought compromises whereby the traditional outline of an attenuated cone could be achieved while adhering to the letter of Nikon's edict. This has been thought to explain the invention of the *kub* churches along the River Onega, of the unique church at Nyonoksa (**83**) with its five tent towers (each crowned with a dome) and of those singular stalked dome clusters in the villages on the Mezen' and Pinega. None the less in the eighteenth century, the old tent church enjoyed a notable revival; by then the late Patriarch's edict had no doubt lost most of its force.

Despite their great variety and exceptional interest these wooden churches of the north attracted little attention in the earlier years of architectural research in Russia. At last, during the years between the Revolutions of 1905 and 1917, several native scholars published studies both of the northern and the Ukrainian wooden styles. It then came to be a generally accepted thesis that the wooden architecture of the north had evolved almost independently of any outside inspiration but had powerfully influenced the development of Muscovite brick architecture in the sixteenth and seventeenth centuries. By the early

113 Vasilyevo, near Kizhi. Eighteenth-century chapel.

1930s, however, a new generation of scholars had begun to reconsider the established doctrine. D. Ainalov (1933), while stressing the contrast between the quiet logic of Byzantine building and the unbridled fantasy of northern timber architecture which it completely failed to subdue, accepted the role of the wooden style in influencing Muscovite architecture. Nevertheless he sought to derive the plans of wooden churches (especially the cruciform plans) from Byzantine sources. But N. Brunov (in Alpatov and Brunov, 1932) treated the traditional thesis with profound scepticism, denied the originality of the northern wooden churches and questioned their influence on the brick architecture of the Muscovite State.

In the years 1942–4, during the occupation by Finland of eastern Karelia, the Finnish scholar Lars Pettersson was able to investigate the wooden architecture of Zaonezhie, the great complex of peninsulas and islands in Lake Onega including Kizhi. This singular area is exceptionally rich in wooden churches and chapels which are reasonably typical of the north Russian style as a whole, even if certain church-types are not represented there. Pettersson made full use of his opportunity, unique for a non-Russian. His published study must be the most exhaustive ever undertaken in the area, running in all to nearly six hundred pages of print (though the purely descriptive first section, being printed in Finnish, is inaccessible to most potentially interested readers). Influenced seemingly by Brunov, Pettersson, while sensitive to the enchanting fantasy of these timber structures, was not prepared to accept the originality of their various constituent elements. On the contrary he sought their prototypes far and wide, in the Gothic, in the brick architecture of Novgorod and Muscovy, in the conventional Byzantine which had given birth to those styles, in the timber Byzantine which he postulates and even in the buildings of the Early Christian and classical worlds. A full summary of this great speculation would be out of place here but it will be referred to again below, as will the divergent views of other authors, including my own.

The discussion may start with the subject of plans. All Orthodox churches have their plans divided obligatorily into three distinct parts these being, from east to west, the sanctuary, the naos and the pronaos or narthex (to which a porch or exonarthex may be added). Throughout the Byzantine world this liturgical requirement became also an architectural tradition and the naos, the central element of the three, was invariably surmounted by the highest or (if there were but one) by the only tall roof or cupola in the composition. In very early times more ambitious churches were given a cross-shaped plan by the addition of north and south arms to the naos – an excellent system from the point of view of building dynamics since the dome was thus buttressed on four sides. This developed in turn into the 'cross-in-square' or 'inscribed cross' church-type (German *Kreuzkuppelkirche*) which possesses even greater mechanical advantages. Here the central square is reduced to four corner-piers only, the angles between the arms are filled up and the arms themselves, in the external view, tend to lose their separate identity. In this later form the cross-in-square

114 Kem'. Eighteenth-century church (photographed 1932).

115 Bell turret of eighteenth-century chapel at Korba, near Kizhi.

became the basis of church architecture throughout Russia, after Christianity was introduced in the tenth century.

Among the wooden churches of north Russia there are, as has been seen, both linear and cruciform plans and some writers have been at pains to identify their prototypes in the masonry churches of Russia and the Balkans. Pettersson has even interpreted the pillarless central rectangle of wooden churches as derived by reduction from the four-pillared cross-in-square of Novgorod. I myself see no need to invoke so devious a pedigree for the simple square *klet* of the northern carpenters, its dimensions determined by the average length of the available timbers. I have no doubt that whenever Christianity penetrated to the northern forest zone, during the heyday of the Novgorodian republic, such plans were already to hand. Builders in timber would already have known that a tall box of horizontal logs, whether square or octagonal, was intrinsically unstable – a fact proved again and again in modern times by the collapse of free-standing wooden belfries. A central rectangle buttressed on two opposing sides by additional rectangular elements formed a relatively stable structure, and such buildings would have been readily available for adaptation as churches. For purely mechanical reasons the cruciform plan, as in the case of Byzantine stone churches, was the best solution of all. It would not be surprising if these too were known before the introduction of the Christian religion, and before foreign prototypes could possibly have played any part. Indeed one might claim that builders in wood had no option but to extend their structures by adding additional elements either on two sides or on four. All the same, masonry buildings did of course exert a parallel influence on wooden plans. This can be seen particularly in the sanctuaries, narrower than the naves from which they project, and usually five-sided in imitation of the semi-circular masonry apse.

Similar considerations apply, in my opinion, to the octagon, whether or not this was developed before the spread of Christianity in the north. Pettersson searched Europe and the Mediterranean as far back as Early Christian times for rotundas and octagons from which those of the northern forests could be derived, and similarly sought alien sources for the tent roof. But here again I feel that they arose by a natural process of evolution among builders who, necessarily restricted to logs alone, and to logs of limited length, had to overcome the shortcomings of their material as best they might. As pointed out earlier, a much larger church could be constructed, given logs of a certain length, by adopting the octagonal plan in preference to the square. It seems to me, too, that the tent roof would have arisen almost of itself, in the first instance simply by giving the upper walls of the octagon an inward inclination until they met at a point. The clue is to be found in their horizontal structure which survives to this day in the older 'tents' (**71**). Refinements would have been introduced later by repeated trial and error. (It may be said in parenthesis that experiments with *reversed* pyramids were made too. They were in their nature unstable and bound to be short-lived. None survive, but seventeenth-century travellers recorded examples, like one visible in **85**.)

The 'sun ceiling', that is the false saucer-dome of the naos which often shuts off the empty spaces above, is another matter. I agree with Pettersson that this is a deliberate imitation of a masonry dome. Yet I feel it was needless to pin down the origin of such ceilings to Byzantine or Balkan ribbed domes built many centuries before, for they appear to be a relatively modern embellishment to the northern wooden churches. Moreover they are largely confined to the Lake Onega area – always, since the eighteenth century, in close touch with St Petersburg where Baroque domes were well known. One may add that anyone imitating a true dome in timber will resort to a framework of ribs almost of necessity. The same happened in Moldavia (p. 259).

An interesting and novel suggestion of Pettersson's was that the influence of German Gothic, penetrating via Novgorod, could be detected in northern wooden churches and belfries. Whether we think of their tent roofs or of the almost equally widespread wedge-shaped pitched roofs, they are often uncommonly steep. Precisely this steepness is attributed to Gothic influence, though one might argue that the same prevalence of heavy rain and deep snow which governed the development of these features in Germany did the same in Russia. It may also be, as suggested above, that tent roofs were of spire-like steepness from the beginning. I am inclined to this view, and see the tall spire as part and parcel of the Russians' urge to build tower-like churches, possibly as an expression of heavenly aspiration, possibly to contrast with the monotony of the forested plains, but certainly to ensure that a church should be visible from afar by travellers and pilgrims. I well remember steaming slowly up the Northern Dvina many years ago, when the top of a tall wooden tent roof appeared again and again over the trees, as the first sign of the next village.

Wooden belfries of the Russian north were thought by Pettersson to be inspired, one and all, by a specific German-built clock tower of 1436, still standing by the Bishop's Palace at Novgorod. The fact that its spire was originally wooden lends some support to the idea. True bell towers succeeded simpler bell-frames or bell-cots at an uncertain period, but none of those now standing are earlier than the mid seventeenth century, nor is there any reason to trace them back to the same early period as the tent church. So this theory of their origin may be substantiated when more is known, even though existing wooden towers bear little resemblance to the supposed prototype. The same author derives other church embellishments ultimately from Byzantine, Early Christian or even classical sources: such are the fretted bargeboards, 'gutter-boards' and matched roof-crestings found in Zaonezhie, chiefly in chapels of modern date. This attractive fretted woodwork closely resembles that found on larger wooden houses of the same area, and has much in common with corresponding adornments surviving today in many parts of central and eastern Europe. All these could owe something to the Byzantine tradition of south-eastern Europe, spreading in ever widening circles. But one wonders if craftsmen working in wood might not have arrived at very similar patterns independently in widely separated areas.

Next I must deal with the two most characteristic architectonic features of the north Russian wooden style – the bulbous dome and the 'barrel roof' or *bochka*. The origin and purposes of the bulb-shaped dome, that hallmark of Russian architecture in general, have been a subject of debate ever since the subject was first studied. Earlier writers proposed an Islamic origin for the bulb. Others suggested that it came in very late as one aspect of Baroque influence. But it would now be generally admitted that the bulb existed too early in Russia for this theory, and in any case the Russian and Baroque 'bulbs' are by no means identical in form. More probably these domes were evolved locally in response to climatic conditions: their steep sides, drawn out to a point at the top, as well as their overhang, helped to shed both rain and snow. The same is true of the *bochka*, a closely related form having the same ogee outline as the dome.

The ogee arch appears in a Russian stone church (at Yuriev Polsky) as early as the thirteenth century, and it seems that both bulbous domes and *bochki* (both of them ogees in profile) became widespread in Muscovite brick architecture from the late fourteenth century onwards. Domes, however, gradually lost their original significance, becoming little more than stalked ornaments set upon the church roof. These features may normally have been constructed on a wooden framework, but it does not necessarily follow that they were as yet absorbed into wooden architecture proper. Such frivolities, unjustified by constructional needs, would probably have been eschewed by the earlier builders in timber. They appear to have capitulated, however, in the sixteenth century. From then on these adornments were assimilated in earnest. Every roof, every tent tower, had to be crowned with a small bulb, while the *bochka* was employed almost as widely, especially for the roofs of sanctuaries and, in cruciform churches, for those of all four arms.

Another, more complicated problem is presented by the 'superposed' or superimposed *bochki* referred to above. The old view was that wooden 'tented' churches had not only influenced Muscovite masonry architecture in their general form but had also handed on specific details, notably the two or three tiers of *bochki* as at Una and Varzuga (**89**, **90**). These features were supposed to have been copied in the Muscovite

116 Kolomenskoye, Moscow. 'Tower' church dedicated to the Ascension, 1532.

117 Chernigov, Ukraine. Church of St Paraskeva (Pyatnitskaya Tserkov') as restored by P. D. Baranovsky. Late twelfth to early thirteenth century.

'tower' churches of the sixteenth century, especially Kolomenskoye (**116**), but the truth cannot be so simple. In the case of superposed *bochki*, it would be idle to claim a purely wooden origin for them, especially as they performed no special structural function in a wooden building.

While *bochki* may well have been invented and developed in wood, I believe that in their 'superimposed' form they betray the influence of a medieval Russian vaulting system. This system, dependent on 'encorbelled' arches, played an essential part in the roofing of brick-built churches and was often preferred to conventional vaulting. The church to be so vaulted was given four broad, round or segmental arches (or narrow barrel vaults) partly supported by the four outside walls and partly by internal piers (but the system could work without internal supports). A second series of four broad arches was 'corbelled out' from the first four, extending the vaulting inwards at a higher level, and a third series, again one step higher, would usually complete the vaulting and support the cupola. Externally these 'stepped' vaults, if left exposed as they originally were, could be both elegant and picturesque. Unfortunately they were seldom weather-proof and therefore almost always covered over at a later date by ugly hipped roofs through which the drum of the dome projects most awkwardly. In recent years, however, several such roofs have been restored to their original state, not only in Novgorod and Pskov (where they were once thought to have been invented) but in the Moscow area, in Smolensk, and as far south as the Kievan kingdom. An interesting example from the latter area is Professor Baranovsky's convincing restoration, undertaken in the 1940s after severe wartime damage, of an early church in Chernigov (**117**). Thus we know that models for multiple wooden *bochki* had been available at least since the thirteenth century and were widespread in Muscovy from the fifteenth century onwards. Their decorative value continued to be exploited in brick architecture up to the seventeenth century, after builders had ceased to employ the system as a constructional expedient. It is no wonder that these attractive forms appealed to the builders of wooden churches too, so superimposed *bochki* became acceptable in the northern forest zone, where single ones were no doubt already a familiar feature.

Evidently the traditional view, that the northern wooden style exerted an overwhelming influence upon the brick-built churches of Muscovy, must now be revised. These influences were reciprocal and could be reflected back and forth between the styles, as was indeed to be expected, in view of their overlapping range. Nevertheless it seems to me unquestionable that other major features of Muscovite architecture from the sixteenth century onwards are indeed attributable to the impact of timber-built forms: especially tall tent towers and decorative covered stairways and galleries. They first appear in the completely non-traditional 'tower' churches of Kolomenskoye (**116**), Dyakovo and Ostrovo in the Moscow area (now engulfed in greater Moscow). They appear too in that famous church of St Basil the Blessed in the Red Square, whose design includes five modified 'tents' in a cruciform layout with four more between the arms of the cross.

Thereafter, a compromise was established between traditional forms of Byzantine derivation and the intrusive elements originating in wooden architecture. The 'tower' churches did not survive as such in masonry but tent towers continued to crown many churches and virtually all belfries, which had become attached to the western end of the church much earlier than in the wooden style. The *kryltso* – the elegant covered stairway complex of the wooden churches – remained popular. The *bochka*, in whose development both wooden and masonry buildings had played a part, was used more and more for the adornment of roofs and towers, becoming indistinguishable from the small decorative arches which adorn the roofs of brick churches and are known as *kokoshniki*. With all these novel elements in their make-up, supplemented by the Ukrainian strain mentioned in Chapter 4, the charming and fanciful Muscovite masonry churches of the seventeenth century diverged widely from their early prototypes. To summarise, one can claim with confidence that these various elements of wooden origin ensured the final severance of Russian church architecture from the sober and logical ancestral style of Byzantium.

3

Ukrainian Galicia and Carpathia

This is the smallest of the main areas into which our subject matter is divided. In terms of modern geography it is however a complex area, including as it does parts of three east European States: Czechoslovakia, Poland and the Soviet Ukraine. Ethnologically it is more complex still, and the three different styles of wooden architecture that must be considered are associated with three different sections of the hill-dwelling Ukrainians or Ruthenians who form the majority of the population. Among minorities one must mention particularly the Hungarians and Rumanians in Trans-Carpathia (the latter very influential in the field of wooden architecture). In Slovakia and Poland the Ruthenians are of course themselves a minority.

Who are these hill-living Ukrainians, Ruthenians or Ruthenes? According to some accounts they are descended from successive waves of nomad herdsmen who, arriving from the south from the fifteenth century onwards, washed up against the Carpathians and tended to settle there. This movement was part of the Vlakh or Wallachian migration, which had already contributed its quota to the population of Rumanian Wallachia. Originating as residual groups of the ancient Thracians, these migrants also included Slav elements from the Balkans. In the Carpathian area there took place in due course an admixture of Ukrainians proper to whom these hill peoples became assimilated and who, at least since the last century, have claimed them all as Ukrainians. Indeed the word Ruthenian is often understood as a synonym of Ukrainian or Little Russian. But in the old kingdom of Hungary, and subsequently in the Austro-Hungarian empire as a whole, it simply meant the non-Catholic inhabitants of Slav affinities in the Galician–Carpathian region.

The political history of the area presents an equally confusing picture. In early historic times the State of Kiev-Rus' would doubtless have laid claim to any Slavs then living in the Carpathian region. But as early as the tenth century the Carpathian watershed had become something of a political barrier, Hungary claiming all territory to the south. To the north, on the other hand, the undulating plateau of eastern Galicia became, from the fifteenth century onward, the stage for Lithuanian and (after the union with Poland) for Polish expansionism. It was under the Polish regime, and with its approval and backing, that the west Ukrainian ecclesiastics, at the Synod of Brest (1596), concluded the union with the Church of Rome, thus establishing the first of the Uniate churches. In 1772 (at the first Partition of Poland) all Galicia was absorbed by that insatiable but relatively benign colossus, the Austro-Hungarian empire, of which it remained a part until the First World War.

After the war, despite short-lived hopes of an independent Ukraine of which Galicia would have formed an integral part, these territories were shared out between Poland and the new State of Czechoslovakia. The Carpathian watershed remained, or became again, the geographically convenient but otherwise artificial dividing line. Russia under its new revolutionary Government was debarred from any share of the spoils, though the Russians (with or without Ukrainian acquiescence) have always claimed Ukrainian territory. It was thus inevitable that Russia should seize the earliest opportunity to gain, or to regain, all the principal territories inhabited by Ukrainians. Their opportunity came, and their claim was duly conceded, after the Second World War. A broad strip of eastern Poland, with its huge Ukrainian population including some of the hill-dwelling Ruthenians (Boyks) to the south, reverted to Russia, as also did considerable parts of northern and eastern Rumania. Sub-Carpathian Ruthenia, which had never belonged to Russia, became Soviet Trans-Carpathia, an *oblast'* of the Ukraine. There remained, however, comparatively small Ukrainian enclaves in the Carpathians and their foothills further west: those north of the watershed are still in Poland, those to the south in Czechoslovakia.

This chapter deals, then, with the wooden churches of those Orthodox peoples, whether rightly called Ukrainians or not, who inhabit the Slavic sector of the eastern Carpathians and the undulating Galician plain to the north. The area extends from the south-eastern corner of Poland, and the contiguous parts of eastern Slovakia, through Soviet Trans-Carpathia to the Rumanian border. Here Rumanian influence has penetrated, adding yet another stylistic element to the architectural complexity of this small area. It is in these wooded hills and isolated valleys, especially among the Boyks, that traditional Slav rural culture remained relatively undisturbed despite all the political upheavals the region has suffered. It is here, therefore, that the basic forms of Slav architecture must be sought, and in this well forested country that architecture was, naturally enough, almost exclusively wooden. It will be left to the next chapter to follow up the evolution of church architecture in the Ukrainian plains to the north and east – a surprising development which owes its inception and its basic character to the beautiful but usually more modest buildings described in this chapter.

CHURCHES OF THE BOYKS AND THEIR KINDRED

It is logical to take these churches first since they seem to represent the aboriginal stock from which the styles of the Lemks, the Hutsuls and eventually the Ukrainian plainsmen developed. The Boyks, Boykians or Boyki have the reputation of being highly conservative, so the conservatism of their architecture forms only one aspect of this people's culture, long wedded to an ancestral, in some ways a primitive, life style. It must be pointed out, however, that a few churches mentioned here, though architecturally of Boyk character, may have been built by neighbouring Ruthene communities rather than by the Boyks themselves.

The Boyk homeland mainly occupies what is now the south-western corner of the Ukraine (territory which between the wars was assigned to Poland) together with the adjoining area to the west which still forms the south-east corner of Poland. On the Soviet side the districts around L'vov,* Busk and Ternopol' still contain an abundance of Boyk churches. They are likewise scattered throughout the foothill country extending thence to the Carpathians, including the districts of Sambor, Drogobych, Stryi, Galich and Ivano-Frankovsk (formerly Stanislavov). In the latter region Boyks and Hutsuls become intermixed, but some churches of more or less typical Boyk character occur further to the east, in and around Chortkov and as far away as Kamenets Podol'sky. Though Boyk villages occur south of the watershed in places (especially in the north-west corner of the region), it is the Lemks who take over in most of Soviet Trans-Carpathia.

Boyk churches, like all those dealt with in this chapter, follow the ancient Orthodox tradition in being divided into three sections. These are the pronaos or narthex (also called *babinets* or 'women's church'), the naos and (beyond the iconostasis) the sanctuary. Typically, a broad cupola or dome is raised upon each of these three sections and the leading characteristic of Boyk churches, distinguishing them sharply from those of the Lemks, is that the middle dome dominates, though seldom raised to any great height. Correspondingly, the central space or naos is a broader element in the plan than either the narthex or the sanctuary which adjoin it to west and east respectively. The visual impact of these churches, as of those in northern Russia, depends largely on roofs and domes, walls playing a minor role. Windows, therefore, contribute little to the general effect, but they do usually occur in pairs on the north and south walls of the naos, generally just above the roof of the surrounding gallery. This three-fold plan with separate domes is to be regarded as the standard arrangement in Boyk architecture. I shall therefore describe these churches first, leaving simplified versions with only one dome, or none at all, for later consideration. Finally, one or two abnormal categories will be mentioned.

A comprehensive range of Boyk ground plans, combined with roof plans, is shown in **118**. These illustrate many points and I shall refer to them frequently. It will be seen at once that all these churches are small, seldom exceeding 20 m in overall length: this is probably associated with the fragmentation of communities into small settlements in hill and forest country. It will also be noticed that the eastern extremities in several of the specimen plans are square, not apsidal: this is a very widespread (and probably archaic) characteristic of Boyk churches in general. Further, it can be seen that external covered galleries are present in every case, their low roofs being mostly supported on brackets made of projecting wall

*L'vov is the Russian form. The others are L'viv (Ukrainian), Lwów (Polish), Lemberg (German) and Leopol (French).

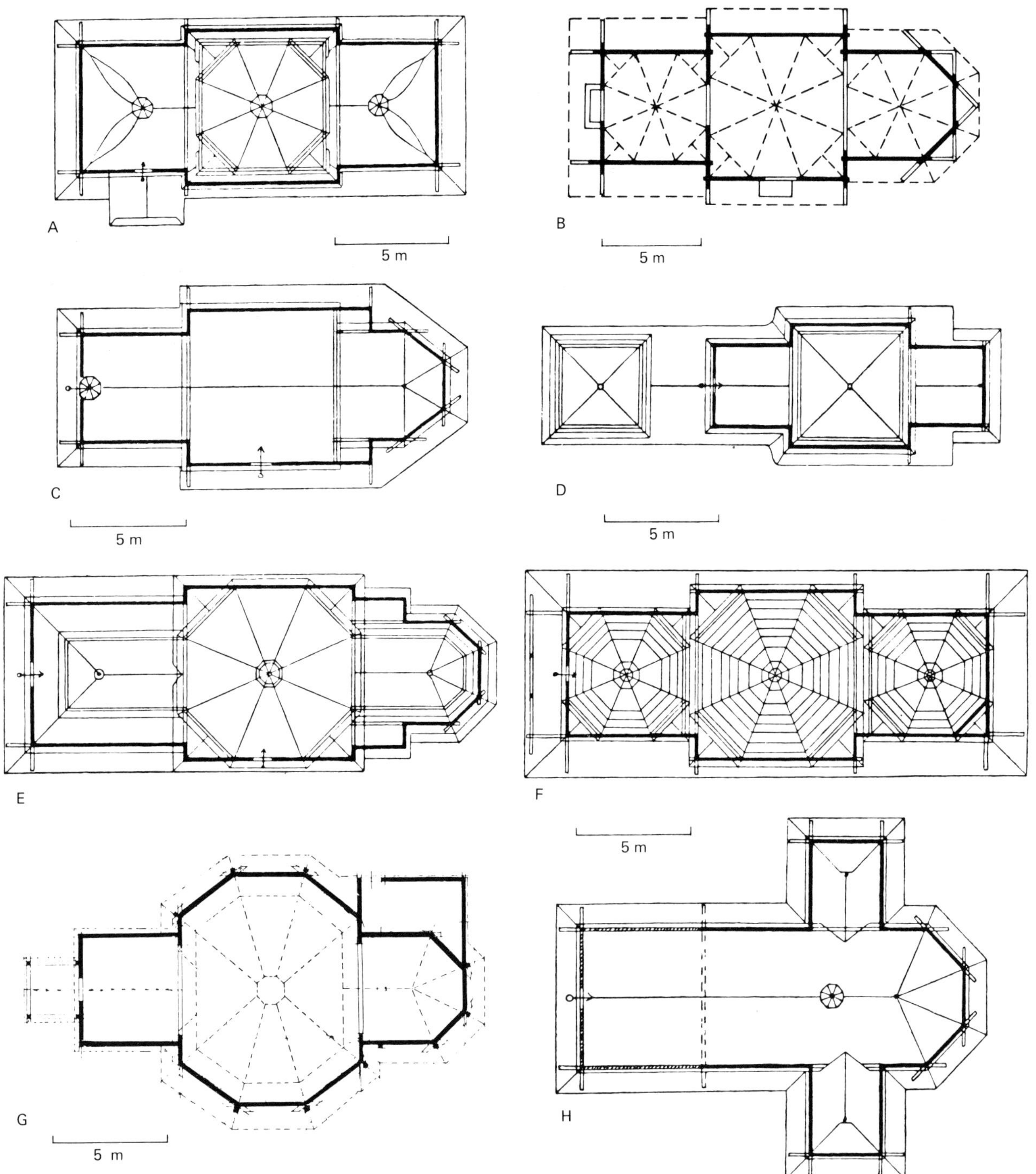

118 Boyk ground and roof plans. A. Biała Czortkowska. B. Gorodok. C. Mostiska. D. Niklowice. E. Sudovaya Vyshnia. F. Matkov. G. Busk. H. Village near Rudki.

timbers (**46**) while others rely wholly or in part on upright posts. The former type of gallery is known in Ukrainian as *opasannya*, the latter as *piddashya*, words which will sometimes be used again for lack of English equivalents. Whichever method of roof support is used, it can be said that the external covered walk is an essential feature of Boyk churches, one which is generally lost in those of the Lemks and in the towering creations of Ukrainian architecture to be discussed in the next chapter.

With few (and late) exceptions the Boyks remained faithful to the old log or blockwork technique which was the common legacy of all the Slavs. One can practically always be sure, even where walls or roofs are concealed by shingles, that they are built up of heavy horizontal timbers jointed at the corners; no framed timber, no raftering of roofs, will be found. Boyk carpenters were masters of all the subtleties of their traditional technique. Walls could be made to converge, and then to rise vertically again; they could be inclined inwards at an increasing angle until they met in the middle line in the form of a vault; or the basic rectangle could be converted at will to an octagon, rising vertically in the form of a drum to be crowned by its broad-based dome.

All wooden churches are extremely perishable. It is doubtful if any of those built by the Boyks date, in their present form, from before the seventeenth century and the majority belong to the eighteenth. Yet they must have been built since the earliest Christian times – about the eighth century in these parts – and no doubt pagan places of worship were being constructed in timber long before that. There are few clues to the aboriginal appearance of such early churches, but in existing ones we can at least distinguish their simpler and presumably earlier elements from those developed later. Thus the faceted or polygonal apse must have been adopted long after the square eastern termination. As far as the superstructure is concerned, one can safely assume that the transition from square to octagon was a comparatively late development; therefore the eight-sided pyramidal roof appeared later than the simple four-sided pyramid, and the dome later than either. Another innovation was the alterna-

119 Cherche, south-western Ukraine. St Basil the Great, 1648. Southern aspect.

120 Gusnoye, Trans-Carpathia. St Nicholas, 1659, from the north.

tion of vertical and sloping sections in roofs, leading to their charming variegation, with tier upon tier of eaves (a 'break' in a roof is locally called a *zalom*, a term I shall use again). It should be added that though domes, eventually bulbous ones, came to be accepted by the Boyks, no real Baroque features penetrated their architecture, except for internal fittings, especially the iconostasis.

Acting on these various assumptions, I can assert that the village church at Cherche (region of Ivano-Frankovsk) is, despite its multiple eaves, the rare survival of an early type, without either octagons or domes, or faceted apse (**119**). Its east and west ends are almost symmetrical. It possesses the obligatory surrounding walkway or *opasannya*, its low roof supported on brackets composed of the structural timbers themselves. As usual, these wall timbers are left exposed under the shelter of the gallery roof whereas at higher levels they are shingled as a protection against the elements. It is interesting to compare the Trans-Carpathian church of Gusnoye, likewise of the mid seventeenth century: here the east and west cupolas are plain pyramids on a square base, but the central one is converted to an octagon (**120**).

Simple pyramidal roofs are retained in many other churches, sometimes in conjunction with features which cannot be regarded as primitive. The 'upper' church of the Assumption at Turka (see below) is one of these: its western division, though barely enlarged, is modified as a belfry (**150** A). Another example is the church from Grąziowo on the Polish side of the border, moved in 1968 to the open-air museum at Sanok, where it is most tastefully positioned (**121**, **122**). It combines an early roof form in the middle, and a rectangular apse, with a two-storeyed pronaos – certainly a comparatively late innovation. This provides an upper chamber for the women of the congregation, who however could observe the progress of the mass only through a narrow slit in its eastern wall. The open gallery which surrounds this upper chamber on three sides partly overhangs the roomy porch space below. The porch and adjacent galleries are here roofed with the aid of stout wooden posts, their place being taken by brackets or consoles at the eastern end of the building. In Ukrainian terminology, the *piddashya* to the west becomes an *opasannya* to the east. Inside, one's attention is at once attracted by a luxuriant Baroque iconostasis (**123**) which will be referred to again at the end of this chapter. A last example drawn from churches of this category is that at Skoriki in western Podolia. Here the cupolas are uniformly octagonal and crowned with eight-sided pyramids (**124**).

We can now trace the transformation of pyramidal roofs into well defined domes (I ignore the miniature domes perched on the summit of such roofs – these are subsequent additions). At Krekhov (L'vov area) the eight-sided pyramids are bulging and beginning to

121 Boyk church from Grąziowo, 1731, eastern aspect. Now at Sanok.

wear the aspect of a dome (**125**). At Chotyniec (Poland, north-east of Przemyśl) there is no doubt about it: the roofs are converted into domes (**126**). As can be seen, this is another of the churches with two-storeyed pronaos. At Piątkowa (Poland) the church, lost in the jungle like a fairy-tale palace, has still better defined domes of depressed bulbous form. It is unusual in possessing masonry piers for roof support in the surrounding *piddashya* (**127**).

Judging by photographs (for foreign visitors are not allowed) one of the most notable of Boyk churches is the one originally built at Dolina in the sixteenth century but moved to Drogobych and re-constructed there with modifications between 1652 and 1656. This church of St George has very well defined domes raised on rather tall drums, the western one surmounting the upper chamber of the pronaos, whose arcade matches the arcading of the external gallery below (**128**). Additional small domes crown side-chapels on the north and south sides, chapels whose projection makes the plan slightly cruciform. Another wooden church (**134**) and, all told, three wooden belfries, make up a unique timber-built complex in this small town.

Many elegant churches continued to be built in this style through the eighteenth and well into the nineteenth century. Ignoring for the moment the more outlandish, which will be referred to later, I

122 Grąziowo from the south-west.

123 Grąziowo. Part of the iconostasis.

124 Church at Skoriki, Podolia, from the north-east, seventeenth century.

must mention here an exceedingly attractive late-eighteenth-century example standing near the village of Równia in Polish territory (**129**). The central octagon with its *zalomy* has extra eaves below the dome and its east and west sections, both square, terminate in beautiful cupolas, more like bells than domes. It has tremendous cantilevered brackets to support the low roof of the *opasannya* (**46**). Such churches represent a very strong tradition, and continued to be built until quite recent times. Those now being maintained in Poland can be visited without any trouble or formality, though some are difficult to find. On the Soviet side, at least two can be seen by travellers driving eastward from the Polish border through the Ukraine: one at Gorodok (Polish Gródek) between the frontier and L'vov (**130**), and another, still in use as a church, at Kizlov west of Busk (**131**). I must admit, however, that neither of these churches is very typical of traditional Boyk architecture: their vertical emphasis, shared by some late churches in Polish territory, betrays east Ukrainian influence.

Many Boyk churches fall short of the standard pattern described above in that they possess but a single external cupola – always the middle one – and even that may be almost eliminated. These reduced versions do not seem to represent an early condition

125 Krekhov. St Paraskeva, 1654, from the south-east.

126 Chotyniec, Rzeszów province, Poland. Church originally built 1613.

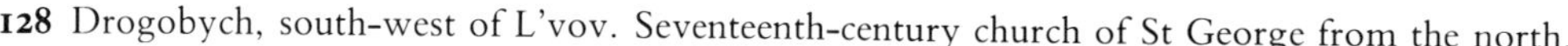

128 Drogobych, south-west of L'vov. Seventeenth-century church of St George from the north.

127 Piątkowa, west of Przemyśl, Poland. South side of the church built 1732.

129 Równia, near Ustrzyki Dolne, Poland. South-eastern view of late-eighteenth-century church.

130 Gorodok, west of L'vov, Ukraine. Former Uniate church.

131 Church at Kizlov, north-east of L'vov.

132 Sokolov. St Nicholas, 1733. Now in the L'vov open-air museum.

133 Chortkov. Eighteenth-century church of the Assumption. South-west view.

which led on later to the greater elaboration of a three-domed plan, but rather a secondary simplification. In most cases the need for economy would have been enough to dictate the adoption of a simpler design. But it does not follow that these churches compare unfavourably with the fully developed model. On the contrary, some of them are an aesthetic delight and, despite their small size, possess the monumental quality of which Strzygowski wrote.

The open-air museum at L'vov contains a wooden church from Sokolov, in the country south of Ternopol', which seems as greatly simplified as a church could be (**132**). Were it not for the miniature stalked dome perched on the principal roof it might almost be mistaken for a house. But the two subsidiary gabled roofs, symmetrically placed to east and west of the higher middle one, and the surrounding *opasannya*, are clues to the real nature of the building. Evidently its parent community could not muster the resources for anything more elaborate or more church-like. One of the wooden churches at Chortkov (also south of Ternopol') hardly even differentiates between the roofs of the different sections (**133**). But a miniature cupola

134 Drogobych. Church of the Raising of the Cross, 1613.

over the naos and a cross standing near by prove again that the structure is a church.

More pleasing to the eye are those churches where a well defined, domed central element is adjoined to east and west by ridged roofs, often of 'hipped' pattern with faceted ends. In the second church at Drogobych, that of the Raising of the Cross, the central element is square with a basically pyramidal roof (**134**). At Poździacz (near Przemyśl, almost on the Soviet frontier) is an attractive specimen whose central element converts to a short octagonal drum carrying a typical broad-based Boyk dome (**135**). I found a similar church, concealed and yet revealed by a tell-tale clump of trees on a knoll, near Busk in the western Ukraine (**136**) and another from that area is now rebuilt, with its free-standing belfry, in the open-air museum at Kiev (**137–138**). It can be seen that these examples show the same gradations between pyramids and domes as were pointed out earlier. One of the most beautiful churches of this type stands at Ulucz, north of Sanok (Poland), the goal, for me, of a long walk down the San valley. Of sixteenth-century origin, the church probably attained its present form in the seventeenth century, the comparatively simple iconostasis being of that period (**139**, **140**). The interior photograph shows also the timbering of the

135 Poździacz. Former church of St Basil, 1777, from the south-west.

136 Village church near Busk in Galicia.

137 Village church from Zelenoye, near Ternopol', 1817. Now in the Kiev open-air museum.

138 The bell tower from Zelenoye.

roofs, the arched partition between narthex and naos, and the conversion of the latter to an octagon. Externally, the western roof is the special feature, combining in one great sweep the main roof and that of the external gallery. Its widely spreading eaves find support, at the western end, in a columned arcade.

Among the Boyks (and the same is true of the Hutsuls) the bell tower is normally a separate structure, sometimes of monumental proportions. A splendid example from Yashenitsa Zamkova is shown in **141**: its three arcaded storeys are almost unique. A modern one in a different but genuine tradition stands at Klimets, a high village in the Carpathians (**142**). In a few untypical cases belfries were attached to the western extremity of a Boyk church, so adding a fourth element to the linear composition (**118** D). In other places – probably under the influence of neighbouring Lemk communities – churches with three cupolas have the western one adapted as a belfry and built in framed timber instead of blockwork. Examples are

139 Ulucz, on the San north of Sanok. Church of the sixteenth/seventeenth century, north-western aspect.

140 Ulucz. Seventeenth-century iconostasis.

141 Storeyed belfry at Yashenitsa Zamkova, Sambor district of Galicia.

143 Uzhok in Trans-Carpathia. St Michael's, 1745.

142 Modern belfry at Klimets in the Carpathians.

found in the north-western corner of Soviet Trans-Carpathia in the hill village of Uzhok (**143**) and at Turka a little further north (**150** A). Kostrino, in the same area, approximates to the Lemk type (**171** D). At Rudka, north of Przeworsk (Poland), I have seen a charming Boyk-type church which shows the same characteristic – in fact the belfry appears slightly taller than the central cupola (**144–145**). This is a miniature church, the main structure being under 15 m long, with a ground plan almost identical to **118** C though the roofs are very different.

The theme of the incorporated belfry brings us to what is possibly the culminating achievement of Boyk architecture. I refer to the extraordinary church brought to L'vov by the Poles in 1928–30 from the village of Krivka, just north of the Carpathian watershed. The drawing (**146**), taken from an old photograph, shows it in its native place in the hills. It now forms the nucleus and the show-piece of the open-air museum established around it at L'vov under Soviet auspices. The late-eighteenth-century architect, while retaining a purely traditional, even archaic ground plan (similar to **118** F), tried to outdo all the efforts of his predecessors. Influenced perhaps by the much taller wooden towers of contemporary east Ukrainian churches (see next chapter), he raised his three cupolas to an unaccustomed height, the central one (still the

144 Rudka, Rzeszów province. Seventeenth-century church from south-east.

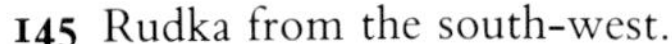

145 Rudka from the south-west.

146 The church of St Nicholas as it stood originally at Krivka in the Carpathians. 1763.

tallest) measuring 17 m (**147–149**). Instead of two or three 'breaks' in the roofs (*zalomy*) he found room for five, and the numerous superimposed eaves give the effect of an oriental pagoda. The narthex has an upper storey with external arcade and, in addition, its cupola served as a belfry. At first-storey level each tower is reduced to an octagon, rising then in steps, to be capped by a bulbous dome.

The main structure and the central and eastern towers are of blockwork throughout. The western tower, however, introduces an element of make-believe: while appearing identical to the other two its upper, octagonal storeys are in fact of framed construction and designed to house the bell chamber (section, **150** B). The openings of the bell chamber had been closed at some period, thus completing the deception, but are revealed again in the building as now re-erected. At ground level there are further interesting details. At the western end, a spacious porch shelters the only door into the church (**151**). Here the wooden uprights with their connecting arches and the cantilevered brackets which jointly support the roof all exhibit decorative carving. The fact that such adornments are not confined to churches is well illustrated by a superb Boyk house from the Skole district of Cis-Carpathia which has been set up near by (**152**). Though of traditional character it was built as recently as 1910.

147 St Nicholas from Krivka now standing in the L'vov open-air museum. South side.

148 Krivka. North-western aspect.

149 Krivka. Upper gallery and belfry surmounting the narthex.

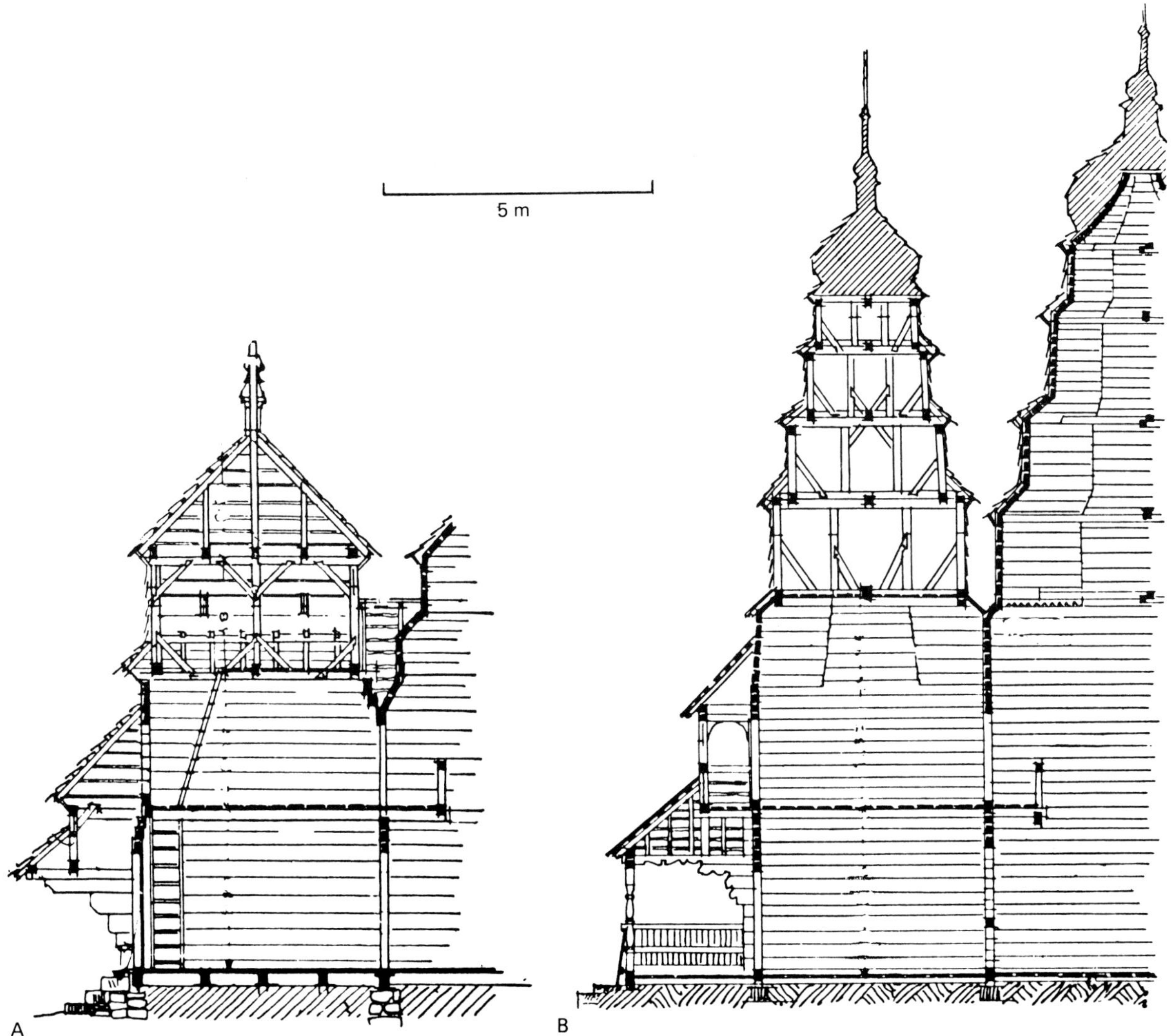

150 Longitudinal sections through narthex and belfry. A. Turka. B. Krivka.

The Krivka church deviates widely from the architectural tradition of sobriety and modesty which is proper to the Boyks. Whether it should be regarded as an outrage or a major masterpiece, or some amalgam of both, must be left to the individual taste and judgment. It certainly inspired a number of successors including what is almost a replica in the neighbouring village of Matkov, west of Tukholka on the main road across the Carpathians (**153**). Still later, but more satisfactory with its well controlled proportions, is the church from Tisovets in the northern Carpathian foothills. Built in 1863 its craftsmanship shows a decline from eighteenth-century standards; it is none the less an exquisite building, re-erected in 1972 in the L'vov open-air museum (**154–155**). The modern wooden church at Verkhnee Sinevidnoye in the same area as Tisovets, close to the trans-Carpathian highway, makes a striking picture viewed from a distance on its hill-top (**156**). It may be cited as belonging (subject, however, to grave deterioration) to the same tradition.

It remains to note that occasional Boyk churches approach the cruciform plan which the Hutsuls, above all, have made their own. The naos of the wooden church at Busk and one of those at Chortkov have faceted extensions bulging out to north and south (**118** G, **157**). Others, like a cemetery church in Podgortsy (near Drogobych), are properly cruciform (**158**). However, the trend towards a real confusion of styles becomes marked only in very recent times. An instance of this occurs at Nižný Komárnik, north-east of Svidník in Slovakia (**159**). The church, evidently built in the present century, is of Boyk character, but stands in a Lemk village.

151 Krivka. Western porch with doorway to the narthex.

152 House from Tukholka, Skole district, south-west of L'vov. 1910.

153 Matkov in the Carpathians. Church of the Nativity, 1838.

154 Tisovets, Skole district, church of 1863 from the north-west. Now in the L'vov museum.

155 Tisovets: south-east corner with corner-jointing and consoles for support of eaves.

156 Modern church at Verkhnee Sinevidnoye near Skole.

157 Chortkov. Church of the Ascension, 1738, from south-west.

158 Podgortsy. Cruciform cemetery church, 1720.

CHURCHES OF THE HUTSULS

The Hutsuls live partly in the eastern end of Soviet Trans-Carpathia (Czechoslovak between the world wars) along the headwaters of the Tissa. Further north, on the other side of the Carpathians, they mostly inhabit the country between the 'Black' Bistritz (a tributary of the Dniester) to the west, and the Cheremosh (a tributary of the Pruth) to the east: this area belonged to Poland between the wars. Some lived further east in north-eastern Bukovina, Rumanian between the wars. Obviously national boundaries have never taken the slightest account of Hutsul territory. Since the Second World War, however, virtually the whole of it has come under Soviet rule. Unfortunately foreigners are not admitted to the Hutsul homeland, and cannot get nearer to it than Chernovtsy (Rumanian Cernăuţi). Material on their wooden churches is therefore more than usually difficult to come by.

These Hutsul churches, unlike those of the Boyks and Lemks, are nearly always of cruciform plan with five divisions instead of three (**160**). Why they adopted this layout, while their near relatives of the other Ruthenian groups generally avoided it, is by no means clear. One may think in terms of possible Byzantine antecedents, but the area where the Hutsuls now live provides no obvious stone prototypes. They did not arrive there, it is true, until the late Middle

159 Nižný Komárnik, eastern Slovakia. Modern church of Boyk style.

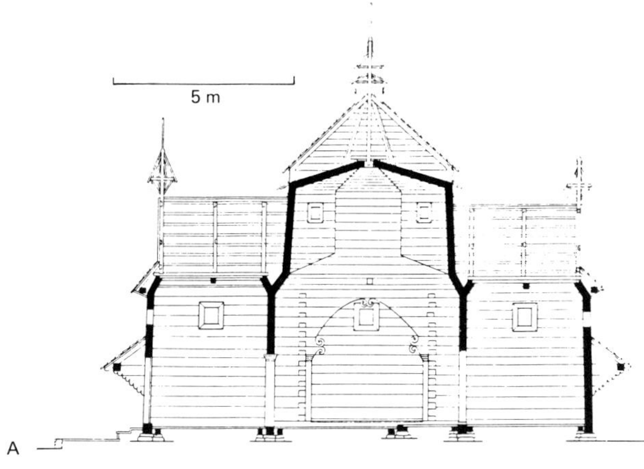

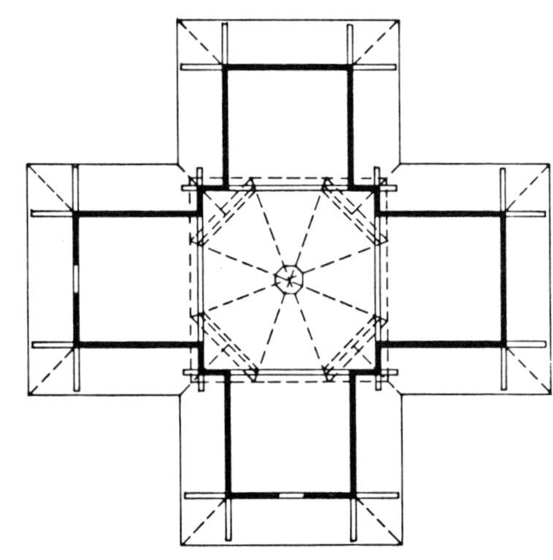

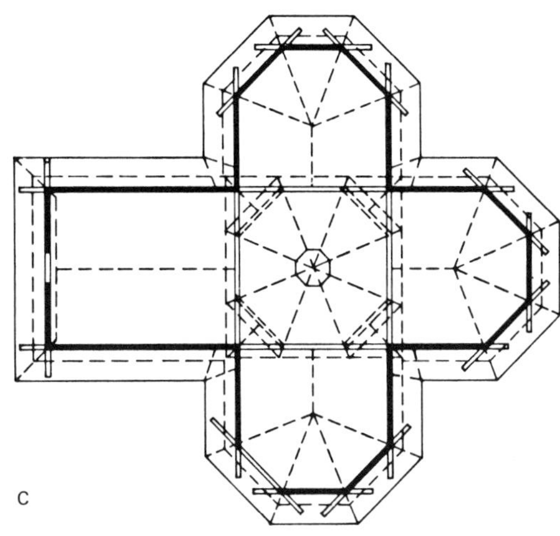

160 Hutsul section and plans. A. Yasinya, section. B. Plan type with squared arms (as Delyatin and Yasinya). C. With faceted arms (as Nadvornaya etc.).

Ages, but we do not know if their wooden churches reach back even that far. It could be suggested that the Hutsuls were at one time more prosperous than their neighbours and could therefore afford the more complex plan, so easily derived from the linear arrangement of three elements in a row. Or again, their settlements may have been more concentrated, so that bigger churches were required, but fewer of them. All these are speculations. In any event, the Hutsuls' adoption of the cruciform plan paralleled, and must have been connected with, the same tendency among the colonists of the 'free Ukraine' beyond the Dnieper. There it becomes the basis of the Ukrainians' most spectacular wooden churches, as shown in the next chapter.

It is probable that simple churches resembling those of the Boyks would have preceded the development in Hutsul country of the cruciform plan, which may have happened no earlier than the seventeenth century. Some churches of this simpler sort probably still stand. However, I can only adduce an intermediate type to underline the probability. This is a church illustrated by Mokłowski at Rovno (Bukovina) whose naos, much like those at Busk and Chortkov, has polygonal, apse-like extensions to north and south, adumbrating a cruciform plan (**161** and **118** G). The other examples illustrated in **160** show the cross fully developed, the north and south arms being approximately equal in size to the narthex (west arm) and sanctuary (east arm). As the two plans show, these churches, like those of the Boyks, have an *opasannya* running all round, its roof supported on brackets built up from the projecting wall timbers. It will also be seen that there are variations depending on whether the arms are square-ended or polygonal. These plans both relate to single-domed churches, one of these (Yasinya) being also seen in section (**160** A). Other examples have domes on each arm as well, making five in all.

The churches at Yasinya and Vorokhta (**162–163**), the former south and the latter north of the main Carpathian range, are both good typical examples of the single-domed model with square-ended arms. They differ of course in proportions; also in the fact that Yasinya has the plan of **160** B, its arms joining the residual central square independently, while at Vorokhta no central square remains, which makes for economy in building. The old illustration (**164**) shows an unidentified but certainly Hutsul church which almost matches plan **160** C, though its west arm too (facing the onlooker) appears to be polygonal and there are subsidiary domes on the arms. As far as I know the churches at Yezupol and Knyazhdvor no longer exist (**165–166**). The drawings are included as

161 Rovno (Bukovina). Semi-cruciform church.

examples of the more pretentious Hutsul church with five fully formed cupolas. Yezupol, where the four domes on the arms were clearly subordinate to the central one, made a not unpleasing composition. Knyazhdvor, on the other hand, where the lofty central cupola was jostled by four others almost as tall, must have been an artistic disaster.

In modern times Hutsul architecture must have made a strong impression on architects seeking inspiration for wooden churches elsewhere. The result has been the appearance of Hutsul-style churches in areas where they do not belong. I give two examples, both from Boyk country: a late-nineteenth-century one from Hoszów near Ustrzyki Dolne (Poland) and a probably still later five-domed structure at Kozevo in Soviet territory, on the main road across the Carpathians (**167–168**).

162 Yasinya, Rakhov district of eastern Trans-Carpathia. Church of the Ascension, 1824.

163 Vorokhta on the Pruth. Church of the Nativity of the Virgin. Eighteenth century.

164 Unknown Hutsul church of eastern Galicia, western view. Eighteenth century?

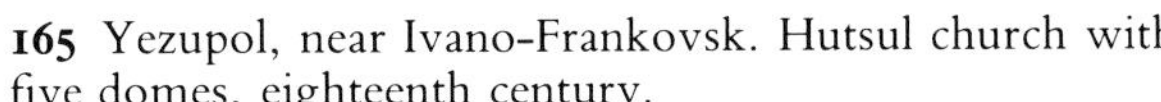

165 Yezupol, near Ivano-Frankovsk. Hutsul church with five domes, eighteenth century.

166 Knyazhdvor, near Kolomya. Five-domed Hutsul church of 1778.

167 Hutsul-style church at Hoszów, south-east Poland. Late nineteenth century.

169 Hutsul belfry at Yasinya. Late eighteenth century?

168 Kozevo in the Soviet Carpathians. Modern Hutsul-style church in Boyk country.

170 Mikulichin, south of Kolomya. Eighteenth-century Hutsul bell tower.

The Hutsuls did not adapt any cupolas of their churches for bells. Belfries stood separately, and some of them, while not differing essentially from those of the Boyks, are among the most imposing ever built in the Ukrainian lands. A great number have been lost, but two fine examples, both thought to be still standing, are illustrated here: Yasinya (next to the church in **162**) and Mikulichin, from the country south of Kolomya (**169**, **170**).

CHURCHES OF THE LEMKS

It is a fact not fully explained that the Lemks (or Lemkians or Lemki), in contrast to their neighbours and kinsmen the Boyks, were quite open to new ideas and influences. In church architecture, those closely related peoples developed styles which are surprisingly different, in that the Boyk style remained static while that of the Lemks, stimulated by outside influences, evolved. In brief, the latter acquired a tall western tower which dominates the whole composition. But both the nature of the towers and the method of mounting them was influenced in the east by Transylvania, in the west by Poland.

These trends in Lemk architecture, probably of fairly recent origin, can be explained in part by their geographical position. Lemks form the bulk of the population of Trans-Carpathia (now Soviet) and have thus been in contact, to the south, with Transylvania and Hungary, from both of which lands the Boyks, mostly living north of the Carpathian watershed, were insulated. Moreover Lemk villages extend much further west than those of the Boyks, both on the Slovak and the Polish side of the hills. They reach almost as far west as the town of Nowy Sącz (Novy Sonch) south-east of Cracow, and thus have long had relations with the Catholic Poles. Throughout their range, in fact, the Lemks were in closer touch with foreign peoples than the Boyks could ever have been. Such contacts may well have been stimulated by a common allegiance to the Pope after the western Ukrainian and Trans-Carpathian Churches accepted the suzerainty of Rome (1596 and after). Political unity may have been another, if only minor factor, since the whole area formed part of the Austro-Hungarian empire throughout the seventeenth and eighteenth centuries.

Lemk master craftsmen, therefore, could have wandered far enough afield to see with their own eyes both Gothic and Baroque churches in Poland, in Hungary proper and in the cities of the Transylvanian Germans. They would certainly have seen the earlier attempts of their neighbours, the Rumanian villagers of Maramureş, on the Transylvanian borders, to interpret these churches in timber. I suspect that this contact was particularly fruitful, but they were seemingly impressed above all by the charms of the Baroque tower which was to become a special feature of their own style.

We must consider the early development of these western belfries, which unlike the remainder of the building are of framed construction. In central and eastern Lemk country they are mounted, Rumanian fashion, on the horizontal beams of the narthex ceiling. The tendency is first seen in some Boyk examples already mentioned above, as at Turka and Uzhok in the upper basin of the River Uzh, near the Polish and Trans-Carpathian borders (**143**, **150** A). Another at Sukhoy, with further developed western tower, is illustrated by Makushenko who does not specify whether it is Boyk or Lemk (**171** A). There is also Kostrino which has been quoted as Boyk in one publication and as Lemk in another, the latter attribution being probably correct (**171** D). This all goes to show that such churches are of intermediate character. They

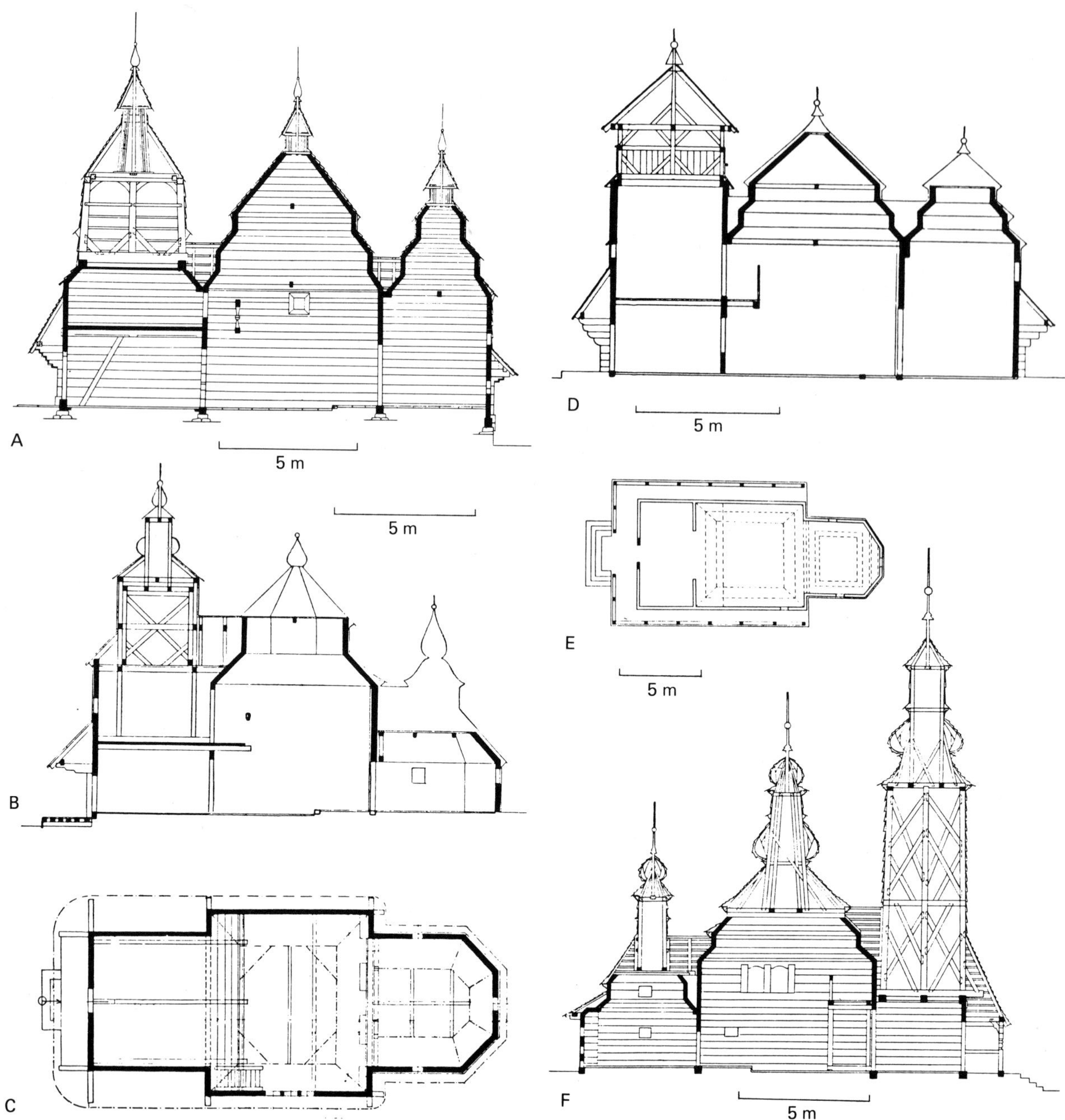

171 Development of the western tower in the eastern Carpathian area. A. Sukhoy (Soviet Trans-Carpathia), west–east section. B, C. Nová Sedlica (eastern Slovakia), west–east section and plan. D. Kostrino (Trans-Carpathia), west–east section. E, F. Kanora (Trans-Carpathia), plan and east–west section.

could pass as examples of either style, but they mark the parting of the ways. As soon as the western belfry becomes appreciably taller than the central cupola, as at Kostrino, the traditional balance of the Boyk church is disturbed and one suspects the influence of the Lemks. The history of their architecture, in fact, consists mainly in the increasing prominence given to the western tower. It brings with it not only a change of balance, but a change of mood. The Boyk church with its subdued symmetrical profile is peaceful and restful; the Lemk church expresses animation and movement.

The central area just spoken of is shared between Soviet Trans-Carpathia and Slovakia, and Lemk villages occur on both sides of the frontier: their churches are of course closely related and cannot be treated apart. On one of the tributaries of the Uzh coming in from the Slovak side, but very close to the Soviet border, there are two villages, Zboj and Nová Sedlica, which both possessed notable wooden churches. In

172 Nová Sedlica, eastern border of Slovakia. Lemk church, eighteenth-century, from the south.

1973 the former had been removed and re-erected at Bardejovské Kúpele; the latter was still *in situ* but its removal too appeared to be imminent (**171** B, C and **172**). These two very similar buildings seem to represent an intermediate stage in the development of a fully fledged Lemk church. In plan they resemble the commonest of Boyk models. The western tower, while Baroque in its detail, has not yet shot up to the imposing height which fashion demanded later in the century but the way it is mounted on the ceiling beams of the pronaos already links it with the eastern, Rumanian-influenced group. The naos and sanctuary cupolas are quite separate but relatively simple, the former an octagon surmounting a square, the latter a small octagon on its own, crowning the polygonal apse. The lowest roof, that of the *opasannya*, surrounds the entire church while the next one above it unites pronaos and naos; the proportions and articulation of the whole building are most satisfying.

One has to enter Soviet territory to examine the finest of these churches in the Mukachevo area. This is in fact the heart of Lemk country, and Mukachevo was the seat of their Orthodox (later Uniate) bishop from the fifteenth century onwards. A particularly beautiful example of a fully fledged Lemk church (and at present the only one in Soviet Trans-Carpathia that foreign travellers can hope to see) was built in the village of Shelestovo, north of Mukachevo, in 1777. Early photographs show it partially plastered over and whitewashed. In 1927, under the Czechoslovak regime, it was taken down and re-erected in Mukachevo. There it stood until about 1974 when it was again dismantled, to be restored and re-erected for the second time at Uzhgorod. It occupies a place of honour in the open-air museum there (**173–175**). A sister church, differing only in detail, still stands at Kanora, high in the hills to the north-east of Mukachevo (**176**).

The plan and section reproduced in **171** E, F indicate how, under the influence of big towers, the pronaos of these churches has been broadened to equal the width of the naos. These two elements together (but not the sanctuary) are surrounded by an open gallery or

173 Shelestovo, now Uzhgorod. Church of the Archangel Michael, 1777, from south-east.

174 Church of the Archangel Michael, western aspect.

175 Church of the Archangel Michael, outer gallery on north side of nave.

176 Kanora in the Soviet Carpathians. St Nicholas, 1792, from the north-east.

177 Chernogolovye, district of Velikobereznyanka. Church of 1794, from the north.

piddashya forming a wide porch at the west end, roofed with the aid of carved posts joined by a balustrade. The tower, of framed timbers throughout, rises vertically from the pronaos ceiling, a projecting bell chamber being present at Shelestovo only. At the summit there follow the twisting curves of a Baroque spirelet, complete with lantern. The middle and eastern roofs are stepped pyramids, the former with two or three breaks or *zalomy*, the latter with one, and the resulting multitude of shingled roofs and domes, with their amply projecting eaves, give a marvellously rich effect (compare **56**). It might be thought that a Baroque

178 Topol'a, eastern Slovakia. Late-seventeenth-century church.

tower would combine ill with the traditional pyramidal roof of the early Boyk model. However, the matching bulbous domes which crown all three elements give a measure of unity to the whole, and this unification is carried further in the western (Slovak) examples to be cited later.

It should not be assumed that all churches from this central area are so fully developed. Many are in fact of much more modest pretensions, possessing a common roof for the two western or even all three divisions. Such churches have a Baroque tower at the western end of the roof and a miniature cupola or *Dachreiter* at its eastern extremity. In marked contrast to the Boyk tradition, where the middle element would always be emphasised, we see here how it is the western tower that enjoys priority and, however greatly reduced, cannot possibly be dispensed with. Examples are plentiful, on both sides of the border. On the Soviet side an attractive one stands at Chernogolovye where the principal roof and that of the outside gallery merge to form a single western roof under the Baroque tower (**177**). On the Slovak side minor churches, while similar in concept, tend to be further simplified, as can be seen from the examples of Topol'a, Hrabová Roztoka and Uličské Krivé (**178–180**). Details of their structure are shown in a view of the western end of the latter church and the eastern end of the neighbouring, almost identical one at Ruský Potok (**181–182**).

To continue this survey we must now travel, in imagination, south-eastwards through Soviet Trans-Carpathia parallel to the crest of the hills. It is an area abounding in wooden churches which come increasingly under Rumanian (or more precisely Transylvanian) influence. I illustrate some striking – even extraordinary – examples from villages on the northern

179 Hrabová Roztoka, eastern Slovakia. Orthodox church of the mid eighteenth century.

180 Uličské Krivé, near the Slovak–Soviet border. Church of 1718 from the south-west.

tributary streams of the Tissa. The first, beautifully embowered among trees, is a church from Rostoka in the upper valley of the Rika (**183**); the others, Kolochava and Kolodnoye (**184–185**), are from the next parallel valley of the Terebla. Their middle and eastern sections have straight, steep, ridged roofs instead of separate cupolas, though Rostoka is said to retain a domed structure, visible only inside. The straight roofs at two levels are very Rumanian, so are the handsome porches with upper arcade at Kolochava and Kolodnoye, so is the method of mounting the uprights of the towers on cross-beams of the pronaos ceiling. A few churches in these valleys even have Gothic-type spires hardly distinguishable from Transylvanian ones, but the favourite Baroque towers have a more decidedly local, and Lemk, character.

Passing finally, on this dream journey, to the southern limits of Soviet Trans-Carpathia we would find ourselves in the main valley of the Tissa. Here, around and between the small towns of Khust, Tyachev and Rakhov, is the source of the powerful Transylvanian influence we have been noticing. This is in fact the northern half of Maramureş (or Maramaros), a largely Rumanian area, though severed from the remainder of the district (only just across the Tissa) since 1918. The wooden churches here are purely Rumanian, belonging to the Gothic-inspired style of northern Transylvania, and will therefore be dealt with in Chapter 5.

From the heartland of the Lemks, bisected by the Soviet–Slovak frontier, we have explored south-eastwards; it remains now to follow up their settlements and their churches in a westerly direction. The Lemks in fact long since extended their range westward along the Carpathians to form a discontinuous belt between

181 Ruský Potok, a church of 1740 very similar to Uličské Krivé. Detail of faceted apse at the east end.

182 Uličské Krivé. Detail of west end.

183 Rostoka, Mezhgorsk district of Soviet Trans-Carpathia. Church of the Presentation of the Virgin Mary, 1759.

184 Kolochava, Mezhgorsk district. Eighteenth-century church of the Holy Ghost.

185 Kolodnoye, Tyachev district. St Nicholas, seventeenth century. Moved to new site, 1800.

Slovaks to the south and Poles to the north. On the Slovak side, where the Ruthenian population is still numerous, such enclaves can be recognised superficially by the appearance of village names and other signs in the Cyrillic alphabet. The principal Lemk areas are centred on the towns of Svidník and Bardejov. On the Polish side, north and north-west of these places, there were many Lemk villages, though their original population was moved elsewhere in the aftermath of the Second World War. Many of the surviving churches, mostly now adapted for Catholic use, lie south-east of Nowy Sącz, near the river Poprad and its tributaries. From the point of view of the Ruthenian hill people the frontier, cutting right through their traditional habitat, must have been an embarrassment, but in former times not a serious one.

Among the wooden churches in this westernmost extremity of the Ruthenian lands none survive from earlier than the seventeenth century and the majority, as so often, date from the eighteenth. We can, however, find evidence of a progression within that period from simpler to more complex models. It is true that their dates of construction do not necessarily fall in with such a progression since a reversion to simpler types could occur at any time in the interests of economy. The series nevertheless affords a picture of the developmental stages which culminated in those delightful, Baroque-tipped fantasies like Mirol'a, Ladomirová and Šemetkovce in the surroundings of Svidník.

In this western area even the humbler churches seem to possess, raised upon the usual three divisions of an Orthodox or Uniate church, three separate roofs or cupolas, including the dominant western tower of the Lemk tradition. It is interesting to observe, however, that these towers – though of framed timber in both cases – are differently constructed from those already described from the central and eastern parts of Lemkland. There, the western towers, Rumanian-fashion, have vertical or near-vertical corner-posts resting on the massive cross-beams of the pronaos ceiling. One object is to prevent the pronaos from being obstructed, as it would be if these corner-posts came down to the ground. In this western area on the other hand, the same object is achieved in a different way. The corner-posts do come down to the ground, but are inclined outward towards the base. Thus their feet stand far enough apart not to encumber the pronaos; they may even straddle it, coming down, instead, into the surrounding covered gallery. Such western belfries, with their inclined sides, are a leading characteristic of the Catholic wooden churches in Poland and Czechoslovakia, and their framed construction is the same. It seems certain that the western Lemks, living as they were in close proximity to the Catholic Poles and Slovaks, adopted this expedient from them. The contrasted structures of main church and tower are well shown in the drawing, **186**.

The simpler Lemk churches in this part of Slovakia

186 Perspective diagram showing structure of a typical western Lemk church.

187 Točany, Bardejov area of eastern Slovakia. Church of 1739 from the south-east.

188 Točany. Part of a Last Judgment scene from the interior.

189 Lukov-Venecia, Bardejov area. Church of 1708, south side.

often show little sign of Baroque embellishment. Tročany has its sanctuary unadorned but tower and naos carry a cap of candle extinguisher shape (**187**). There are rustic paintings inside, a lurid detail from the Last Judgment being shown in **188**. At Tročany the western tower is built partly over the porch but at Lukov-Venecia entirely, which results in a lengthened composition (**189**). In this church the tower has an overhanging bell chamber to compensate for its inwardly sloping walls, and the naos roof is stepped. In the quaint church at Kožany the tower is further elaborated (**190**). External galleries are now no longer obligatory; their roofs may be combined with the main roof, or reduced to a western porch, or altogether absent, as the illustrations show.

Wherever bulbous shapes appear in these more western regions, where Russian influence is unlikely, one senses the onset of the Baroque. Domes of this form, commonly on stalks rather than drums, and sometimes accompanied by odd little disks or aprons above or below, often occur in this area as a capping to pyramidal roofs and towers. They mark a stage in the 'Baroquisation' of the style, yet may accompany modest towers and simple unstepped roofs as at Korejovce (**191**). Other churches show towers of increased prominence, and stepped roofs either for the naos as at Bodružal' or for the sanctuary as at Jedlinka (**192–193**). With the heightening of the western belfries the full-blown Baroque takes over and we find all three divisions of the church finished off with slender dome-cum-lantern pinnacles, conferring that unity on the building which was spoken of in an earlier paragraph (pp. 126–7). At the same time the external gallery tends to disappear. The taller the building the less interest was shown in this attractive feature, which often survives only in the form of a western porch.

In this last, most highly evolved category of the western Lemk school we may place the best known Polish specimen – Powroźnik (**194**) – as well as Kwiaton, whose interior is also shown (**195–196**). A rare cruciform example, Dobroslava from the Svidník area of Slovakia, may also be mentioned at this point (**197**). Most memorable, however, are a whole group of churches around Svidník, all of the usual tripartite plan and with a square, not apsidal sanctuary. They date in their present form from the middle to late eighteenth century. A longitudinal section and three representative plans are given here (**198**). The section again illustrates the contrast between the framed construction of the belfry, an imported technique, and the

190 Kožany, Svidník area. Late-eighteenth-century church viewed from the north-west.

age-old log structure of the naos and sanctuary, which extends also to their pyramidal roofs. The same point was made by the perspective diagram (**186**) which, though based on the Lemk system, could apply equally to related Catholic wooden churches. In overall plan these churches usually follow the ancestral Boyk model, the middle section (the naos) being broader than either narthex or sanctuary. Sometimes however (**198** B) the narthex equals the naos in width – a consequence of the preponderant role of the western tower in Lemk churches, as was also seen in the more ambitious specimens of the central zone (**171** E). The feature distinguishing these plans from those of the Boyks is that they reveal various methods of

191 Korejovce, Svidník area. Church of 1761, south-eastern view.

192 Bodružal', Svidník area. Church of 1658, from the west.

193 Jedlinka, Bardejov area, near the Polish border. Church of 1763, from the south-east.

194 Powroźnik, south-east of Nowy Sącz, Poland. Lemk church of 1643.

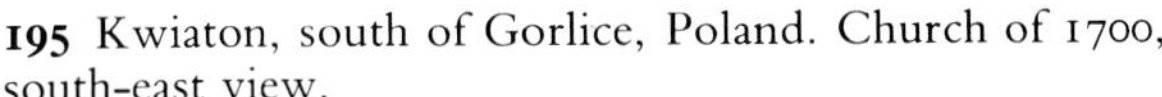

195 Kwiaton, south of Gorlice, Poland. Church of 1700, south-east view.

197 Dobroslava, Svidník area. Cruciform Lemk church of 1705, from the east.

accommodating the massive corner-posts of the western tower which in this area (as explained above) come down to the ground. In B, though widely separated, they all stand within the spacious narthex; in C two stand inside and two outside in the porch; in D all four are outside. Still other solutions were attempted, and it has to be admitted that the problem of incorporating an alien type of tower in these churches found no consistent or wholly satisfactory answer.

Despite these comments, the churches of the Svidník group must be numbered among the most delightful creations of Ruthenian wooden architecture. While enjoying the matching Baroque spires or cupolas, so nicely graded in descending order from west to east, one forgets any awkwardness in the articulation of the tower. Of the examples illustrated Ladomirová, which happens to retain a Boyk-type plan, is the earliest (**198** D, **199**). Mikulášová with its broadened west end has been re-erected in the health resort, Bardejovské Kúpele (**198** A, B, **200**). Mirol'a is one of those still standing in the charming and variegated natural landscape of northern Slovakia (**201**). The interior of Šemetkovce, another church of the same group, is shown here and will be described below (**202**).

Internally, the various church types dealt with in this chapter differ from each other only in so far as outward architectural features are necessarily reflected

196 Kwiaton, interior looking east.

199 Ladomirová, Svidník area. Church of 1742, south side.

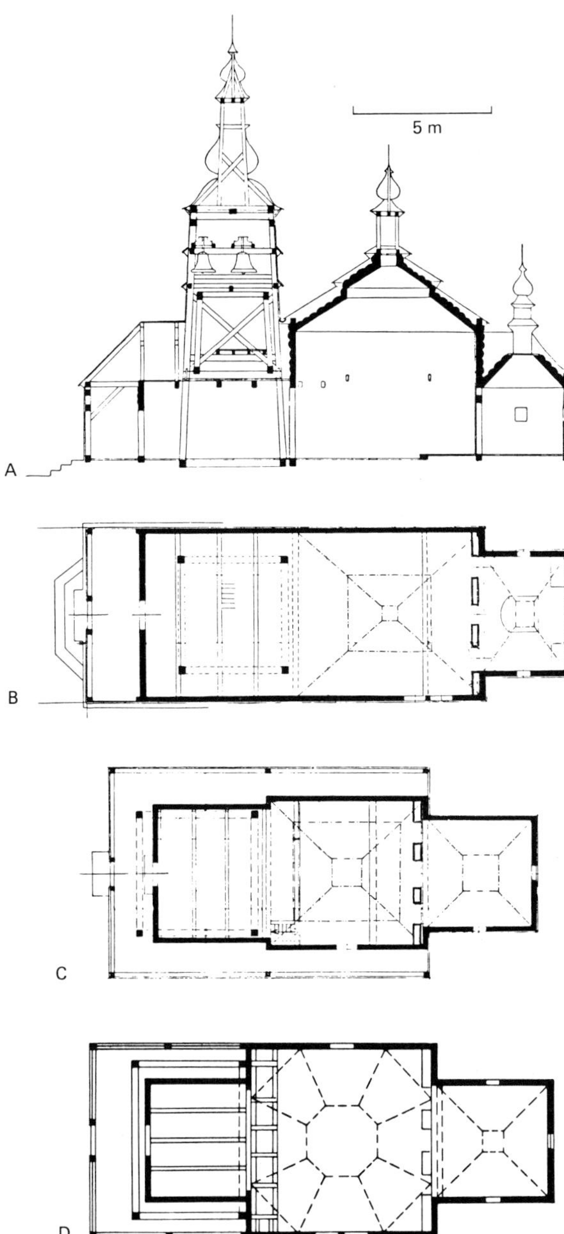

198 Western Lemk churches. A,B. Mikulášová, west–east section and plan. C. Nižný Orlyk. D. Ladomirová.

inside. The interiors, therefore, are much less distinctive than the exteriors. All of them, judged by the standards set in masonry architecture, seem very small and cramped, but at the same time endearingly intimate. As can be seen from the plans, the overall length of these churches rarely exceeds 20 m and is often no more than 15 or 16 m. The main internal space, the naos, may measure up to 7 m square but in smaller churches will be of the order of 5 or 6 m square; only Hutsul churches, in view of their north and south arms, are more spacious. The sanctuary and the narthex or pronaos are of course smaller still. The latter in some Boyk and practically all Lemk churches is further constricted by a low ceiling, which may constitute the floor of an upper-storey *babinets* for women of the congregation. Frequently (especially in Lemk churches) this upper floor extends eastwards in the form of an open gallery projecting into the naos, whose open spaces are thus further restricted.

Narthex and naos are partially separated by a solid timber, arched partition which is visible, for instance, in **140**. As a rule it does not obstruct the view from the western threshold so that, on entering, one is immediately aware of the iconostasis which is the principal feature of every Orthodox interior. There is a great measure of uniformity in the overall design of the iconostasis throughout the Orthodox (including the Greek Catholic) world. Those of the little Ruthenian wooden churches can hardly compete in magnificence with, say, the great five-tiered iconostases of Moscow and Yaroslavl. Nor are the icons themselves the work of masters. Yet these modest iconostases possess the same essential elements as the most splendid ones, and however rustic their execution they seldom lack that subdued and solemn radiance which draws the eye and holds the attention of the worshipper wherever the eastern rite is celebrated. Four beautiful examples – two from Boyk and two from Lemk churches – are reproduced in this chapter and will serve to illustrate the description which follows (**123**, **140**, **196**, **202**). In the next two chapters there will only be shorter references to the iconostasis, for purposes of comparison.

The iconostasis or icon-screen can be compared to the rood-screen common in English churches before the Reformation. But it conceals the sanctuary more effectively than any western equivalent, so increasing the sense of mystery that surrounds it. Existing iconostases almost always have three doors (in a few small churches only two). The central one, through which only priests may pass (though in old Russia the Tsar had this privilege), is the Royal or Holy Door. Its two leaves, elaborately carved in open-work,

200 Mikulášová (now Bardejovské Kúpele). Church of 1760s, from the east.

201 Mirol'a, Svidník area. Church of 1770, south-eastern aspect.

202 Šemetkovce, Svidník area. Interior with iconostasis, 1752.

generally incorporate panels depicting the Evangelists, though if six panels are present the top two show the Annunciation. In the course of the service the priest passes through this door from time to time; when it is open one can glimpse the altar behind (**196**). The two side openings may be closed with curtains or may have wooden doors, often adorned with archangels. Beside and between these doors are the large, important icons of the lower tier, normally four in number (and there may be an extra set below them). The Holy Door is flanked invariably by Christ Pantocrator (to the right) and the Virgin and Child (to the left). At the far left one most often finds St Nicholas and far right (as a rule) an icon depicting the patronal saint or festival.

In all Ukrainian lands the Last Supper is represented immediately above the Holy Door in reference to the symbolism of the liturgy. At the same level, to left and right, come at least twelve smaller panels with icons depicting the great festivals of the Church calendar. These include, from the life of the Virgin Mary: her Nativity, Presentation in the Temple, Annunciation, Assumption; from the life of Christ: Nativity, Presentation, Baptism, Transfiguration, Entry into Jerusalem, Ascension. Besides these, panels are often devoted to Pentecost and the Elevation (or Exaltation) of the Cross; and, when additional spaces are available, to other christological scenes such as the Crucifixion and the Raising of Lazarus. Artistically and iconographically these small panels generally form the most interesting series in the whole iconostasis.

Above the tier of festivals comes a series of tall, arched panels framing figures of the Apostles (with St Paul taking the place of Judas). They are moving in procession or at least casting their eyes inwards towards the larger, central panel where the *Deesis* is represented: Christ enthroned, flanked by the Virgin Mary and St John the Baptist. These flanking figures are seen as the two principal intercessors on behalf of humanity. The whole row of panels at this level forms in fact an extended *Deesis*, the additional figures all joining in the act of supplication. As the photographs show, no further tiers of icons are fully developed in the smaller wooden churches. But some additional panels, variously arranged, will usually be present at the top of the screen, and these contain figures or busts of Old Testament prophets and patriarchs. Surmounting the whole is a Crucifixion with Adam's skull at the foot of the cross. It cannot be properly seen in the illustrations to this chapter for these very cramped interiors make photography difficult, but is shown in **211** and **359**. (I may add that pews are, from the point of view of taking pictures, another severe impediment: they are found in Uniate churches and in those now used for normal Roman Catholic worship.)

The iconostasis commenced its career in the Orthodox lands around the fifteenth century when it took the form of a low barrier, not yet a high screen between naos and sanctuary. It was primarily a 'stand' for icons, which only gradually came to occupy set positions. By the sixteenth century the pattern described above was well established. Records show, however, that the iconostasis as a whole took a 'stepped' form earlier in that century: its lowest storey extended right across the church, but the festival tier was shorter and the *Deesis* tier shorter still. Later both these tiers were extended so that the iconostasis became approximately rectangular and filled the whole of the available space between floor and ceiling. This arrangement remained obligatory from the seventeenth century onwards. Two of the iconostases illustrated, with the icons they carry, are thought to date basically from the latter part of that century (**140**, **202**). Both have been carefully restored. Their icons, though of vernacular character, belong to the genuine Byzantine tradition and build up superb colour harmonies. In the case of Šemetkovce there is an additional large movable icon of the same period in the left-hand corner, representing that popular favourite, St Nicholas. It is typical of many such portraits where the principal figure of the saint is flanked or surrounded by scenes from his legend.

The eighteenth-century iconostases shown in **123** and **196** incorporate ebullient Rococo detail of the kind that, carried on the crest of the wave of the Counter-Reformation, swept the western world of the period. Naturally, the Uniate churches were particularly susceptible to this artistic movement, though in the case of the Boyks its effect was limited to the iconostasis, making little impact on architecture proper. We see twisted columns, spiral volutes, ingenious combinations of concave and convex curves, medallions wrapped in fruit and foliage, winged putti. At the same time the style of the icons, heavily tinged with the art of the Catholic west, is now losing its traditional character; indeed in **196**, though the usual subjects are all there, they are fluffy and over-naturalistic and, to the devotee of things Byzantine, not really icons at all. Notwithstanding these reservations I find every iconostasis an object of beauty and fascination, as the end-product of a tradition centuries old, and as the joint work of a whole team of committed artists and craftsmen. The iconostasis is more than a complex and subtle work of art: it is also a reflection and an epitome of the people's faith.

Besides those forming part of the iconostasis itself, many separate icons, like the St Nicholas at Šemetkovce, have been found in the wooden churches dealt with in this chapter, especially in eastern Slovakia and Trans-Carpathia. Those of notable quality have mostly been removed to museums. Many of these icons came originally from professional workshops active in the seventeenth century in Polish (now partly Soviet) territory, but later on the icon became an object of local handicraft production. Some of these churches are, in addition, adorned inside with religious paintings of 'folk' character painted directly on the wooden walls (**188**). They complete an ensemble which owes its character to the rural architectural traditions of the area, coupled with the persistent, omni-present legacy of Byzantine art.

4

The Ukrainian plains

The Ukrainians equate their homeland with 'Kievan Rus'', the first Russian State, based then as now on the middle reaches of the Dnieper (the Borysthenes of the ancients) and the city of Kiev. The Kievan State owed its origin to one of the great trade routes of early Europe, that which, pioneered by the Norsemen, connected the Baltic with the Black Sea and hence with Constantinople. The Dnieper formed part of this trade route which consisted almost entirely of waterways. Old Novgorod, far to the north on the Volkhov, was likewise a city of the waterways controlling the northern end of the same trade route, including its exit via Lake Ladoga and the Svir' to the Gulf of Finland. Inevitably, Novgorod was in close touch with Kiev for centuries and for a while formed part of her dominions. Thus an early link was forged between northern and southern Russia, which however did not alter the fact that their traditions were very different in architecture as in other fields.

Though the first prince of a Kievan State was the Norseman (or Varangian) Rurik, who took control in A.D. 862, his dynasty soon became assimilated to the Slavs. Links with Constantinople existed from the first but it was in 988 that the Christian religion of the Eastern Empire was officially embraced by Prince Vladimir (Ukrainian Volodymyr). His statue today overlooks the majestic river in whose waters his people were baptised *en masse*. Thus the first brilliant period of Ukrainian Christian civilisation was inaugurated, and some major churches on the Byzantine model were erected in the eleventh and twelfth centuries, beginning with the famous St Sophia of Kiev, founded by Vladimir's successor, Yaroslav the Great, about 1037. At that period, however, most churches in towns and all those in country places would have been wooden, and references in early chronicles indicate that the three-frame plan, so important throughout later history, existed at least as early as the eleventh century. This early civilisation, long harassed by tribes of nomadic horsemen invading from the east, was destined to be blotted out by the last and most catastrophic of these invasions, that of the Mongols in 1240–1. This brought all cultural advance to a standstill for more than a century and contributed to the transfer of political authority to new, less exposed centres in the north-east. The earliest of these were Vladimir and Suzdal'; the foundation of Moscow came later.

Both Kiev and Novgorod had grown old long before the rise of Moscow which was gathering momentum in the fourteenth century, especially after the defeat of the Mongols in 1390, at Kulikovo on the Don. Muscovy, becoming a power in the land so late in history, was regarded as an upstart principality by both the ancient States. The Ukrainians have indeed always claimed to be the real Russians, to whom Muscovites – their oppressors of later times – remained an object of dislike not unmixed with contempt. Yet it was inevitable that the Muscovite principality should aspire to extend its sway throughout the lands of its Slavic kinsmen and, eventually, establish a maritime frontier both in the north and the south. Novgorod, with its vast 'colonial' possessions in the far north, was taken over (not without much bloodshed and brutality) as early as the fifteenth century. But the Ukraine, with its ancient culture and different language, and stronger sense of a separate identity, struggled to maintain or to re-assert its independence all through history. It was in vain, for Lithuanian and Polish imperialism on the one hand, and relentless pressure from Tsarist Russia on the other, were to obliterate the Ukrainian State and lead to partitions as tragic and damaging as those of Poland itself.

We must revert, however, to events of the later Middle Ages, more relevant to the architectural history of the country. By the end of the fourteenth

203 Cossack camp with wooden church on Khortitsa island. Drawn by de Beauplan about 1650.

century the great Lithuanian expansion had already engulfed the whole basin of the Dnieper and its big eastern tributary, the Desna, with such cities as Smolensk, Bryansk, Chernigov and Poltava. Two hundred years later, after the Union of Lublin between Lithuania and Poland had given a fresh impetus to these conquests, the combined State could even claim the territory of the Zaporozhian Cossacks on the lower Dnieper. They had also advanced into Moldavia to the south-west, but the Black Sea coasts were still held by the Crimean Tartars. So it came about that for centuries Poland was in control of White Russia (Belorussia), the whole of the Right-Bank Ukraine (west of the Dnieper) and part of the Left-Bank or eastern Ukraine. Inevitably, this resulted in the penetration of western influences into the Ukraine, including architectural influences. Both the Gothic and the Renaissance appeared in the west, especially in L'vov. From the mid seventeenth century onwards the impact of the Baroque was widespread. In wooden architecture it was perhaps stronger in the eastern Ukraine (then an architectural vacuum) than in the west where (as shown in the last chapter) ancient traditions were firmly established.

The Cossacks have just been mentioned and will be mentioned again since they played so large a part in Ukrainian history. The word *kozak* is said to be Turkish for lawless people living by war and robbery. This may have been a true enough description of some of those disaffected people who, in the fifteenth century, joined in bands in the southern Ukrainian steppes and established the first 'Cossack' settlements. Others were hunters and fishermen who returned in winter to their home villages further north. Soon these settlements attracted all those whose main concern was to escape from Polish or Russian domination, and even many foreign freebooters and malcontents seeking refuge and freedom. For those benefits they risked a dangerous life in perennial conflict with the Tartars of the Crimea. From an early date these Cossack communities gained a romantic image and began to attract recruits even from noble families. They came to be recognised as a buffer force shielding the Ukraine (still under Polish control) from Tartar aggression.

By degrees these communities of fighting men organised themselves on a democratic basis, and in 1552 a headquarters camp, the *sich*, was established on the island of Khortitsa in the lower Dnieper. This was the same island which in earlier times had served as a staging point on the old trade route from the Baltic to the Black Sea. It lies just below the main rapids of the Dnieper (submerged since the great 'Dneproges' barrage was built) at the place still called Zaporozhie ('beyond the rapids'), and the whole community were known thereafter as the Zaporozhian Cossacks. It was an armed, stockaded camp complete with wooden church (**203**) and it was a celibate community, though the warriors based there had families in neighbouring villages. The elected rulers of the Cossack 'host', known as Hetmans, included many remarkable and powerful personalities who acted as Heads of State, conducting their own diplomacy with Poland, Muscovy, the Crimea and Turkey. Attempts by Poland to subdue and control the Zaporozhians long remained fruitless, though other large Cossack groups became, in effect, mercenaries in the Polish service. Both Poland and later Muscovy found the Cossacks a thorn in their flesh, but at the same time came to depend upon them for defence. Their onslaughts on the Turks were more particularly popular, and the Zaporozhians launched attacks on Constantinople three times in the seventeenth century, returning thence with enormous booty.

By the middle of the seventeenth century the Cossacks had become to a great extent identified with the Ukraine as a whole where they assumed the position of an upper class. That part of the country not under Polish rule became known as the Cossack State, and its rulers, usually Cossacks themselves, adopted the title of Hetman. Some of them were figures of outstanding gifts and great erudition, speaking various languages both ancient and modern. They also expressed their piety by founding churches and monasteries. They were great champions of the Orthodox against the Uniate Church which had become dominant in the western Ukraine. Kiev during this period regained much of the lustre it had lost during the previous centuries, becoming again a great cultural and religious centre, especially after the appointment of Peter Mogila, a talented Moldavian, as Metropolitan of Kiev in 1633. From the mid seventeenth century onwards, the Baroque became well established in masonry architecture, gaining the name, owing to its local characteristics, of Ukrainian or Cossack Baroque. And many wooden churches in outlying places are to this day – in so far as they still survive – commonly referred to as Cossack churches.

In 1648, under one of the best-remembered Ukrainian rulers, Bohdan Khmelnytsky, came a spirited but inconclusive insurrection against the Poles. In 1654 Khmelnytsky, casting around for allies, concluded the Treaty of Pereyaslav with Moscow. Though his motives were those of a Ukrainian patriot, subsequent generations saw this treaty as the beginning of the end of Ukrainian independence. From then on, in fact, Muscovy started eroding the independence of the Ukraine and the liberties of its citizens, an aim relentlessly pursued through the remainder of the seventeenth and on into the eighteenth century, until by 1746 the country was reduced to the status of a Tsarist province. In the midst of this period of declining Ukrainian fortunes Hetman Ivan Mazepa (1687–1709), another great patriot, sought to arrest the trend by throwing in his lot with Charles XII of Sweden, then on one of his extraordinary forays in the far south. So in 1709 Charles, with Mazepa's troops in support, met the forces of Peter I (the Great) near Poltava. The outcome – a resounding victory for Peter the Great – was always remembered by Muscovy as a triumph, but by Ukrainians as a tragedy. Under the present regime Khmelnytsky's name is widely glorified, while Mazepa's is better left unmentioned.

From the seventeenth century onwards many foreign travellers recorded impressions of the Ukrainians and their country, often drawing contrasts with Muscovy, most unfavourable to the latter. 'What a blessed land; what a blessed people!' wrote Paul of Aleppo as long ago as 1656. He could not bear Muscovy where, he continues, 'a padlock had been set on our hearts . . . for in that country no person can feel anything of freedom or cheerfulness'.* Descriptions of the Ukrainian scene speak of a refined and sensitive people, of cleanliness and order, of handsome men who wore only the moustache (unlike the 'bearded Muscovites') and singularly beautiful women. In most areas the land was cultivated by independent peasant farmers. Their houses, tastefully set in the landscape, had log walls coated inside and out with clay or plaster and whitewashed. Some of these impressions might well be repeated even today but the real Ukrainian countryside (as distinct from a few main roads) is not at present accessible to visitors from abroad.

Against the background of these conditions and events we have to visualise the architecture of the area. Whether thinking of masonry or wooden architecture one is struck, first of all, by the complete difference between the styles of Muscovy and northern Russia and that of the Ukraine, a fact which underlines the independence of the Ukrainian cultural tradition. One is struck too by the irrelevance of the unstable political frontiers between the eastern or 'free' Ukraine and its western parts under Poland: in architecture, they correspond to no dividing line. It is true, however, that primitive architectural forms tended to be preserved in less accessible areas, especially in Galicia and the Carpathians (previous chapter) and in the swampy forest-lands of Volhynia, and these areas fell within the Hungarian or the Polish, later wholly Austro-Hungarian, spheres of influence. On the other hand it was also true, as remarked above, that the Baroque style, propagated above all by the Jesuits, crept in through these western marches. The omnipresence of the Catholic Poles as a governing class ensured it, but the style was eventually adopted with enthusiasm by the Ukrainians themselves.

As regards the unique later developments of Ukrainian wooden architecture, to be described in the remainder of this chapter, it is noteworthy that they took place in the seventeenth and the first sixty years

* Quoted from V. Sichynsky, *Ukraine in Foreign Comments and Descriptions*, New York, 1953.

of the eighteenth century, while the Ukraine still clung precariously to some measure of independence. Thereafter, though some fine churches were still erected, they showed no originality of design, while the general tendency was one of decline and decay.

The earliest wooden churches of the Orthodox Slavs in this part of Europe are represented today by those of the Boyks described in the last chapter. They were modest, squat, tripartite structures, typically with three separate roofs or cupolas, the middle one being invariably dominant; and an encircling roofed gallery provided shelter for the lower walls, as also for people attending church. Such, one may suppose, was the basic church type among the Ukrainians living in what is now the western Ukraine, that is the plains extending north to the Pripet and east to the Dnieper. In any case this three-frame church-type represents the point of departure for their architecture. As mentioned above, it must have existed in the western Ukraine as early as the eleventh century – practically from the beginnings of Ukrainian Christianity – and its basic techniques were no doubt well known before that. The cruciform plan with arms added to north and south and five cupolas instead of three certainly made its appearance at almost as early a date and some churches of particular importance were apparently still more complex. The simplest forms of three- and five-fold church, surviving in the Galician–Carpathian area, are almost absent today from the Ukraine proper, though a few of those in Volhynia, as a result no doubt of its isolation, do approach the old Boyk pattern.

It is in Volhynia, too, that some evidence can be found of those tendencies which in time turned Ukrainian architecture into something very different from that of the hill country of Galicia and Carpathia. The old province of Volhynia was the northern half of the western extremity of Ukraine between the uplands to the south and the River Pripet to the north. It consisted very largely of marshland and forest, the great forested tract being still called Polesie (Ukrainian

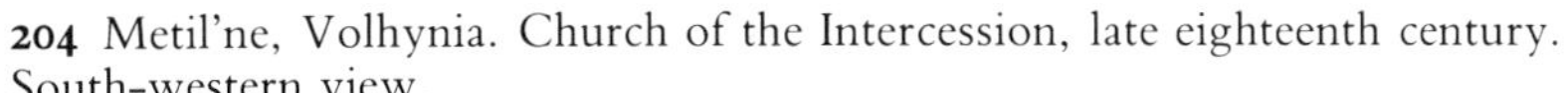
204 Metil'ne, Volhynia. Church of the Intercession, late eighteenth century. South-western view.

Polissia) from *les*, a forest. Volhynia therefore had poor communications and was traversed by no important routes. It stood aside from the main stream of events and tended, like the mountains, to preserve an early culture. Today it is broken up into the *oblasti* (regions) of Volhynia and Rovno and the more northerly parts of Zhitomir. Its main towns include Kovel', Lutsk, Rovno, Novograd Volynski and Ovruch.

Wooden churches here are interesting but not particularly beautiful. They have lost the *opasannya* and the overhanging eaves which were such attractive features of the primitive model. They have been somewhat elongated vertically; not enough to produce a striking effect, but on the other hand more interest is shown in windows to relieve the blankness of the walls and the cupolas above. In plan they normally show the expected three rectangular frames (the central one being the broadest), a faceted apse and the obligatory western door with porch (**204–205**). As a rule, domes are of ample diameter like those of the Boyks, and there may be either three or one, or roofs may be tentatively 'stepped'. The semi-cruciform church, with naos extended polygonally to north and south, also occurs; in this case an additional door with its own porch is likely to be added on the south side (**206**). The traveller by road between L'vov and Kiev has the opportunity to view one of these, still in use as a church, at Rovno (**207–208**). It has a single, stepped cupola, a polygonal apse, a two-storeyed narthex with gallery overlooking the naos, and a typical separate belfry. There are also examples of the full cruciform plan in Volhynia (**209**). In this particular case the ill-constructed external gallery is evidently a subsequent addition, but it is interesting to see windows in two tiers on the main walls, foreshadowing developments further east.

Internal views of two of these same churches are shown here. That of Kamen'-Kashirsky, with its curiously shaped partition between narthex and naos, differs little from a Boyk interior, though the greater internal height accommodates an iconostasis of four instead of three well defined tiers (**210**). The inside view of an octagonal pyramid rising from a square base, also showing the top storey of an iconostasis (**211**), is said to represent the central cupola at Stepan', north of Rovno. If so, the broad dome seen externally

205 Kamen'-Kashirsky, Volhynia. Church of the Nativity of the Virgin Mary, 1723, from south-east.

206 Serniki, Volhynia. St Demetrius from the west. Early eighteenth century.

207 Rovno (Polish Równe). Semi-cruciform church of the eighteenth century (?).

(**209**) must be a sham, merely disguising the pyramid. In any case such log-built, eight-sided pyramids are widespread in these parts, and they lead on to the tall stepped cupolas of the more highly evolved Ukrainian wooden churches (compare **223**).

Two more wooden churches from other parts of the Ukraine are illustrated here and exemplify the same stage of development as the Volhynian ones. Both now stand in open-air museums so the interested visitor may succeed in seeing them. The church from Doroginka (near Fastov, south-west of Kiev) now stands in the Kiev folk museum (**212**). That from Ostriiky, now at Pereyaslav-Khmelnytsky, is from the area of Belotserkovka west of Poltava (**213**). They show the same essential characteristics already met with in Volhynia: rectangular plan with faceted apse; loss of external gallery; some heightening of the whole church; and in the case of Ostriiky a stepped middle cupola as at Rovno. Both churches have west and south doors with cut-off upper corners, a peculiarly Ukrainian shape; the frames at Doroginka have been re-carved with the original motifs (**214**).

To the east of Galicia and south of Volhynia lies the region traditionally known as Podolia, the heart of it lying between the southern Bug and the Dniester. The latter river forms the northern boundary of Bessarabia, Rumanian between the wars, now the Soviet Republic of Moldavia. Administratively Podolia is now shared between the regions of Khmelnytsky (formerly Proskurov) and Vinnitsa; besides those towns it includes, as their names indicate, Kamenets Podol'sky and Mogilev Podol'sky. Podolia was very much more involved in affairs and events, in comings and goings, than Volhynia. In architectural development, correspondingly, it was no backwater, but the scene of numerous experiments which have left their traces in a variety of forms and plans. In these ways Podolia did not lag behind the Kiev region: in both areas, churches are becoming more distinctively Ukrainian. The wooden churches of the remaining

208 Rovno. Church door with typical Volhynian belfry.

Right-Bank areas, that is those west of the Dnieper, can therefore be considered together. Some typical plans are shown in **215**.

The pleasing Podolian church at Zin'kov, south of Khmelnytsky (**216**), resembles in its plan and proportions a Volhynian church like Serniki (**206**). In Podolia, however, these linear, three-frame churches turn up in greater variety as the plans show. It is interesting, too, that several of them have an open gallery, completely surrounding the building. One of them is the imposing specimen at Vinnitsa which still stands and which visitors from abroad should normally be able to see (**215** C, D and **217**). The surrounding gallery, in this case a *piddashya*, reminds one of the ancestral Boyk church. It is to be explained, no doubt, by the proximity of Galicia to the west; further east it is found no more. The plan of Vinnitsa is also unusual in that each section is rigorously octagonal so that re-entrant angles are formed at the junctions, two on each side. The contrasted plan of Chemerisi, being entirely rectangular at ground level, looks at first sight archaic, but each element was converted to an octagon at the first opportunity – at the base of each tall, tower-like cupola (**215** G, H). This was one of those Podolian churches which had attained the same

209 Stepan', Volhynia. Church of the Trinity, late seventeenth to beginning of the eighteenth century.

210 Kamen'-Kashirsky. The interior, looking eastwards to the iconostasis.

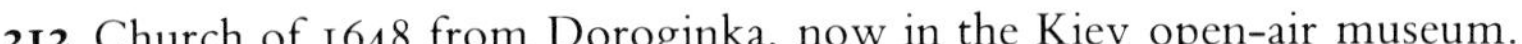

212 Church of 1648 from Doroginka, now in the Kiev open-air museum.

211 Stepan' (?). An eight-sided pyramidal cupola surmounting the nave, with part of the iconostasis.

213 Church of 1606 from Ostriiky, now in the open-air museum at Pereyaslav-Khmelnytsky.

degree of vertical elongation, and therefore the same uniquely Ukrainian character, as those in the neighbourhood of Kiev.

The church of St Paraskeva from Zarubintsy, south of Kiev, is typical of these singularly attenuated churches which became widely popular in eighteenth-century Ukraine (**218**). It now stands in the recently founded Museum of Folk Architecture and Life of the Ukrainian Republic. This covers 180 hectares of open countryside where each natural-looking hamlet among the fields consists in fact of re-assembled buildings from some particular part of the Ukraine. The church in question, the most conspicuous of three so far erected there, has a plan resembling that of Sinyava in the same neighbourhood, though here the pronaos is faceted like the apse and porches are wanting (**215** F). The winter view shows how the narrowness of the east and west extremities contributes to the effect of height. There are south and west doors, the

214 South door from Doroginka.

219 St Paraskeva, the west door.

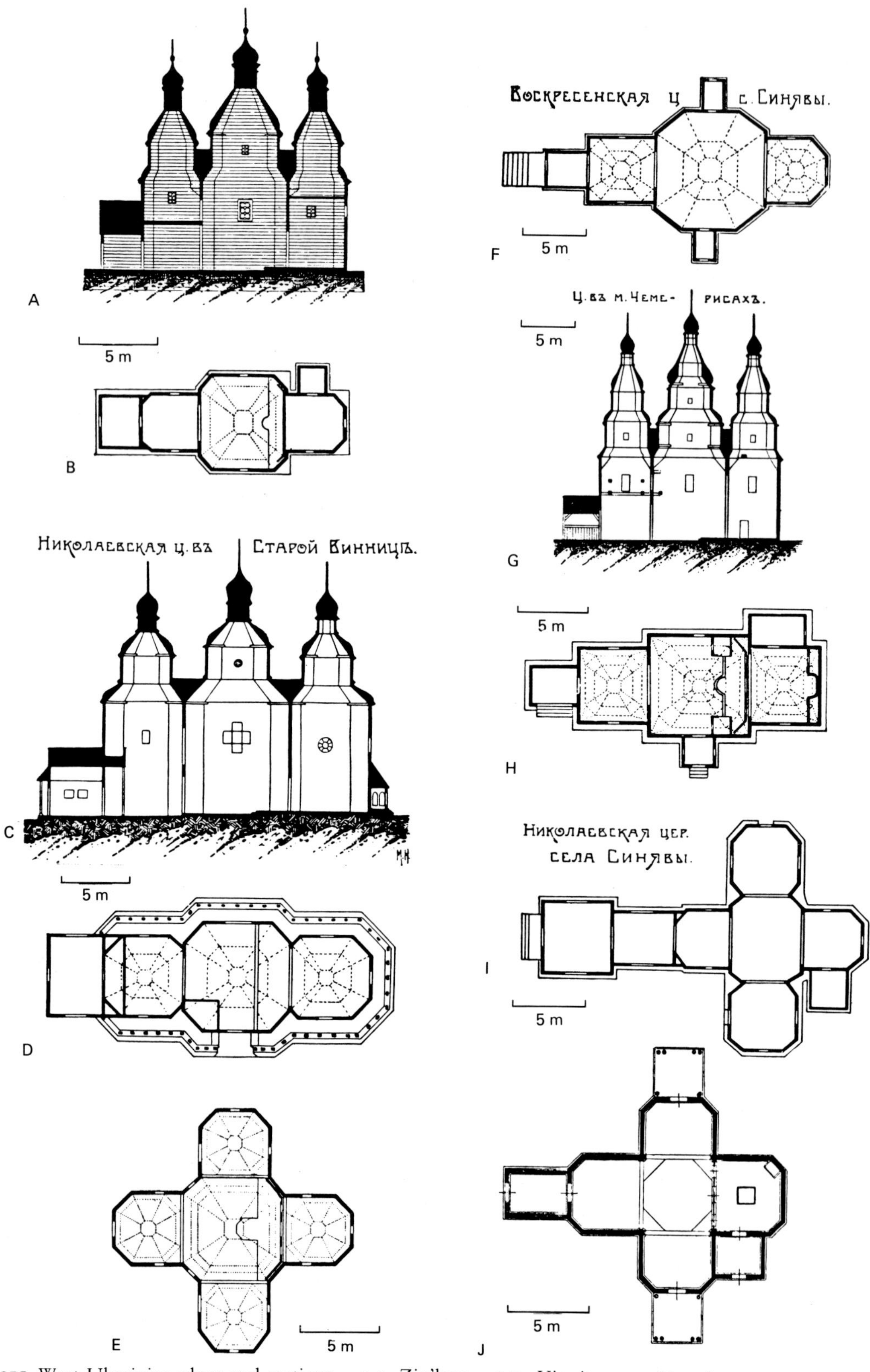

215 West Ukrainian plans and sections. A,B. Zin'kov. C,D. Vinnitsa. E. Yaryshev. F. Sinyava (church of the Resurrection). G,H. Chemerisi. I. Sinyava (St Nicholas). J. Khadorov.

216 Zin'kov, Podolia. Church of the Archangel Michael, 1767. South facade.

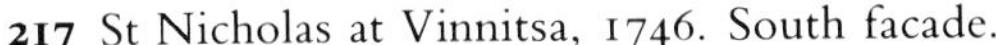

217 St Nicholas at Vinnitsa, 1746. South facade.

218 St Paraskeva from Zarubintsy, eighteenth century. Moved in 1974 to the Kiev open-air museum.

220 St Paraskeva in course of re-erection, seen from the south.

latter being shown in detail (**219**): its frame, of the special six-sided Ukrainian shape, is re-carved to the original design. The special attention paid to doors extends also to windows, likewise designed henceforth for external effect as well as for improved lighting within (some are now round, cross-shaped, quatrefoiled or arranged in triplets).

The photograph of this church in course of re-erection is most instructive as showing very clearly the essential log construction which, in nearly every case, disappears in the finished product under a protective cladding of thin vertical boards (**220**). The tall cupolas or towers are treated in the regular Ukrainian fashion, inclined stages alternating with vertical steps. The 'breaks' so produced in what would otherwise be a continuous roof surface are the *zalomy* already met with in Boyk and Lemk roofs, but here they are more drawn out, in proportion to the great elongation of the cupola. The Zarubintsy church has two *zalomy* to the middle cupola, one each to the flanking ones.

At the time of my visit in 1977 the interior was unfurbished, all constructional timbers exposed, and no iconostasis as yet in position. The interiors of the three tall cupolas were open to the eye right up to their summits – as is normal in Ukrainian churches, unlike those of northern Russia. The pronaos, however, often has an upper storey with open gallery looking eastward, and it is possible that this was still to be built in. The central section, the naos, is eight sided from the foundations upward in this particular church and therefore shows no transition from square to octagon. Such transitions are however visible, high above eye level, in the two eastern angles of the pronaos and the two western angles of the sanctuary.

Before moving on from the western to the eastern

Ukraine we need to take a short look at the cruciform churches of Podolia and the Kiev area. These too show inventiveness and experimentation, even if the cruciform plan was more persistently used, and its possibilities more fully explored, beyond the Dnieper. One pleasing cruciform church at Yaryshev near Mogilev Podol'sky has (if it still stands) a central octagon with four short sides and four alternating long ones to which the four arms, all with faceted ends, are attached (**215** E). This logical plan appears, surprisingly, never to have been used in the eastern Ukraine though the churches of the Liman School (see below) come close to it. It must possess some magic being known as far afield as Moravia and Finland (pp. 313, 383). Another plan which did not find acceptance further east was that of the second church at Sinyava, with indented walls corresponding to the linear plan at Vinnitsa (**215** I). It was otherwise with the plan at Khodorov, also from the Kiev area. This was an example of the cross reduced to its simplest terms – that is, to arms only, attached to each other but not to any central figure (**215** J). This shape of church, in view of its stability and comparative ease of construction, was bound to meet with success, and in the eastern Ukraine there were once many more. The finest cruciform church of the Right Bank stood literally on the right bank of the river, on a site now probably inundated by one of the great Dnieper reservoirs; but it was more nearly related to the Left-Bank group and will be described with them. I refer to the long-lost church of the Vedmedovsky monastery (**234**).

It was in the wide-spreading plains of the Left Bank – that is, the Ukraine east of the Dnieper – that Ukrainian architecture really came into its own in the seventeenth and eighteenth centuries. Much of this considerable area, as large as Britain, had been something of a no-man's-land since the Mongol invasions of the thirteenth century and its southern marches had long since been claimed by the Tartars of the Crimea, who intermittently raided inland. Cossack bands had established settlements at certain points in the area, especially (as mentioned earlier) on the lower Dnieper, from the late fifteenth and sixteenth centuries onwards. They were the pioneers of Ukrainian recolonisation in these potentially rich and fertile plains, but there was no general settlement until the seventeenth century. The extraordinary developments here of late Ukrainian wooden architecture were taking place, therefore, in a region cut off, architecturally speaking, from its roots, but not unaffected by Baroque influence. Perhaps for these reasons was that development so strange and extravagant. Or maybe these towering cupolas expressed a sense of euphoria in a land not only new and desirable but 'free' – for much of it had not known Lithuanian or Polish rule, at least not for long. In any case it is probably an instinctive urge among designers to erect lofty buildings in flat country. So the tendencies already foreshadowed in the western Ukraine were consummated here in the east.

The distribution of these wooden churches in the eastern Ukraine was far from uniform and probably determined mainly by the abundance or otherwise of timber. The great majority were found in a broad band extending from the area of Chernigov, north of Kiev, south-eastwards to Khar'kov and beyond. In terms of the modern *oblasti* or regions they were most abundant in those of Chernigov, Sumy, Khar'kov, and the northern parts of Poltava and Dnepropetrovsk. One has to write of the past as few of these churches survive. Most of those that were still standing in the 1920s, including practically all the finest examples, are now lost, whether through accident or the vicissitudes of war or the misplaced fervour of Stalin's anti-religious and anti-Ukrainian drive of the early and middle 1930s. I was unable to establish the facts in the Soviet Union itself, where the subject is understandably embarrassing, now that the best specimens of folk architecture are eagerly sought out for re-erection in open-air museums. Nor are local publications a reliable guide, as they often fail to indicate whether a given building is still standing or not. The fate of these churches is one of the most grievous architectural tragedies of modern Europe, to be compared only with the loss of the wooden synagogues in Poland and Belorussia during the Second World War.

About sixty of these wooden churches survived long enough to be documented in the last few decades, latterly in the comprehensive work by the late S. A. Taranushenko. The great majority dated from the second half of the eighteenth century. This fact alone proves that the expectation of life of these wooden churches was never long. Travellers' records and old drawings prove that many such churches – of the same types that continued to be built into modern times – were already standing in the seventeenth century, yet scarcely any lasted even two hundred years and most disappeared without a trace. The conclusion to be drawn is that most of the late examples described below belonged to types devised at least as early as the previous century. The fact remains that the eighteenth century, here as elsewhere in eastern Europe, marked the high tide of carpentering skills.

The earliest east Ukrainian wooden church of which a more or less reliable picture exists had a plan of the familiar three-frame type. This was the

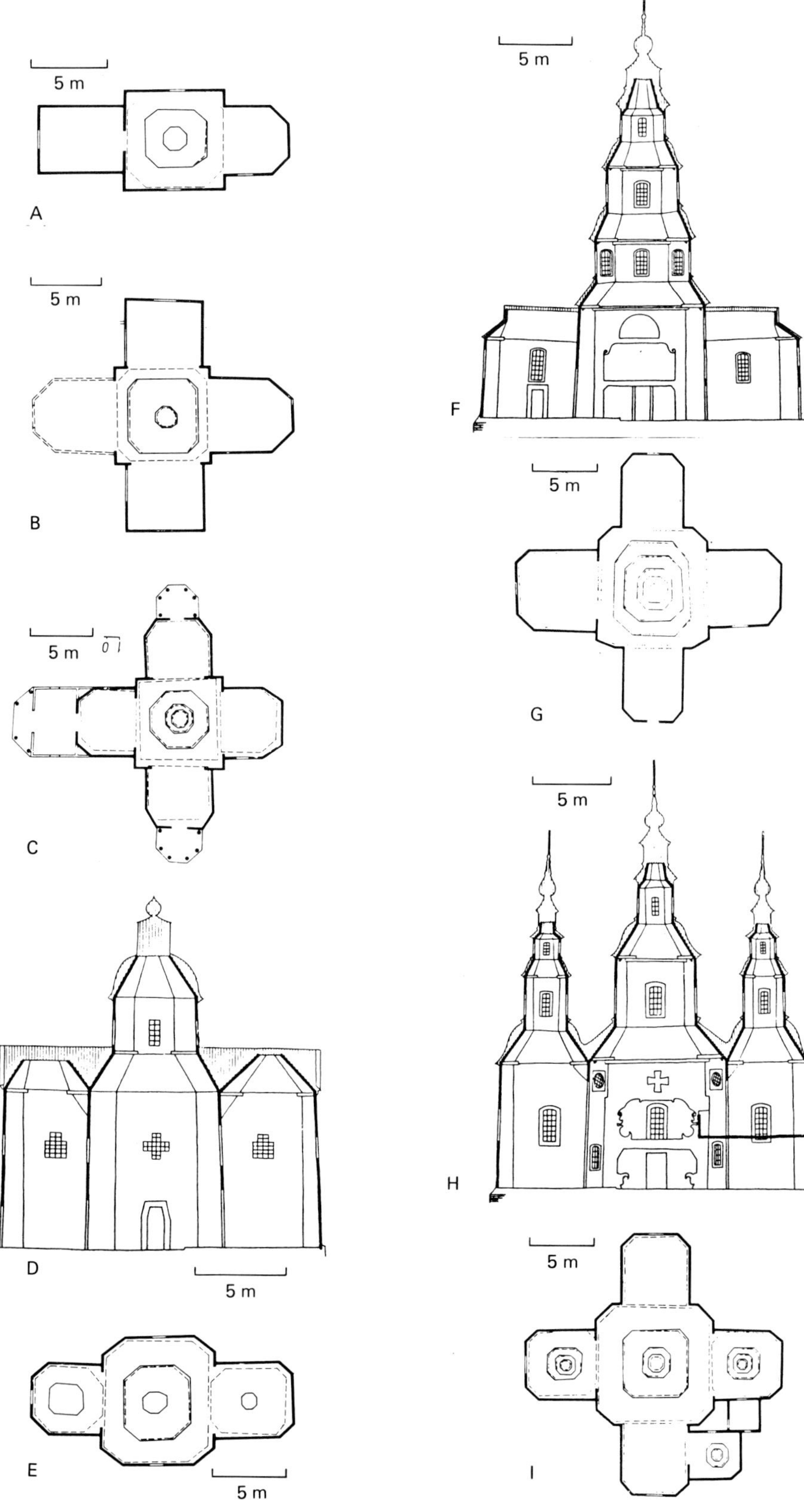

221 East Ukrainian plans and sections A. Sedniv. B. Gusarivka. C. Lebedin. D,E. Sosnitsia. F,G. Verkhny Byshkyn. H,I. Cherkas'ky Byshkyn.

222 Lebedin. St Nicholas, 1783, from south-west.

225 Osinove, *oblast'* of Voroshilovgrad. St Michael's church, 1789.

223 St Nicholas. Upward view inside the single tower.

224 Verkhny Byshkyn, *oblast'* of Khar'kov. Church of the Archangel Michael, 1772.

226 Cherkas'ky Byshkyn, *oblast'* of Khar'kov. Church of the Trinity, 1751.

227 Cherkas'ky Byshkyn. The interior from a painting by G. N. Logvin.

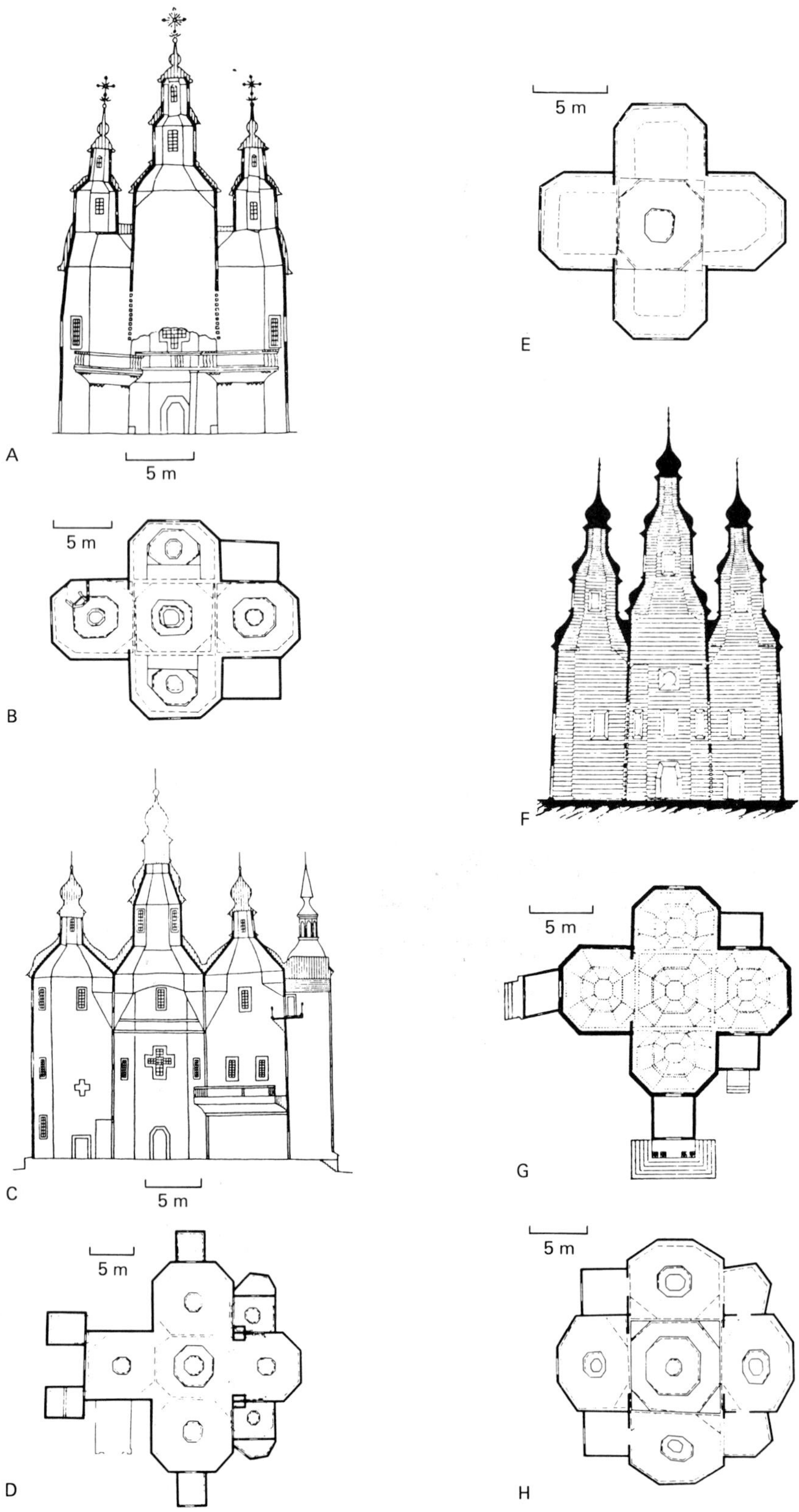

228 East Ukrainian plans and sections. A,B. Pakul': south-north section and plan. C,D. Berezna: east-west section and plan. E. Svirzh. F,G. Romny (afterwards Poltava), west–east section and plan. H. Korop.

Cossacks' church at their headquarters camp, the Zaporozhskaya Sich, on Khortitsa island (**203**). The drawing is due to de Beauplan, a French military engineer in the Polish service who was stationed in the Ukraine between 1630 and 1647. Evidently at that time the traditional linear plan still enjoyed esteem. In the eighteenth century, however, this church-type no longer represented the norm in the eastern Ukraine. It accounted, it is true, for about half the recorded churches, but they repeated long-familiar designs, were generally undistinguished, and became really numerous only in the latter part of the century, a period of decline. On the contrary, among the recorded churches it is those of cruciform plan that so often show originality of conception and audacity in execution.

The known cruciform churches – some of them extraordinary masterpieces of timber construction – exhibited a variety of plans which can be placed in an evolutionary sequence. They are best dealt with in that order, although it does not necessarily coincide with the order in which the recorded examples were built. I must point out once again that archaic plans, though they played their part centuries ago in the evolution of the style, had a way of reappearing again and again, even into modern times. This was true in the Ukraine and equally true in other provinces of timber architecture. A similar observation applies to the cupolas. Simple ones with one step or *zalom* obviously ante-dated tall, complex ones which might have three or four *zalomy*, and were certainly a late development. Yet many late churches reverted, probably for reasons of economy, to the simple, ancestral cupola which therefore affords no clue to the date of construction of the church.

Representative plans are given in **221**. The normal three-part church plan had, as in the styles of Galicia and the Carpathians, a rectangular central frame to which the narrower west and east arms were attached (**221** A). The earliest cruciform plans were certainly produced simply by building similar north and south arms against the two free faces of the central rectangle. This left the corners of that rectangle exposed – the corners, in fact, were all that remained of it. Gusarivka, south-east of Khar'kov (1690), is a relatively early example of such a plan, to which a polygonal apse was added (**221** B). A seventeenth-century church at Lebedin (Sumy region) possessed the additional refinement that all the arms terminated polygonally. This plan was apparently copied in the church of St Nicholas (1783) in the same town, which in turn has disappeared (**221** C, **222**). This was one of those cruciform churches which possessed but a single tall, central cupola, completely open to view inside. An interior photograph survives, showing the conversion of square to octagon and the convergence of the walls between the first and second octagons (**223**).

Plans based upon a central square lead on to those with a central octagon. This is built up of four short sides, alternating with four long sides to which the arms of the church are applied. The linear version is shown in **221** E. The construction of cruciform versions evidently involved enormous labour since they possessed no less than thirty-two angles at which all the timbers had to be jointed. Yet this plan was the special characteristic of the School of Liman, so called after the small town of that name beyond Izyum, south-east of Khar'kov. Some of these churches had a single towering cupola in the middle with as many as four *zalomy*; the striking example once standing at Verkhny Byshkyn, 29m tall, is illustrated here (**221** F, G and **224**). Some, like Osinove, were planned with the traditional five cupolas, though one of them remained unbuilt (**225**). A few had three, though the example at Cherkas'ky Byshkyn was embellished by a fourth, crowning a chapel in the south-east corner (**221** H, I and **226**). The wash painting gives a realistic impression of the view from the central space into one of the arms (**227**). This was clearly a well lit interior, and in fact all these churches were provided with large windows in the main walls and at every step in the cupolas. The strong tradition of the Liman School, which stuck resolutely to its difficult and laborious plan of construction, did not falter until the first years of the nineteenth century. Their churches were widespread in the Khar'kov area, many of them in the basin of the Donets and its tributaries to the east. I cannot say how many survive. One can only hope that one or two may still be found for the open-air museum now planned for Khar'kov, and thus be saved for posterity.

In all the churches of the Liman School the four short walls of the central octagon showed up outside between the arms of the cross, and they added one more facet to diversify the interior scene. Aesthetically, these were great advantages – advantages sacrificed, however, whenever builders adopted the simplified cruciform plan as in **228** B, E and G. This is the plan from which all trace of the original square or octagon has been eliminated and where the four arms meet each other at right angles. Churches built on this plan lost nothing in stability, while labour and resources were saved and could be devoted instead to other desirable ends, like the enlargement of the whole structure, the improvement of interior vistas and the building of ever more graceful cupolas. It is not known when this plan was first used, and the

229 Pakul', Trinity church, 1710.

recorded examples can tell us nothing of chronology. In the seventeenth and eighteenth centuries it was simply one of the available alternatives. It must also be said, however, that the most imposing of Ukrainian churches of the eighteenth century were all built on this principle. Some had one single central cupola, but all the more important examples were given a full complement of five.

The earliest of the major documented specimens was the church of the Trinity at Pakul' in the Chernigov area (**228–230**). Its five cupolas formed a graceful cluster, the central one, about 30 m high, considerably overtopping the other four surrounding it. Windows were inserted in the cupolas at each level, and the cross-shaped ones in the end facets of the arms prove that these openings were designed for effect as well as for utility. The plan was not exactly equal-armed so that the transverse section (**228** A) is appreciably narrower than the longitudinal. As in all the taller churches of the region the western arm had an upper storey with gallery overhanging the central space. Subject to this, the cupolas were fully visible internally and offered remarkable vistas: **230**, for instance, shows the transition from square to octagon in the western and middle sections, with the faceted extremity of the northern arm beyond.

In the tremendous church of the Ascension at Berezna in the same area (**228** C, D and **231**) the architect, one Panas Sholud'ko, succeeded in further improving the interior both by heightening the common space below the cupolas and by reducing the partitions between these to an absolute minimum.

230 Pakul', interior.

The old photograph (**232**) gives an idea of the carpenters' daring and virtuosity. It must be admitted that these amazing inside effects were achieved at the cost of the outside which, with its cliff-like walls (and windows at three levels), had become rather ungainly. The church had another individual character – two towers attached to the western arm, one of them accommodating a spiral staircase, and each crowned with an extra cupola. (These could have been inspired by the twin towers of many western churches.) All in all, this was one of the most outstanding achievements in timber construction in the Ukraine, or indeed anywhere in Europe.

Another splendid wooden church, dedicated to the Virgin of the Intercession, was built at the expense of a Cossack dignitary at Romny (Sumy region) in 1764 (**228** F, G and **233**). In 1900 it was taken to pieces and re-erected at Poltava where it survived the troubled 1930s and stood unharmed until the Second World War. In 1941 the city was set on fire in the course of Hitler's thrust to Stalingrad and the great church perished in the flames. It had a certain gauntness and purity of line in the tradition of Pakul', with its five cupolas arranged in the same way, but as a compensation for this severity there was an incredibly luxuriant Rococo iconostasis within. The church showed an interesting feature shared with some others in the Ukraine: the arms with their cupolas were deliberately built to lean inwards, a device which enhances the impression of height in the external view. This design was nothing new, for an engraving dated 1706, showing churches built by Hetman Mazepa, includes an almost identical one (and another, possibly also wooden, not unlike Berezna). Obviously both designs go back at least to the seventeenth century.

My last example of the cross-shaped plan with five cupolas will be the one mentioned earlier which stood near the bank of the Dnieper south-east of Kiev (strictly speaking on the wrong side to be numbered among Left-Bank monuments). This church of the Vedmedovsky monastery was originally built in 1735, was modified sixty years later and survived until 1910, when it was thought unsafe and pulled down. The old photograph, together with the plan and section (**234–235**), show several features which differentiated this remarkable building from the others of its class. The five cupolas were even more slender than usual, the central one with its extra storey and three *zalomy* measuring 37 m. These extra-tall towers, as well as the large classical porch with its own dome, probably date from the second period of building. The arms, it will be noticed, are not polygonal but square-ended. The

231 Berezna, Chernigov *oblast'*. Church of the Ascension, 1759. South-western aspect.

232 Berezna. West, south and central cupolas.

233 Romny (later Poltava). Church of the Virgin of the Intercession, 1764, from the south-west.

plan and photograph both show another feature of particular interest: the prominent rectangular angle-chambers placed between the arms of the cross, making up a plan of nine compartments instead of five. These were not merely separate rooms built into the corners (as in other such plans) but an integral part of the main interior space, with which they communicated through wide openings.

It was just such a plan that led on to the even more complex composition of nine cupolas at Novomoskovsk (previously called Novoselytsia, or Samara after the local river). It is still in existence (**235–239**). This most ambitious of all 'Cossack churches', dedicated to the Trinity, was the work of a master carpenter named Yakim Pogribniak and was built in the years 1775–8. It is true that the existing church is a virtual reconstruction of 1887, but this fact is not unduly disturbing, the building being, I believe, a faithful replica of the original. To the traveller searching for what little remains of Ukrainian folk architecture it is no small comfort, after many frustrations and disappointments, to find one major example intact, in a place one is allowed to pass through. In my own case, it was the main justification for extending my journey to the eastern Ukraine. And I can assure others who venture to linger in this small town – between Khar'kov and Zaporozhie – that they will not forget the experience.

At first sight the church may be a bewildering array of massed cupolas grouping themselves in fascinating and ever-changing patterns as one moves around. But in fact this is a perfectly logical extension of the now

234 Trinity church of the Vedmedovsky monastery, 1735 and 1795.

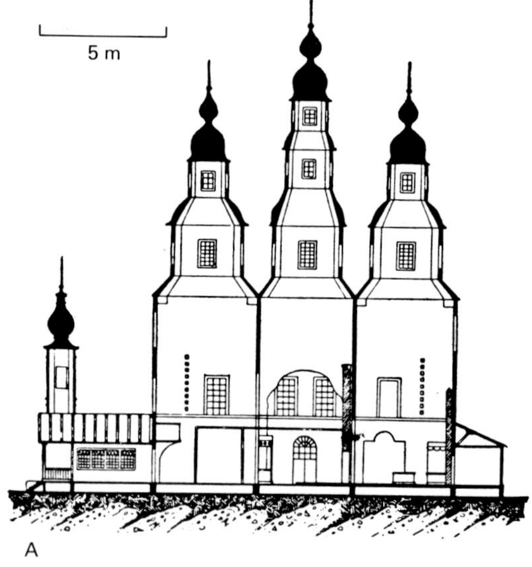

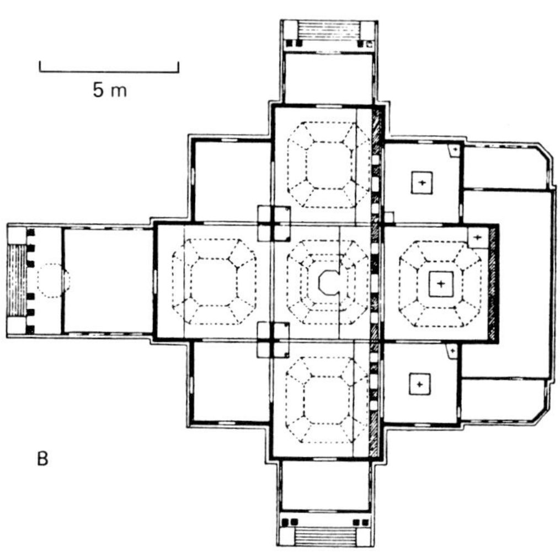

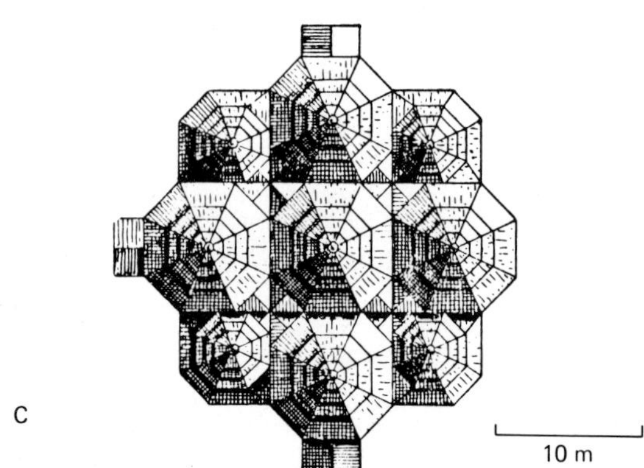

235 East Ukrainian plans and sections
A,B. Vedmedovsky monastery, west–east section and plan. C. Novomoskovsk, roof plan.

familiar cruciform plan with five towering cupolas, plus four additional elements filling the angles between the arms. The novelty is simply that these corner chambers carry the four additional cupolas. Their roofs alternate in a very satisfactory way with those of the four axial cupolas, which spring from the higher base of the arms. There is, in addition, a modern free-standing belfry with a much larger dome, seen to the left in the distant view (**237**). The plan of this church makes an interesting parallel (probably developed quite independently) to that of the famous 'St Basil' (officially the church of the Trinity) in the Red Square at Moscow, itself inspired by wooden prototypes. That church, however, consists of nine practically separate chapels, which lack any common interior space.

The interior at Novomoskovsk, of which I was allowed a brief glimpse by a startled and worried custodian, unexpectedly gives the impression of a single, almost uninterrupted space. This is because the openings between the central square and the four arms are both wide and tall, though traversed high up by horizontal beams at two levels, required in the interests of stability. The four corner spaces communicating with the adjacent arms of the cross through lower, arched openings do not strike the eye as separate chambers but substantially extend the general interior space. The whole is well lit by numerous

236 Novomoskovsk, *oblast'* of Dnepropetrovsk. Church of the Trinity, 1775–8 and 1887. South-east view taken in winter.

237 Novomoskovsk. Distant view from the east.

238 Novomoskovsk from due north.

windows in the outer walls and also from above, since all the nine cupolas, with their octagons pierced at two levels, act as light wells. The architect thus managed to reconcile a spacious interior with an outside appearance which, crowning and even surpassing the Ukrainian tradition, resembled a clustered fungoid growth of jostling, pinnacled towers.

The Trinity church at Novomoskovsk, despite its long and logical pedigree, was an almost unique manifestation of eighteenth-century exuberance. Among more modest and less conspicuous church-types there was another which appears to have originated in the same century. Based likewise on the cross, it had one central cupola and one over the western arm – a non-traditional arrangement. The open-air museum at Pereyaslav-Khmelnytsky, south-east of Kiev, possesses two such churches from the surrounding country, though at first sight they seem to have little in common. One of these, from the village of Vyunishcha, looks like a copy of a small masonry church and offers little of interest though the interior, with octagon raised on a square base, is a nice example of local timber construction (**240**, **241**). The church from Andrushi, on the other hand, is of unmistakable Ukrainian character (**242**). The tall, stepped, central cupola is without a doubt of traditional log construction but the very slender belfry surmounting the western arm may well be framed – a point I was unable to check as the church could not be opened.

In the same open-air museum a fine example of a three-storeyed, free-standing bell tower has been re-erected (**243**). It stands now, as it originally did, near the church brought from Ostriiky (**213**) but was built about 150 years later, in the eighteenth century. (Note that the constructional horizontal timbers of the bottom storey are here left exposed, owing to the protection afforded by the colonnaded gallery.) Old drawings of two other types of Ukrainian bell tower are given in **244**. Still more interesting is the detail from an engraving of 1677 showing buildings in the Monastery of the Caves (the Pecherskaya Lavra) at Kiev (**245**). The storeyed tower labelled *Zvonnitsa* (belfry) is clearly timber-built and it is a more elaborate structure of its kind than any known to have been built since. These towers would make an interesting study on their own but, like the churches themselves, they have become a rarity in the Ukrainian plains.

Before concluding this survey I must mention some outlying wooden churches which are related to the Ukrainian group but fall outside its main range as shown on the map. The fact that they do fit in to the general Ukrainian pattern is shown by the three- or five-part plans and by the disposition of the cupolas, whether there be five, three, or only one. For instance the still existing church at Berislav near Kherson has a single central cupola flanked by almost symmetrical eastern and western arms (**246**). The pattern is perfectly Ukrainian but this church lies far to the south in the steppe region, so that one presumes that its timbers had to be floated down the Dnieper. The same may well have been true of some churches of similar layout which once stood on or near the River Don, well outside Ukrainian territory to the east. There are few records of these interesting buildings and one old drawing must suffice as an example (**247**).

Lastly there is White Russia or Belorussia which lies immediately north of the western Ukraine and shares

239 Novomoskovsk: jostling cupolas from the north-west.

240 Church from Vyunishcha now at Pereyaslav-Khmelnytsky, eighteenth century. South-east view.

241 Vyunishcha. The cupola seen internally.

242 Church from Andrushi, now in the open-air museum at Pereyaslav-Khmelnytsky. 1768.

243 Bell tower from Ostriiky, Belotserkovka district. Eighteenth century.

244 Ukrainian wooden belfries drawn by D. Savitsky. The lower example is identified as Volhynian.

a long frontier with Poland, to which it belonged between the wars. It possesses a few scattered wooden churches mostly of minor interest, some of them, with their western towers, frankly copied from stone or brick prototypes. Among more traditional types there are tripartite churches resembling some of the simpler as well as some of the more complex Ukrainian ones (**248**). More interesting are the cruciform five-part churches, especially an excellent specimen as far north as Vitebsk, which none the less shows kinship with the south, not with northern Russia (**249**). It is not clear whether this church still exists. In any case its influence has persisted, an example being the still surviving church at Novoropsk (**250**). Belorussia did possess some wonderful wooden synagogues, which are all believed to have perished tragically at the hands of Hitlerite forces in the Second World War. A brief account of these is given in Appendix II.

Ukrainian wooden architecture of the seventeenth and eighteenth centuries is distinguished above all by the development of multi-storeyed tower-like cupolas, sometimes reaching a height of 30 m or more. Were they invented spontaneously by the Ukrainian builders on the basis of traditional forms? My own view, as already suggested, is that Renaissance and Baroque towers in Poland and Silesia played some part in this development – which seems the more likely since Baroque decorative details were certainly adopted in the Ukrainian brick architecture of the same period. Yet one must recognise that these towers of west European derivation not only looked very different when interpreted in log construction but were used quite differently in the country of their adoption. They had to fit the traditional three- and five-fold plans (which remained unaffected by outside influences) and so had to be grouped in threes or fives, while a single tower could only be placed in the middle, never at the west end.

The interaction between timber and masonry architecture always makes a rewarding study. In the case of the Ukraine it has long been the accepted view of Ukrainian and Russian writers that the Ukrainian Baroque (sometimes called 'Cossack Baroque') was strongly influenced by the local timber architecture, which had itself absorbed Baroque features. I find this view reiterated in contemporary publications and I personally find it convincing, even if it is difficult to prove conclusively that the requisite wooden prototypes existed early enough. However that may be, the principal wooden church-types can be closely paralleled among brick structures of the Ukrainian Baroque and most scholars will probably continue to

245 The great bell tower in the Monastery of the Caves, Kiev, in an engraving of 1677.

246 Berislav on the lower Dnieper. Church of the Presentation of the Virgin from the south. 1726.

247 Cossack church of St Demetrius at Stanitsa Petrovskaya on the lower Don.

248 Rubel', Brest region, Belorussia. North elevation of St Michael's church, 1796.

249 Vitebsk, Belorussia. Church of the Prophet Elijah, seventeenth century. From a watercolour by I. Trutnev.

regard the brick-built versions as derivatives of the wooden.

The linear, tripartite plan with three cupolas is reflected in several brick-built Kiev churches including that of the Exaltation of the Cross within the precincts of the Lavra and that of St Theodosius just outside it, both dating from about 1700. Others are a church of the Resurrection at Sumy (1702) and a very late one, St Michael's at Polonky, north-east of Kiev (1777). But the example most often quoted in the literature is the well known church of the Intercession (Pokrov) in Khar'kov, eastern Ukraine, dated 1689. It is shown in **251–252**. The upper storeys of its three graceful cupolas are in fact a perfect replica of the corresponding type of wooden church, together with an arcaded gallery all round its base, reminiscent of Vinnitsa. But this gallery (which is in fact wooden), instead of being at ground level, runs high above one's head since the whole building is raised on a massive basement storey which has no equivalent in local timber architecture. The church is clothed, of course, in Baroque detail including broken window pediments very curious to western eyes: these have nothing to do with the wooden prototype nor, of course, do the high decorative courses composed of bricks set corner-wise. A general view of this interesting and beautiful building is impossible, at least in the leafy season. My long-range photograph (**251**) shows its upper storeys only, together with another oddly alien feature – the purely north Russian belfry (left) which surmounts the west end. On the right an ex-monastic,

250 Novoropsk, Belorussia. St Nicholas from the south-west. 1732.

now museum building of indescribable style completes an architectural ensemble which is unusual, to say the least.

Derivatives of wooden cruciform plans also exist in Kiev, one with a single cupola being St Nicholas Pritiska (1631). Most, however, are five-domed. Two of these are very closely related to wooden prototypes: All Saints 'at the Trading Gates' which surmounts a big entrance gate to the Lavra, and the Cathedral of St George at the Vydubitsky monastery (**253**), both built at the very end of the seventeenth century. Many others of similar plan and with five cupolas can be found by combing through illustrated books. There are, for instance, the churches at Nizkenichi in Volhynia (1653) and others north-east of Kiev, in the *oblast'* of Chernigov: the Gustyn monastery (1672–6), Nezhin (late seventeenth century), Novgorod Seversky (early eighteenth), Priluky (c. 1716), St Catherine's at Chernigov itself (1715). In the Poltava area there are at least two notable churches of this category – the Assumption at Lyutenka (1686) and the Transfiguration at Sorochinski (1732). Yet another is the Transfiguration at Izyum, south-east of Khar'kov.

It is not difficult to identify these churches of the wooden tradition. Their plans are the same as those of the three-frame and five-frame wooden churches and their cupolas are placed on the axes. In the cruciform

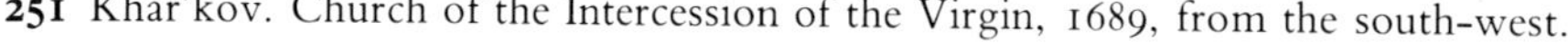

251 Khar'kov. Church of the Intercession of the Virgin, 1689, from the south-west.

252 Khar'kov, Intercession: eastern cupola with part of the surrounding wooden gallery.

253 Kiev. St George in the Vydubitsky monastery, 1696–1701. East end.

variety the arms stand out clearly both internally and externally, and they have faceted extremities. If additional chambers are built in the angles between the arms (making a nine-part plan) they are low and inconspicuous and never crowned with cupolas. This contrasts entirely with the Russian 'cross-in-square' system where the corners are filled right up, the arms disappear in the external view, and the four subsidiary domes sit on the corners, that is on the diagonals. In the seventeenth and eighteenth centuries there were, of course, reciprocal influences. Many churches of the Russian type were built in the Ukraine (but decorated in the local Baroque manner). More importantly, Ukrainian architects were summoned to Moscow, especially after the Treaty of Union in 1654. They took with them the style and the system of ornamentation they knew, and were thus instrumental in establishing the style known as the Moscow Baroque. So the influence of Ukrainian Baroque and consequently of its wooden prototypes extended even to Muscovy. Ukrainian-type plans, axial domes, storeyed towers and Baroque detail – all complete novelties – appeared in and around Moscow. Some of these churches and towers have been demolished, others remain on the outskirts of the old city, as at Fili and the Don and Novodevichy monasteries.

When the Christianity of Byzantium was adopted in Kiev-Rus' in the tenth century, it was natural and inevitable that the architecture of the Byzantines should come in too. In fact, in the two centuries following the conversion a number of domed churches were built in the Kievan State itself and in the outlying possessions of Smolensk and Novgorod. In the Ukraine of today examples stand (or at least are known from foundations) not only in the principal cities of Kiev and Chernigov, but in smaller places like Kanev, Pereyaslav and Ovruch, also at Galich and Vladimir Volynsky further west. All the same, the vast majority of churches at that early period were timber-built, and one would expect them to have been influenced by these newly introduced Byzantine churches, so conspicuous at the time for their size and their novelty. Surprisingly, perhaps, such influences had little or no effect on the essential layout of the wooden churches, which thus demonstrated the strength of the tradition they embodied.

This chapter has shown that practically all Ukrainian wooden plans were either longitudinal, with three cupolas, or cruciform, with five; and in the second case the domes stood on the axes, i.e. on the arms of the cross. This arrangement did exist at Constantinople in the lost church of the Holy Apostles, which is thought to have inspired St Mark's at Venice and St Front at Périgueux. But it did not become popular in the Byzantine world and was not even represented among the Ukrainian stone-built churches. The majority of these are (or were) single-domed, but if additional domes are present they stand on the corners, i.e. on the diagonals. It is evident, therefore, that the five-fold plan with axial domes, a very natural one in wooden architecture, developed in the Ukraine independently of Byzantine influence. It may still be maintained that Ukrainian solid-timber cupolas represent an attempt to imitate Byzantine domical structures, but it seems more probable that these too had been handed down locally from early, possibly even pre-Christian times. The one feature of Ukrainian wooden churches that can be attributed with more confidence to the Byzantine inheritance is the onion dome in its outward aspect. Introduced in its later Byzantine form, raised on a drum, the dome gradually assumed the bulbous shape so familiar in all the Russias. Its function in Ukrainian (as in north Russian) wooden churches is not structural but purely aesthetic: it gives a culminating flourish to every tower and cupola.

Whether the Ukrainian wooden churches had anything more than local significance in architectural history remains an open question. Strzygowski certainly believed that they did. One of the recurrent themes of his writings was his theory on the derivation from Asiatic sources of the cupola raised on a square base – a key architectural form which came to dominate Byzantine building and eventually made its way to western Europe. In Strzygowski's belief the problem of converting a square to a circular (or octagonal) dome-base was solved in the first instance in log buildings, by experiments with diagonal timbers laid across the corners of the square (*Übereckung*). And he believed that the Ukrainian wooden churches of today were the descendants of these early wooden domes-on-the-square, which led to similar structures being evolved in other materials – sun-dried brick, adobe (pisé) and stone. Facilitated by the Indo-Aryan migrations, this would have happened in various countries from India to Iran and Armenia, especially in those regions where timber was scarce. The squinch (according to this theory) was the first expedient to be developed, being followed later by the more efficient pendentive.

I suppose few architectural historians would now question the eastern derivation of various elements in Byzantine art and architecture, including the dome raised on a square. But I see no good reason for postulating a timber origin either for this feature or (as Strzygowski does) for the square as such. This is surely one of the more obvious plan forms to adopt, whatever the material in use, and if the builders have a dome in mind, a circular, polygonal or square base are the only alternatives open to them. I therefore feel it is unrealistic to link the timbered solutions found in the Ukraine with any early experiments in dome design carried out in countries further south-east (even if Ukrainian-type wooden buildings ever extended so far afield). Their real links, I am sure, are with the ancestral wooden architecture of the old Slav homeland, best represented today by the more primitive churches of the Boyks, as described in the previous chapter.

5

Rumania, Hungary and Yugoslavia

This chapter relates mainly to Rumania, a country both humanly and scenically among the most attractive in eastern Europe. Moreover it looms large in this survey: it is exceptionally rich in wooden churches and these, far from being uniform in character, belong to three different styles which must be dealt with separately. We shall also find that these three styles are not confined to Rumanian soil but extend beyond the present borders proving once again – if proof were needed – that the political frontiers existing at any particular moment in history play but a minor role in a study of this kind. The geography of the country is dominated by the Carpathians. They form a huge arc traversing Rumania from the north in a south-easterly direction, then turning directly westward to cut across the country again. Between the eastern limb of this range and the River Pruth lies Moldavia; between the southern range and the Danube lies Wallachia; within the arc is Transylvania. These three principal divisions of the country are therefore very well defined geographical entities, and their histories too have been largely distinct.

Moldavia and Wallachia remained separate principalities (though for centuries dominated by the Ottoman Turks) until 1860, while Transylvania, despite its predominantly Rumanian population, did not join the Rumanian State until 1918. The country's frontiers since then have corresponded to a great extent with the historical habitat of the Rumanian people. What has happened, however, is that border areas, mostly of mixed population, which were assigned to Rumania after the First World War, were lost to her again after the Second. Ethnic purity is an unrealistic and unattainable ideal in Rumania as in most countries. On the one hand, great numbers of Rumanians find themselves living outside the borders of the State, mostly in what is now the Ukraine and Soviet Moldavia (or Bessarabia). On the other hand, minorities of very long standing – especially Hungarian and German – live inside Rumania, mostly in Transylvania. As will be seen, both factors have influenced the character and the distribution of the different types of wooden architecture discussed in this chapter.

These three styles, though sharing some common characteristics, and though subject in some degree to mutual influences, developed independently in the three main regions. The sequel will show that both the Moldavian and the Transylvanian styles were very distinctive and highly specialised, for in the first case the Byzantine, in the second the Gothic, contended with local tradition for mastery. This was not true, however, in Wallachia, which for uncertain reasons remained faithful to the more basic, the less differentiated style from which the other two so conspicuously diverged. It is also true that the Wallachian-type wooden churches are closely related to those found in Yugoslavia, especially in Serbia and Croatia. For these reasons I have used the term 'Basic Balkan' for the wooden churches of the three last-mentioned areas.

The Rumanians regard their country as an outpost of Latin culture hemmed in by Slavs to the north and east, by Bulgars to the south, by Magyars to the west. Certainly the occupation of Dacia by the Romans about A.D. 105 and their presence there for more than 160 years did much to shape the early history of the country. In particular, the basic Latin of the retired legionaries who settled and inter-married there (men of various origins and nationalities) was of tremendous influence – to the point of superseding the local language or languages. The various stages of the occupation are recorded in graphic (if biassed) detail in the long spiral of reliefs which adorn Trajan's column in Rome. Despite all the barbarities of the conquest, despite the destruction of the Dacians' own promising civilisation, the Rumanians (rather like the British) revere the Roman tradition and have identified them-

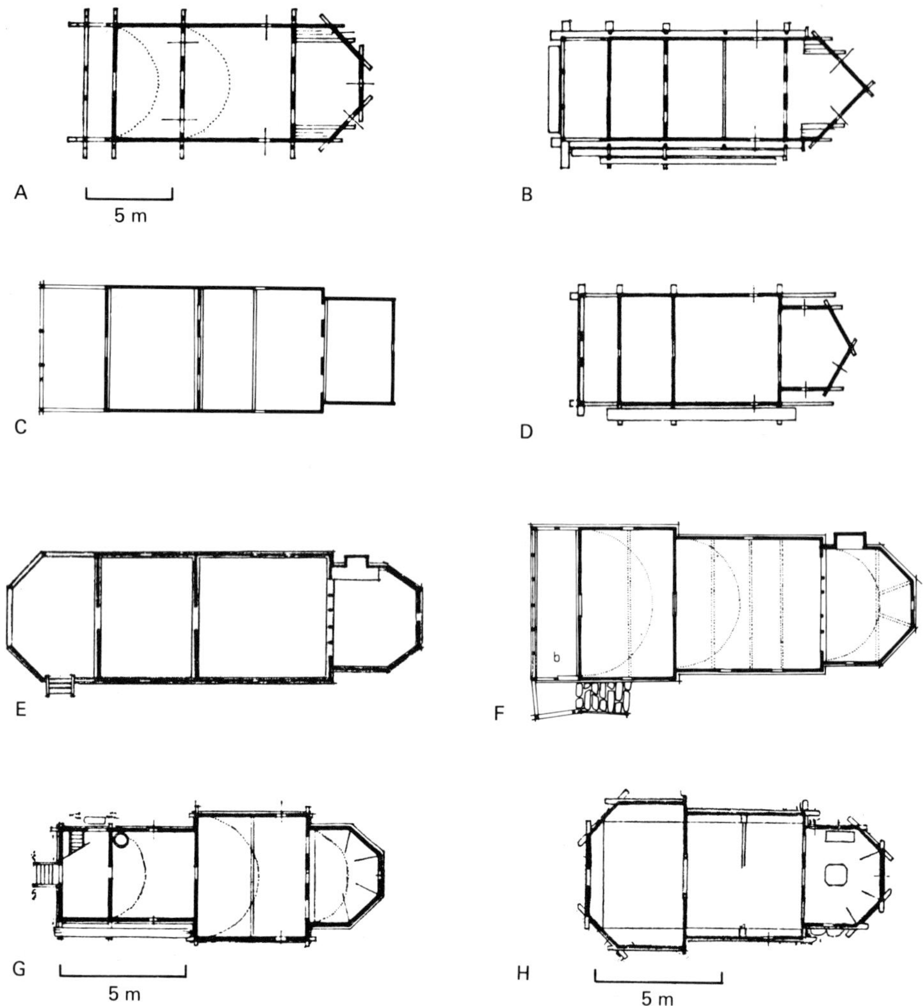

254 Wallachian plans. A. Dealul Glodenilor, Gorj. B. Dealul Pietrişului-Scoarţa, Gorj. C. Ştefăneşti, Vîlcea. D. Comăneşti-Pojogeni, Gorj. E. Zătreni, Vîlcea. F. Grămeşti-Costeşti, Vîlcea. G. Frasin-Deal, Dîmboviţa. H. Cărpinişu-Pietrari, Vîlcea.

selves with it. For this reason, perhaps, the Rumanians, though located so far east geographically, are in many ways a westward-looking people. It seems therefore paradoxical that their principal links, from the fourteenth century onwards, were with the Byzantine empire and their religion, as a natural consequence, Orthodox. As further consequences, the masonry architecture of Wallachia and Moldavia became Byzantine (as it still was until the eighteenth century) and the language of their literature, as of their liturgy, long remained Old Slavonic. The Cyrillic alphabet, even for writings and inscriptions in the Rumanian language, was not given up until the middle of the nineteenth century.

The Orthodox Church of Rumania is accepted today by the country's rulers as an aspect of the national culture and tradition (though the Uniate Church, which had accepted the supremacy of Rome, is no longer tolerated). As every visitor to Rumania knows, the Church is very much alive and plays an essential part in the life of the people, especially in the villages. To the student of church architecture it is, I must say, a great satisfaction to find most of the objects of his study still in use for their intended purpose. Monasteries too still exist, though in small numbers. Nuns, on the other hand, seem to be ubiquitous, combining the exercise of their vocation with custodial duties in nearly all the old monuments of monastic architecture in the country. All travellers must have experienced their modest charm, wide knowledge, linguistic gifts and almost invariable helpfulness.

Looking back on several journeys in Rumania I remember with particular pleasure the hospitality I have experienced there, especially among priests and

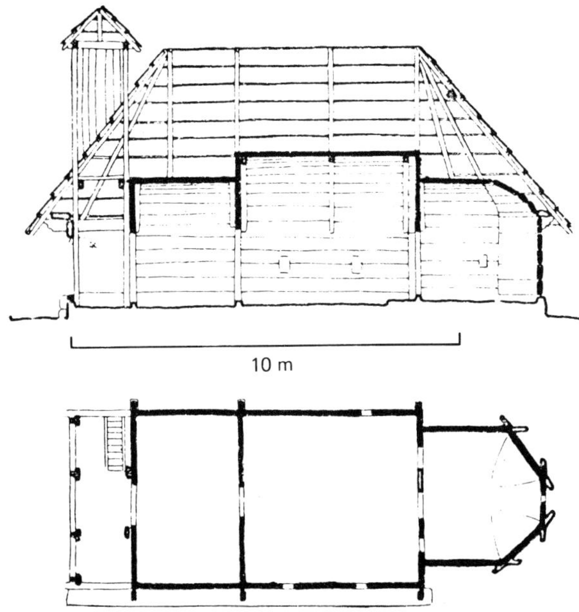

255 Broşteni, Gorj county. Representative Wallachian plan and longitudinal (west–east) section.

country people, and the many occasions when they welcomed me to village ceremonies – weddings, baptisms, commemorations and festivals of the Church. Of course Rumania is not very different, in this respect, from other east European countries where the foreigner is free to go where he likes: the less sophisticated the community, the more spontaneous the welcome will be. But there is another characteristic of the Rumanians which cannot escape the visitor's notice and seems to me unique, and that is their innate aesthetic sense. In the villages every house, no matter how modest, is adorned in some way – walls are painted or patterned in relief, verandahs, balconies and pillared porches have their woodwork decoratively carved, roofs have an ornamental turret in one corner. Perhaps it is the same artistic instinct that makes these people cling, more than in any country I know, to their traditional costume. The scene on a sunny Sunday in the Maramureş, when all the inhabitants are out in the village street in their embroidered finery, is something the foreign traveller can never forget.

This chapter is based on Rumania, a country uniquely favoured, as far as wooden architecture is concerned, in south-eastern Europe. The second section deals, however, with two groups of wooden churches in Yugoslavia whose architectural links are with Wallachia. Similarly, the fourth section is devoted to wooden belfries in Hungary, the most important of which are indubitably related to Transylvanian examples dealt with in the immediately preceding pages. As will be seen, these excursions beyond the geographical borders of Rumania also involve crossing the religious divide between Orthodoxy and Catholicism (in Croatia) and Protestantism (in Hungary). In addition, the scope of this chapter extends to some smaller areas bordering on Rumania which are now under Soviet administration. The inclusion here of wooden buildings from so many territories is not, of course, an arbitrary act. All are inter-related and, as I see it, can only be dealt with together.

THE BASIC BALKAN IN WALLACHIA AND THE BANAT

Many unassuming wooden churches are to be found in the old principality of Wallachia lying between the Southern Carpathians (or Transylvanian Alps) and the Danube. Very similar churches occur in central and south-western Transylvania, for they represent the parent stock from which the remarkable style of northern Transylvania descended. This section, however, is mainly concerned with Wallachia where the style is best represented. In Muntenia alone (that is, Wallachia east of the River Olt) 130 wooden churches have been described in recent years and they represent only a fraction of those that once existed. As might be expected, most of them are located in the forested country of the Carpathian foothills, but a few still stand in the lowlands too, even down to the Danubian plain (e.g. Vidra, **256**). My examples come mostly from the general area of Piteşti (Argeş county) and, further west in Oltenia, from the area of Tîrgu-Jiu (Gorj county). Only a few now surviving date from the seventeenth century, the great majority from the eighteenth or early nineteenth, but they are unadulterated specimens of folk architecture.

Wallachia emerges clearly in history only in the fourteenth century when its links with Constantinople were established, its first Byzantine churches built, and its first Metropolitan appointed by the Byzantine ecclesiastical authorities. Almost from the beginning the threat of the Ottoman Turks to the principality was steadily growing, and their armies finally subdued it in 1462, led by the same Sultan Mehmet II to whom Constantinople itself had fallen only nine years before. The popular reputation of successive Wallachian princes depended of course in part on their personal and diplomatic qualities, but most of all on the extent to which they staved off the Turks, or resisted their pretensions after the conquest. If just one among them is to be mentioned by name it

256 Vidra, Ilfov county. Church of 1795, south-west corner.

must be Michael the Brave (1593–1601), a thorn in the flesh of the Turks, who in 1600 brought about a short-lived union of all the Rumanian lands – something never achieved again until 1918. Like many rulers of the Rumanian principalities he was active too in the religious and cultural spheres, being remembered especially for his promotion (for the first time) of the Rumanian vernacular as a literary tongue. Michael's equestrian statue now stands in Bucharest, which however did not become the Wallachian capital until half a century after his death, following Curtea de Argeş and Tîrgovişte.

It is doubtful whether the overlordship of the Ottoman Turks was here an inhibiting factor as far as church-building was concerned. This was certainly the case in Serbia (next section) under direct Turkish rule, but in a vassal State like Wallachia the Turks were very much more tolerant. The princes of Wallachia were even able to build some grandiose palaces and monasteries in the very period we are considering – that of the Brancovan princes whose favourite style of architecture represents the last flowering of the Byzantine tradition in Rumania. But the countryside at large was generally impoverished, bled by the Ottomans whether directly or indirectly and too often the stamping ground of contending armies. Churches, therefore, including the wooden ones which alone could be afforded by the rural population, were small and unpretentious. Nevertheless in Wallachia (and, as we shall see, in Croatia) they are generally distinguished by a small bell turret at the west end, a feature which links this architectural province with western rather than eastern Europe. It is a curious fact that the wooden churches of Wallachia, in contrast to those of Moldavia, normally show no Byzantine influence despite the fact that masonry architecture in both principalities was Byzantine. There are indeed some intermediate types north-east of Bucharest near the Moldavian border, but they are of no special importance and are not illustrated here.

It is time to consider the ground plans of these churches. Rumanian authors are obsessed with the 'typology' of plans, to the extent that G. Ionescu has proposed a series of five classificatory tables, each with vertical and horizontal coordinates, providing slots for about one hundred theoretically feasible plan types, to be expressed by combinations of figures. If his system were generally accepted it might be useful as a shorthand method of recording plans. In a broad survey of this kind I prefer to follow the simpler classification published earlier by R. Creţeanu with particular reference to Muntenia (eastern Wallachia). I

257 Frasin-Deal (Copacei), Dîmbovița county. Church from second half of the eighteenth century.

shall however limit myself to a verbal description with illustrations of some common and some curious types (**254**).

Virtually all Orthodox (or ex-Uniate) churches in Rumania have the obligatory three sections: narthex (or pronaos), naos (or nave) and sanctuary. The porch is an optional (but aesthetically very important) addition which did not become general until the eighteenth century. In its simplest possible form (known only from two examples in central Transylvania) the plan is just an oblong like a house, but this is a rare exception which can be ignored. The first and simplest group of plans in Rumania – quite common in Wallachia and Transylvania – is based on the plain oblong but the east end is faceted. So the north and south walls form an uninterrupted line from west to east with no narrowing of the apse (**254** A, B). These plans are considered archaic but since they were also economical to build they might be used at any time and do not necessarily afford a clue to the age of

258 Cîrstieni, Argeş county. Church of 1759 from south-west.

churches. The second group, to which most wooden churches in both Wallachia and Transylvania belong, comprises plans where the apse is reduced, that is narrower than the remainder of the church (**254** C–E and **255**). In the small third group narthex and naos are of unequal width: most often the nave is broader, giving a plan mistakenly described by some Rumanian writers as cruciform, as in **254** G. (It is noteworthy that this latter variety, standard among the Ukrainians, accounts for only a minute proportion of Wallachian or Transylvanian plans.) The fourth, trefoiled group is diagnostic of Moldavia or Moldavian influence and can be forgotten for the moment.

The other main features of the layout are variable and can be found in different combinations with any of the basic plan types set out above. The sanctuary apse may have anything from three to seven sides, five being standard. If the number is even there will be a median angle at the east end. Such four- and six-faceted apses are known, but are distinctly unusual (**254** B, D). Another uncommon form is the rectangular sanctuary projecting from a broader naos as in C: it can be considered a reversion to an early and primitive condition. In the Banat both seven-sided apses and perfectly semi-circular ones, composed of segmental timbers, occur. Though rare in Rumania these form a link with neighbouring Serbia where both are known (cf. **272**). Sometimes there is a small extension on the north side of the apse, resulting in asymmetry. This represents the prothesis, used in the preparation of the Elements for Communion (**254** E, F). The church door is usually at the west end but can be on the south side, which is considered an earlier position. The porch, if present, is normally western and rectangular. Porches can also be polygonal (E) and this is one of the features which, uncommon in Rumania, assumes importance in the related churches of Serbia. Occasionally, if a porch is lacking, the narthex itself may be polygonal (H), but this form is better known in Moldavia.

259 Drăguţeşti, Argeş. Church of 1814 now at Goleşti.

260 Jupîneşti, Argeş. Church of 1742 with polygonal porch.

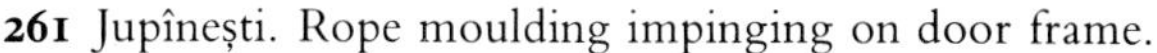

261 Jupîneşti. Rope moulding impinging on door frame.

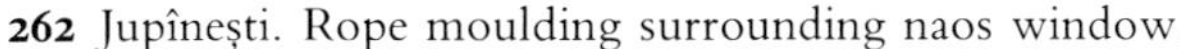

262 Jupîneşti. Rope moulding surrounding naos window.

263 Morăreşti, Argeş, church of 1832. Rope moulding diverted around west door.

Such are the main features to be deduced from ground plans. Some authors have made them the basis of classifications which I consider artificial, for the fact is that almost the same range of plan types are often common to obviously different styles. I can now pass on to the superstructures whose characters are far more distinctive and really do determine the various divergent styles in a given area, Rumania being a case in point. For Wallachia the longitudinal section and plan given in **255** are alike typical. They can serve to illustrate the 'Basic Balkan' style in general, which I have called by this name for the very reason that it is basic and ancestral and lacks any extraordinary modifications.

The plan shows the three obligatory divisions of the church plus a western porch, and a 'reduced' apse of five facets. The section shows that all these divisions are covered by a common outer roof. The naos is somewhat higher than either narthex or sanctuary. All three are closed in by simulated barrel vaults, above which there is empty roof space (cf. **267**). In this particular case the bell turret surmounts the porch but many are built over the narthex or straddle porch and narthex. It is noteworthy that the ceiling under the belfry is invariably flat; elsewhere it is likely to be vaulted. Some bell turrets are a little more prominent and may have quite a large bell chamber, still others rise in two stages. On the other hand a few of these churches have plain roofs without any turret, in which case there may be a separate belfry.

The illustrations accompanying this section give examples of the various structural, and at the same time decorative features that meet the eye around a Wallachian church. Consoles, fashioned from the projecting timbers of outer walls and internal partitions, are used to support the eaves. At the west end it is the open porch that attracts ornamental treatment. Its roof is generally raised on four wooden posts or

264 Morărești. The extended western porch.

265 Drăganu-Olteni, Argeş, church of 1785. Details of the west end.

266 Drăganu-Olteni. Roof structure in south-west corner.

colonnettes which may be carved in a variety of devices, all probably rustic interpretations of the Baroque. An attractive feature – decorative but not functional – is the horizontal rope moulding or girdle (*brîu*) which completely surrounds many of these churches. It is not attached to the wall timbers but forms part of them from the beginning. It seems to be inspired by a similar moulding first used in sixteenth-century masonry churches in Wallachia, whence the idea spread into Moldavia. This is therefore a distinctively Rumanian feature which became popular in wooden churches throughout the country. The rope moulding often strays from its normal horizontal course to form surrounds for doors, and occasionally also for the small windows positioned immediately above it (**262–263**).

The photographs form a series progressing westwards from the Bucharest area, and begin with Vidra, in the plains south of the capital (**256**). The church is notable for its exceptional length and very roomy porch, but is visually impaired by the loss of its shingles, replaced by unsightly metal sheeting. From Frasin-Deal (county of Dîmboviţa) north-west of Bucharest, I give an entirely typical example of a modest Wallachian church, its basic plainness relieved by the beautiful wooden head-pieces in the surrounding graveyard (**254** G and **257**).

267 Drăganu-Olteni. Barrel vault seen inside the roof space.

From Argeş district, further west, the first example is Cîrstieni: with its plain roof unbroken by any tower it looks very like a Serbian church, and here, as there, a free-standing belfry stands close by (**258**). The slightly broadened naos and the rope moulding are visible, and there is no porch. However, the great majority of these churches have both a western bell turret, sometimes rising in two stages, and a simple western porch. A good example from Drăguţeşti now stands in the Museum of Viticulture and Arboriculture at Goleşti (**259**). Jupîneşti is interesting for its polygonal porch, surmounted by a larger-than-usual bell chamber (**260**). Its rope moulding too has individuality. In abutting against the western door frame it forms a serpent's head, and when passing below the windows it is diverted around them (**261–262**). At Morăreşti the moulding similarly makes a detour over the western door (**263**). This is one of several late churches in the area where the western roofs project so far that extra supporting posts are needed, standing outside the porch proper; all are carved, and the general effect is most decorative (**264**).

Drăganu-Olteni in the same countryside has a church with several attractive features (**265–267**). The first view through its western porch shows massive basement timbers, carved columns with the arches linking them, the west door, the rope moulding, a typical ladder, and corner-jointing (**265**). The second shows how upright posts and cantilevered brackets can be combined to form a support system for the porch roof (**266**). The projecting 'horsehead' bracket is supporting nothing, but it may have had a magical function, for such horseheads were believed to ward off evil spirits. The ladder in **265** gave access to the roof space which afforded an external view of the simulated barrel vault (here set in, so as not to occupy the full width of the naos). Its planks are fixed at the ends by means of wooden pegs and supported internally by semi-circular wooden ribs (**267**).

The remaining photographs were taken in the county of Gorj in Oltenia (Wallachia west of the River Olt). There is no change of style as the typical church of Colibaş makes clear (**268**). In **269–270** there are two sculptured details of western porches in the *comuna* of Peştişani: the second of these villages (Hobiţa) has another association as the birth place of the sculptor Brancuşi, who may well have been influenced by these rustic carvings. Finally, **271** shows a

268 Colibaş, Gorj county. Church of 1797 from the west.

269 Peştişani, Gorj. Carved detail of western porch.

270 Peştişani-Hobiţa. Carved 'capital' of porch column.

271 Peştişani-Boasca. Consoles or 'wings' of apse.

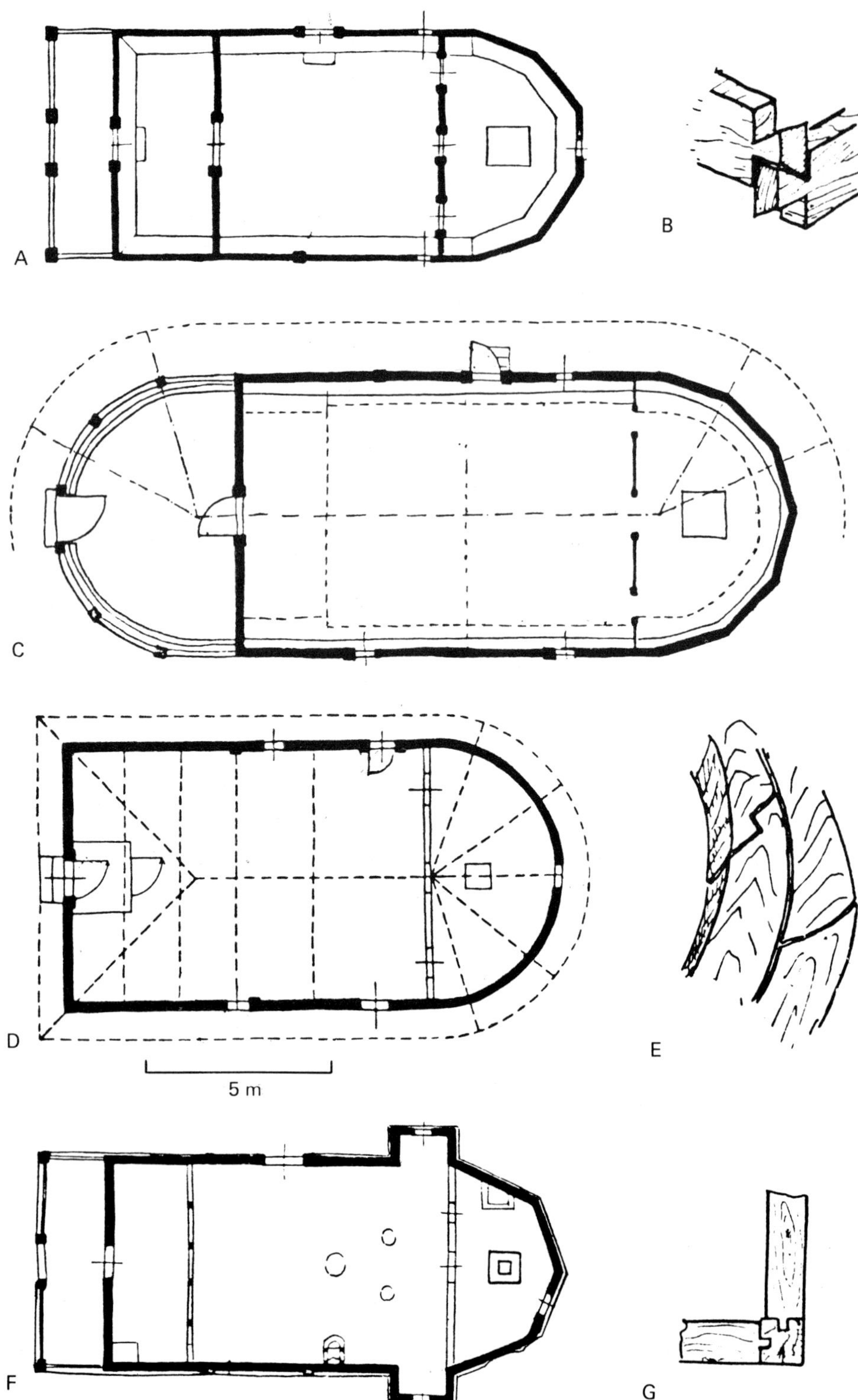

272 Plans and sections of Serbian wooden churches to uniform scale. All built between 1830 and 1832. A. Lozovik, Smederevo district. B. The same, corner-jointing. C. Selevats, Smederevo district. D. Vrba, Kralyevo district. E. Dobroselitsa, jointing in the semi-circular apse. F. Popovitsa, Zayechar district. G. The same, corner-jointing in horizontal section.

274 The 'Pokaynitsa' (church of Atonement), 1818. Western view with base of belfry in the foreground.

nice specimen of brackets or consoles, supporting the eastern eaves of the church at Boasca, a village of the same group. In such positions, owing to the obtuse angles of the apse facets, these form interesting paired 'wings'. Such brackets are not, of course, confined to Wallachia but occur in various forms throughout Rumania and other Orthodox regions.

After the collapse of Turkish rule in 1718 the Austrians took possession both of Oltenia (which they called the Banat of Craiova) and of the Banat proper 'of Temesvar' (now Timişoara) further to the west and north-west. The former area was held only for about twenty years while the latter remained part of the empire until the First World War. The Austro-Hungarian presence, long or short, made no difference to the folk architecture of these regions. Today, the Banat technically forms part of Transylvania. Its twenty-eight wooden churches have been written up so we know that they bear a general resemblance to those of Wallachia, and that the surviving examples date from the same period. Their particular interest lies, however, in the fact that they form a link with the wooden churches of the Serbian hill country not far away – separated from Rumania, in fact, only by the great gorge of the Danube (the Iron Gates). The linking features have been mentioned above and relate especially to the apse, which can be six- or seven-faceted or even perfectly semi-circular. By this logical transition we can go on to consider the Serbian churches.

THE BASIC BALKAN IN SERBIA AND CROATIA

Yugoslavia enters into this study, marginally at least, for there are many unpretentious wooden churches in Serbia and Croatia, and a few both in Slovenia and in Bosnia (where some small wooden mosques are also said to exist). My samples come from Serbia and Croatia only, but I believe them to be representative. The relationship of these churches to those of southern Rumania is unquestionable. They belong to the same widespread and unspecialised type of western

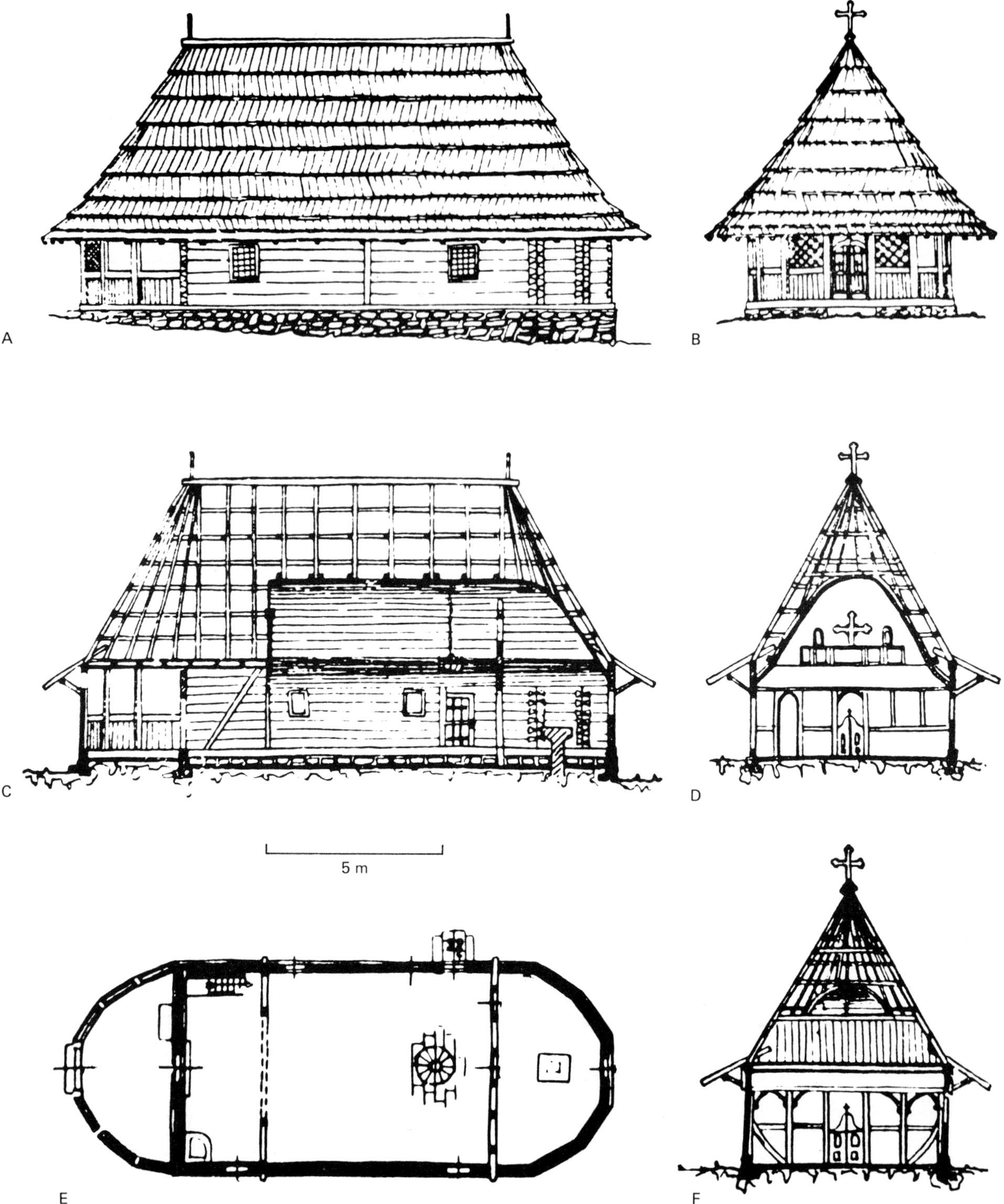

273 The 'Pokaynitsa' near Velika Plana, Smederevo. A. South elevation. B. West elevation. C. Longitudinal (west–east) section. D. Transverse section through naos. E. Plan. F. Transverse section through porch.

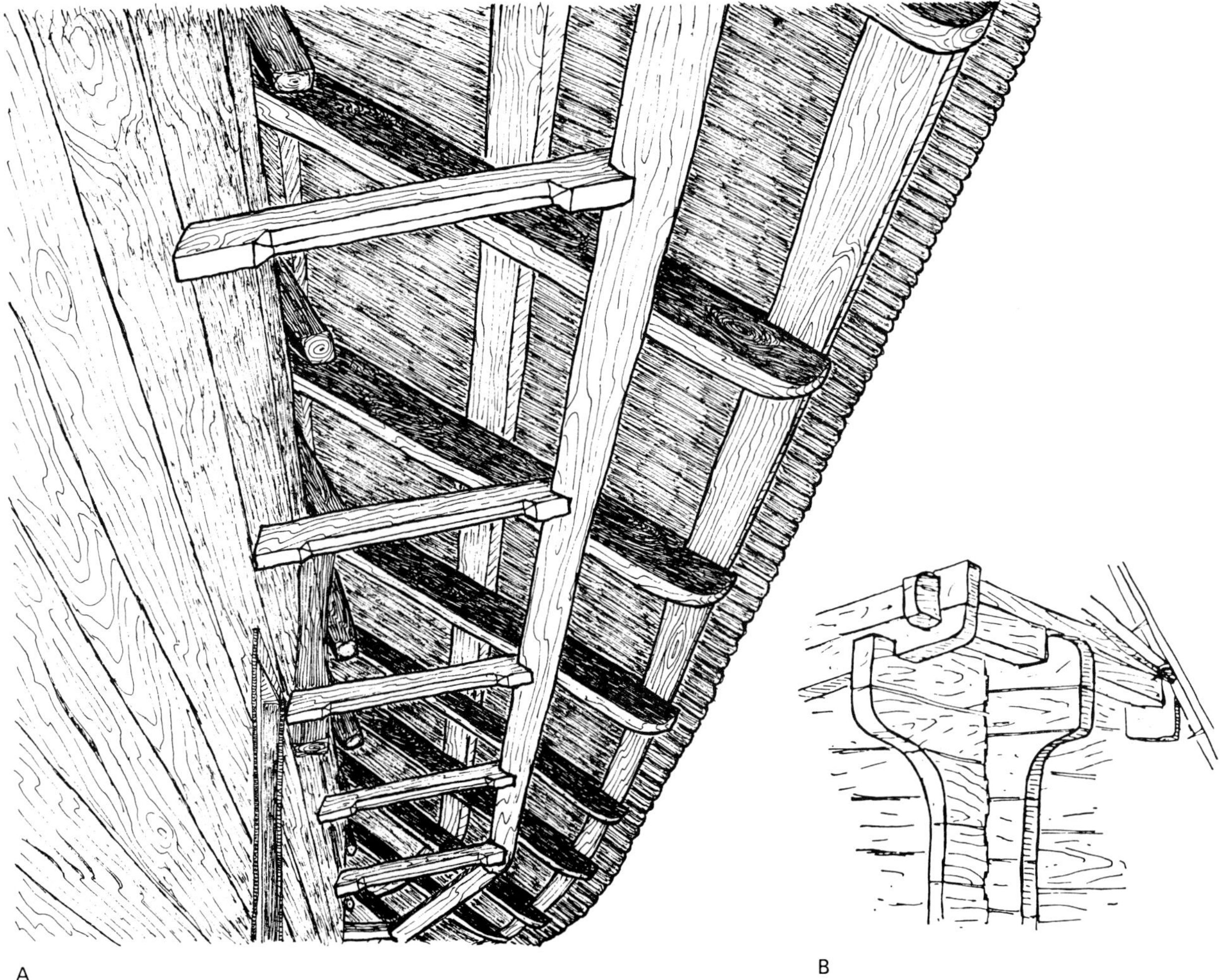

275 Serbian methods of supporting eaves: A by struts (Pokaynitsa); B by brackets (Dobroselitsa).

rather than eastern affiliations. These churches are very simple and there is little difference (architecturally) between those of Orthodox Serbia and Catholic Croatia. I shall take Serbia first, where the surviving churches are all of very late (early-nineteenth-century) date.

Five centuries of Ottoman domination (tyranny, the Serbs would say) were a sad sequel to the proud and splendid years of the medieval Christian kingdom. Nothing like the great Byzantine churches of the golden age could ever be built again. Though the Christian faith survived, the modest rural church architecture which survived with it owed nothing to the Byzantine tradition. As in any other country, wherever forests abounded village architecture would be based on timber. So it was in the wooded, hilly regions of old Serbia, south of Belgrade, both east and west of the Morava valley, that most of the wooden churches were built. Their survival, however, appears to have been beset with even more hazards here than in neighbouring countries. Since the Middle Ages many generations of wooden churches must have been built only to be destroyed or abandoned in the perpetual unrest. During the centuries of Turkish rule – far longer in duration and far more heavy-handed than their 'indirect rule' in Wallachia – the Serbs found it expedient to keep their churches as small and inconspicuous as possible. They had no towers at all – nor was there any point in building a belfry, since bells were not allowed to be rung.

Conditions became more favourable under the Austrian regime which lasted (as in Oltenia) from 1718 to 1739. But the Turks then regained the country for another fifty years. Meanwhile there was a revival of national consciousness leading to major insurrections in the late eighteenth century. It led also to a renewal of activity in church-building, the motives being at once religious and patriotic. But even those churches

276 'Pokaynitsa'. Elderly monk in the semi-circular western porch.

have mostly disappeared. Independence was achieved by the Serbs – at least for some part of the territory they claimed – only after 1815, under Prince Miloš Obrenović. The wooden churches now standing in Serbia (just over forty are described in the monograph by Pavlowitch) nearly all date from Miloš's time. They still follow the tradition – though it was no longer imposed by a hostile occupying power – of the inconspicuous house-like roof unbroken by tower or turret. But these churches, however modern their date, are genuine examples of traditional Serbian folk architecture. Many are in use, while some have been restored and are maintained as historical monuments.

In principle these Serbian churches have the usual three sections with the addition of a porch, but there may be no porch, and in small churches or chapels the narthex may not be clearly differentiated. The diversity of plans found in Serbia (in view of the small number of surviving churches) is surprising, but all are characterised by the simplicity of the basic layout, with no narrowing-down of the sanctuary (**272**). Some of those with simpler eastern terminations, far from being earlier efforts, are reversions of the mid nineteenth century. Some combine such apses with north and south projections which produce a semi-cruciform plan (**272** F). But most of the churches built between 1810 and 1830 specialised in many-sided apses, with seven or eight facets. They looked almost semi-circular and the ideal of the time was evidently the perfect semi-circle, inspired by masonry apses (D, E). These were laboriously pieced together from curved timber sections, their junctions so arranged as

277 'Pokaynitsa'. Interior facing iconostasis (note that this has middle and north doors only).

278 Typical Croatian church at Draganički Goljak near Karlovac, 1689. Longitudinal (east–west) section and plan.

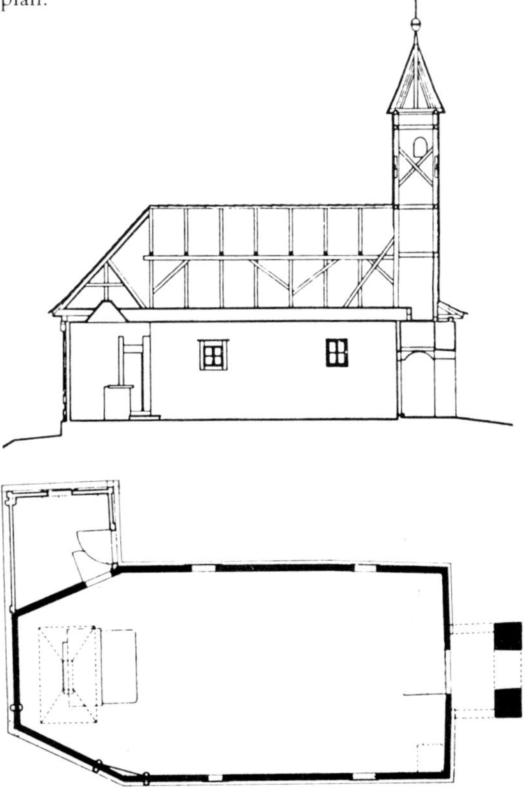

279 Free-standing bell tower at Čačinci in Slavonia (north-eastern Croatia).

280 St Barbara, Velika Mlaka, Zagreb. Eighteenth/nineteenth centuries.

not to lie directly one above another. I mentioned earlier that the Serbian liking for round apses is paralleled in the Banat; elsewhere in Rumania this technique is rare. Another structural oddity seen in a few of these churches is the avoidance of proper jointing by the use of grooved uprights at the angles, into which the horizontal timbers are slotted (G). This ancient technique is likewise known in Bulgaria and Rumania (cf. **35** and **39**).

Porches also were the subject of special attention. Many of them are rectangular as in Wallachia, with balustrade and four uprights. The polygonal porch, however, proved more popular in Serbia and there achieved the same precisely rounded form that was sought after for apses, with the result that the most characteristic of all Serbian plans made its appearance – semi-circular at both ends (**272** C). An example better known than most is the church at Velika Plana in the Smederevo district, some 80 km south-east of Belgrade. Being entirely typical of its genre, it is here illustrated in detail so that any verbal description seems superfluous (**273–277**). Known as the Pokaynitsa (Pokajnica) or church of Atonement, it was built in 1818 by the Voivode Vuytsa after he had, on the orders of Prince Miloš, murdered his own godfather, Karageorghe Petrovich. The latter had led the first Serbian rebellion and was a political rival of the Prince, who however associated himself with the building of the church and thus with Vuytsa's act of contrition.

From Belgrade to Zagreb, the Croatian capital, is a distance of 400 km. Croatia is not only distant from Serbia but different, a fact of which those peoples are very much aware, despite their close relationship and a shared Slav language (written however in different alphabets). Their divergent traditions arise largely from history, for Croatia, long part of the Austrian but only partially and briefly of the Ottoman empire, was more in touch with the west and became a Catholic, not an Orthodox country.

It has been said already that the Byzantine tradition of the old Serbian kingdom apparently left no traces in the wooden architecture of later centuries. I have also tried to show that all the 'Basic Balkan' churches, whether Orthodox or Catholic and wherever they occur in Yugoslavia or Rumania, are closely related to each other and to the architecture of western rather than eastern Europe. It is natural, therefore, to find the Croatian churches conforming to the already familiar type; at most one can say that they are rather taller than average in relation to their width or length. Some of them have the narrowed apse which is normal in Wallachia but wanting in Serbia. Apart from the fact that nearly all are Catholic, these basic little churches, adorned with simple bell turrets at their western ends, would cause little surprise if they stood on Wallachian soil – less than in Serbia, where belfries were generally taboo.

The Croatian Catholic churches here presented come from the rural triangle formed by Zagreb and the small towns of Karlovac and Sisak. Otherwise defined, it is the area between the Sava and its tributary the Kupa including the plain known as Turopolye (from the bison, *tur*, that once lived there) and some minor hills. Some of the prosperous citizens of this fertile area used to live in a type of two-storeyed log house with outside stairway known as the *čardak*, some good examples of which can still be seen in the villages.

281 Cerje Pokupsko, south of Zagreb. Church built c. 1725 from the south-west.

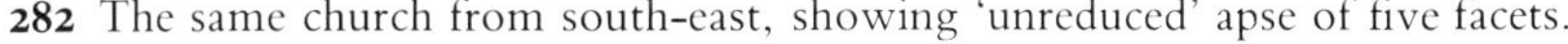

282 The same church from south-east, showing 'unreduced' apse of five facets.

283 St John the Baptist, Buševec, 1768. South side with 'reduced' apse to the right.

284 Ljevi Štefanki in Turopolye. Church of 1725 seen from the west.

285 Ljevi Štefanki from the east, showing reduced, three-sided apse.

286 Interior of Ljevi Štefanki, view eastward to the altar.

The wooden churches here are often less conspicuous than the finer private dwellings. But under the Austrian regime there was no need to hide or disguise churches so they were generally embellished with small western belfries. Plans can be matched among those known from Serbia and Wallachia except that, in these Catholic churches, nave and sanctuary did not have to be so sharply separated, nor was there necessarily a western vestibule. The plan and section of a comparatively early surviving example (1689) shown in **278** are typical, except that the base of the tower is here partly built in masonry. The apse is three-sided with annexed sacristy. Other apses are five-sided and in some cases narrower than the nave but never, as far as I know, with the more numerous facets that found favour in Serbia. In some areas free-standing belfries are found (**279**).

Among wooden churches in Croatia the one most often seen, because it stands on the outskirts of Zagreb near the airport, is St Barbara at Velika Mlaka (**280**). Though of very simple plan terminating in an unnarrowed, three-faceted apse, it is quite imposing, thanks to a more than usually substantial (and probably modern) western tower built in blockwork. The country chapels, on the other hand, have small turrets in framed construction which may crown the gable-

287 Ljevi Štefanki. Baroque detail in the chancel.

end directly over the porch as at Cerje Pokupsko (**281–282**), or stand further back at the forward shoulder of a hipped roof as at Buševec and Ljevi Štefanki (**283–285**). The interior views of this last little church show that the nave has a flat ceiling of painted panels while the miniature sanctuary rejoices in a high Baroque altar, fitting into a more elaborate ceiling of trapezoidal form (**286–287**). It is interesting to find that the churches belonging to immigrant Orthodox communities in Croatia are indistinguishable, externally, from those of the Catholics. The pleasing and nicely shingled example shown in **288**, with reduced, five-sided apse, is at Buzeta near Glina, about 60 km south of Zagreb.

THE NORTHERN TRANSYLVANIAN STYLE

It was the unwelcome destiny of the Rumanians of Transylvania to be ruled almost throughout their history by a foreign power. Yet Transylvania had been the heart of the Dacian kingdom (whose capital, Sarmizagetusa, was near the modern city of Hunedoara) and after the conquest it remained the heart of the Roman colony. During the obscure centuries of the great migrations the Magyars were tending to push eastwards towards Transylvania, 'beyond the forests', and by c. A.D. 1000 their rule was established there. The settlers first sent in by the Hungarian kings were however Szeklers (a related Finno-Ugrian tribe) and

288 Buzeta, near Glina. Orthodox church of the Prophet Elijah, 1813.

Germans, and it was these latter who founded the principal towns of Transylvania – to them Siebenbürgen. Great numbers of Hungarian colonists followed later and during the Turkish domination of their country (sixteenth–seventeenth century) the Transylvanian principality became the one refuge of a free Hungary. It is understandable therefore that the Hungarians have always regarded this desirable territory as by rights their own. Nevertheless the mass of the population remains Rumanian and many eminent Rumanians have been Transylvanian-born. So the boundaries of greater Rumania as drawn in 1918, which at last included Transylvania, did make a reasonably convincing geographical as well as ethnographical unit, despite the large Hungarian communities included unwillingly within it.

The unique wooden churches of north-western Transylvania including Maramureş evolved, under the influence of masonry architecture, from simple prototypes like those described earlier in this chapter. This evolution occurred in comparatively modern times – in the seventeenth and above all the eighteenth century when, over wide areas of eastern Europe, the skills of the carpenter reached their zenith. And it occurred in a region which formed part of the Austro-Hungarian empire for centuries, until the disintegration of that empire in 1918. Except in the south, Transylvania is rich in wooden churches. I cannot give a figure for their numbers, but 1274 were said to be still standing in the 1930s.

Some reference has already been made to wooden churches in the Banat, in south-western Transylvania. They clearly formed part of the south Rumanian 'Basic Balkan' group. The same can be said of many individual churches in central Transylvania – the area around Tîrgu Mureş and thence eastward to the Carpathians which has been studied in detail by E. Greceanu. In fact many of these churches lack bell turrets (though they may have free-standing belfries instead) and some possess the supposedly archaic plan of the apsed oblong, without any narrowing of the sanctuary. Others lacked porches, or had them added subsequently. The reasons in each case were simply economic: the Rumanians in this area were in the position of serfs on big Hungarian estates and did not possess the resources to build more ambitiously. Another factor was the proximity of Moldavia, and a few churches are thus of trefoiled Moldavian plan. A certain number, however, have sizeable Baroque or Gothic belfries which seem to place this group in an intermediate position between the 'Basic Balkan' in the south and the fully fledged Transylvanian further north.

Only by moving further north-west do we reach that exciting country where many a tall, slender spire appears on the distant horizon, piercing the sky. This will mark yet another wooden church, displaying yet another master carpenter's skill, audacity and individual artistic sense. One can still enjoy the experience in favoured parts of the counties of Bihor and Sălaj, best of all in Maramureş, using that district name in its geographically wider sense. But even in these districts the simpler, ancestral types of church are not unknown, and one from Maramureş is shown here (**289**). By including an example from Hungarian territory further down the Tisza I wish to stress the wide extension of these basic types: the Mándok church (now in the village museum at Szentendre) could reasonably be identified as Wallachian (**290**). It is also true, as will be shown below, that the real Transylvanian style extends into territory which, though inhabited at least in part by Rumanians, has never formed part of the Rumanian State.

The churches of this fully mature style are characterised by the inordinate vertical extension of their roofs and towers. Towers are the dominant feature and may, in extreme cases, be of such tremendous height as to dwarf the church below. They are undoubtedly inspired by Gothic or Baroque models existing in the masonry architecture of the Transylvanian cities: Gothic prototypes had been available here ever since the Middle Ages. If there could be any doubt about this dependence the corner-pinnacles clinch the matter. Many Transylvanian masonry steeples have four pinnacles at the base of the spire, and similar ones appear again in the wooden churches of the Rumanian villagers. These are to be seen not as copies but rather as re-interpretations in timber of the Gothic churches long familiar to the rural population. And yet, surprisingly enough, there is no evidence of wooden church towers being built earlier than the seventeenth century. The vast majority – and all the more imposing examples – date from the eighteenth century. Monumental porches – another attractive feature – were developed at the same period.

Reverting now to the typology of plans, I am reproducing a selection here from northern and north-western Transylvania (**291**). It will be noticed that all these plans could be matched in Wallachia. Conversely, nearly all Wallachian plans have counterparts somewhere in Transylvania. Only the types with broadened naos or narthex are very rare there and not represented in the figure. There are many examples of the unreduced apse (A–D), and square sanctuaries are common (E, J). There are also seven-faceted examples (C), a few with a median angle (D), and I believe only a

289 Small country church near Moisei, Maramureş.

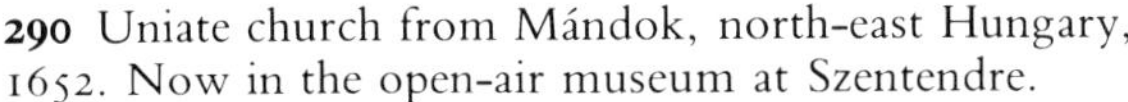

290 Uniate church from Mándok, north-east Hungary, 1652. Now in the open-air museum at Szentendre.

single semi-circular one. The trefoiled plan (not illustrated) is an interloper from Moldavia. In spite of these exceptional occurrences, nearly all major churches share the most frequent of 'Basic Balkan' plans – that having an apse of reduced diameter and of five facets (F–I). As these plans show, porches, and the associated open galleries, may follow the south wall, or both north and south walls, or may wrap right round the western end of the church, occasionally right round the whole church (H). More often there is a western porch only, which however may be much elaborated; it may also become polygonal (G) or very large and square (I).

Unlike the widely distributed plans, north Transylvanian superstructures are absolutely distinctive. An analysis of the most advanced type will be given later but some general points, applicable to the style as a whole, can be made here. The steep raftered roofs immediately attract attention as do the tall Baroque or Gothic-type towers which emerge through the roof towards its western end. The principal roof covers both narthex and naos while an independent, lower one is usually provided for the sanctuary. The towers, western in inspiration, are likewise western in their framed construction which contrasts with the solid blockwork of the churches themselves – a contrast paralleled in the churches of the Lemks (Chapter 3)

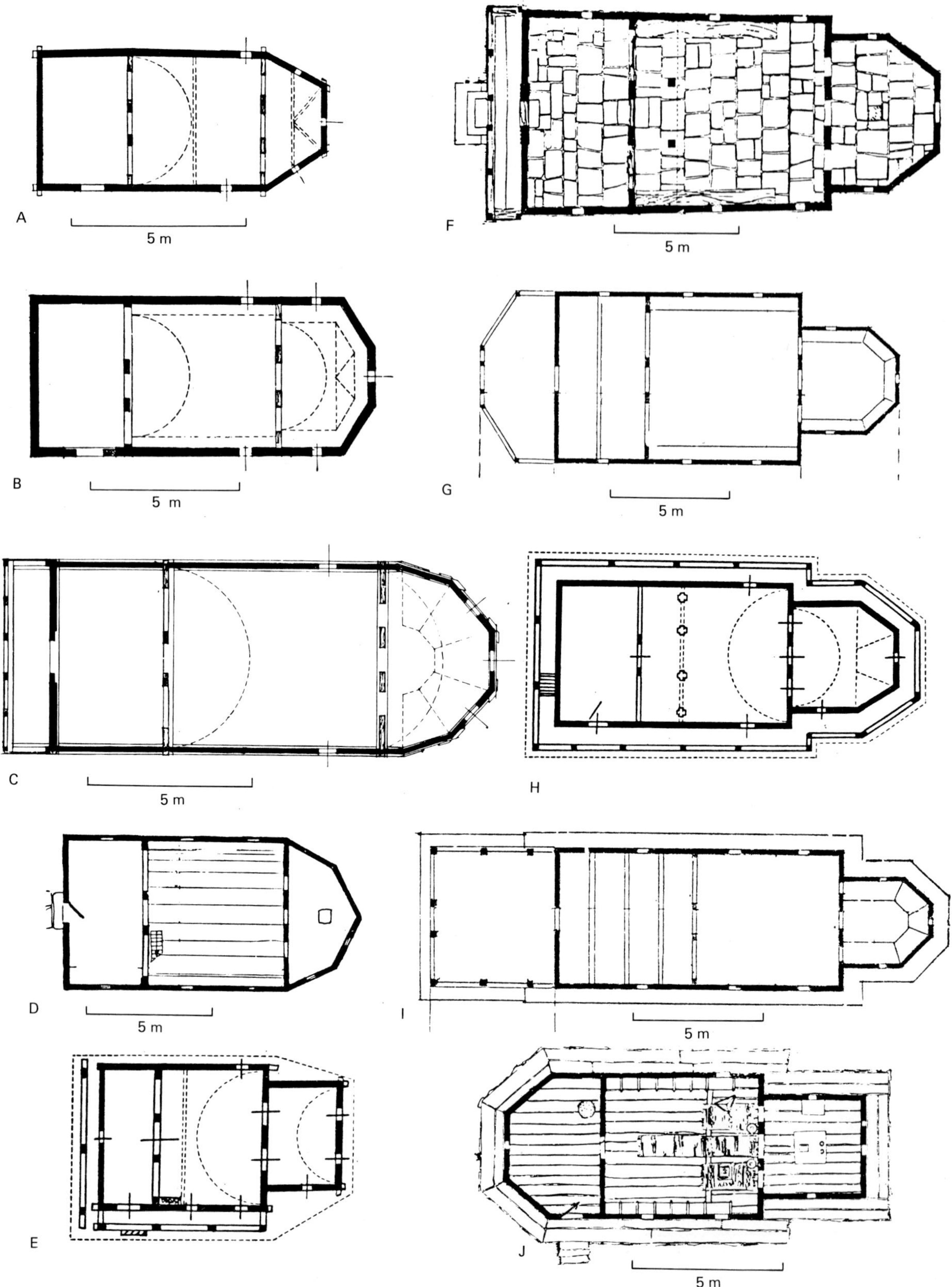

291 Wooden church plans in Transylvania including Maramureş. A. Cupşeni, Lăpuş. B. Dobricul Lăpuşului. C. Costeni, Lăpuş. D. Stobor, Sălaj. E. Sacalaşău, Bihor. F. Şurdeşti, Maramureş. G. Glod, Maramureş. H. Boianul Mare, Bihor. I. Văleni, Maramureş. J. Rebrişoara, Bistriţa-Nasaud.

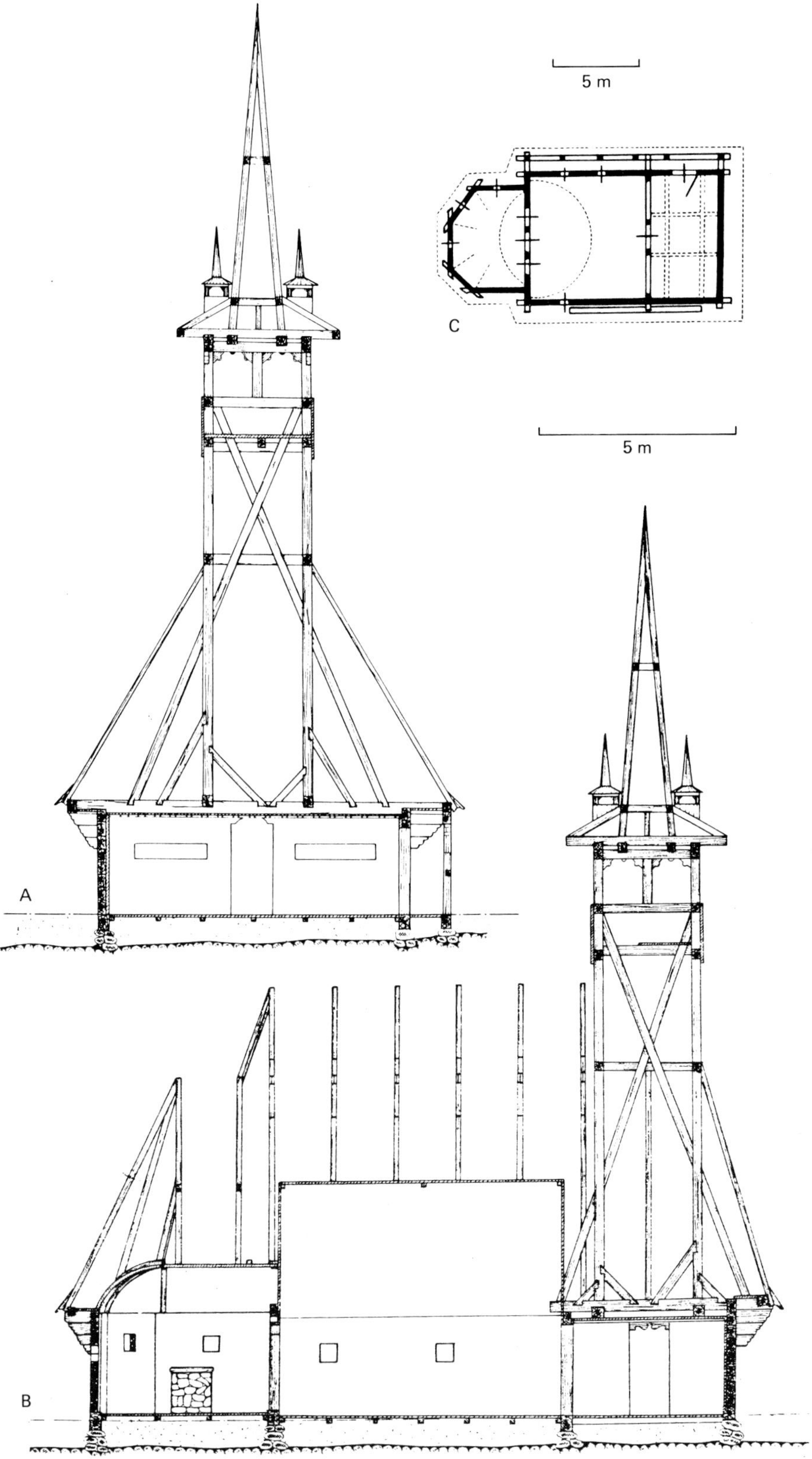

292 Brusturi (now Oradea). Plan, transverse section through porch and longitudinal section to show method of mounting the tower.

and of the Catholic Poles (Chapter 6). The narthex of these churches lies directly below the tower, but is not encumbered, as one might expect, by the tower's corner uprights. The means adopted to avoid this must be regarded as a triumph of rural carpentry and are explained in **292**. The corner-posts of the tower are in fact made to stand on the horizontal timbers in (or immediately over) the low narthex ceiling. This of course greatly increased the difficulty of ensuring the stability of the structure. The problem was solved by the use of diagonal timbers, concealed within the roof space, running from points outside the tower to the uprights of the opposite side – an inverse system of buttressing. At the same time these diagonals served to deflect part of the heavy burden of the tower from the narthex ceiling onto the solid walls of the church.

Spires of one sort or another are the most conspicuous external feature and one's mental classification of the churches tends to be governed by them. On the western margins of the area, in the counties of Arad and Bihor adjoining Hungary, we find that Baroque spires are (or were) very numerous and sometimes in a majority. Some typical examples taken from Petranu's work on Bihor are shown in **293**. Further east a sprinkling of wooden Baroque towers may still be found. A splendidly bulbous one, out of all proportion to the size of the church, stands at Lăschia on the western outskirts of Maramureş (**294**). Another is set on the masonry church at Valea Chioarului south of Baia Mare in the same general area (**295**). In the region as a whole, however, it is the Gothic influence that predominates overwhelmingly. I must add that this applies not only to wooden churches as a whole, but to wooden spires standing on stone- or brick-built bases. An interesting example is the medieval church at Gurasada with its central and western towers both finished off in timber (**296**).

In Bihor, where this brief survey of Gothic-type spires begins, there are several varieties. Generally they are angled, spreading out abruptly near the base as at Surduc, a simple example of early type (**297**). Where corner turrets are present, as in the church from Brusturi (**292**, **298**), they stand on this expanded base. Where the spire spreads out gradually, is octagonal in section and overhangs its base it resembles nothing so much as the mouth of a trumpet (Sacalaşău, **291** E, **299**). In the Beiuş area south of Oradea there are slender spires broken by a projecting collar, sure sign of Baroque contamination. These may be rather oddly combined with an overhanging bell chamber, an element (very common in Transylvania) derived from medieval castle towers. The church at Brădet standing sentinel above the village is

294 Lăschia. Wooden church with Baroque tower.

295 Valea Chioarului. Brick-built church with Baroque tower in timber.

293 Typical Baroque towers from Bihor county.

296 Gurasada, Hunedoara county. Church of the Archangel Michael with timber-capped towers.

297 Surduc, Bihor county, Western tower.

301 Stînceşti (formerly Broaşte), Bihor. South-west view.

298 The church from Brusturi, now at Oradea, glimpsed from the south-east. 1785.

299 Sacalaşău, Bihor. West end of the church built 1721 and 1756.

300 Brădet, Bihor. St John the Evangelist as seen from the village below. 1733.

302 Church from Petrind, Sălaj, now in the open-air museum at Cluj-Napoca. Early eighteenth century.

a fine specimen of this type (**300**) and there is a very similar one at Rieni. Stînceşti (formerly Broaşte) also has a collar, but no overhanging bell chamber (**301**).

East of Bihor comes the county of Sălaj (centred on Zalău) where about sixty wooden churches survive. They represent similar types to those of Bihor subject to the waning of Baroque influence. The plans recorded here include several examples with unreduced apse and all the less usual variants of the *reduced* apse: round (Bulgari); square (Sighetul Silvaniei); four-sided with median angle (Dragu). Two churches from this district can be seen re-erected in the open-air museum at Cluj. One of them (Cizer) is rather unusual in having a polygonal narthex and an open gallery encircling the whole church, except for the sanctuary. The other, brought in from Petrind, has a prominent tower with low-placed, overhanging bell

303 The church from Petrind: western silhouette.

chamber (**302–303**). In the extreme gloom which prevailed on the afternoon of my visit only its distinctive silhouette could be appreciated. The outlines of this and similar village churches make one of the most memorable visual images I associate with Rumania.

Another such church, with the low bell chamber typical of this area and even taller spire, still stands in

304 Fildu de Sus, Sălaj. The church of 1727 overlooked from the north-west.

305 Fildu de Sus: extended porch on the south side.

307 Rogoz. Main door with carved cross and 'horse-head' consoles.

306 St Paraskiva at Rogoz, Lăpuş district. Top of eighteenth-century tower.

its native village of Fildu de Sus. It certainly rewards a pilgrimage, along rough and dusty country roads (**304–305**). Moreover an excellent scale model in the Cluj museum is a great help in understanding its construction. The church stands on sloping ground above the village, on a rubble-built plinth which, quite high at the eastern, down-hill end, tapers off to the west as the ground rises. The church itself is quite small and unremarkable, with rope moulding all around and open porch along the south side. But the tower is amazing, especially when one realises that it does not rest on the ground. It rises from the narthex, whose massive ceiling timbers, together with its eastern wall, form a square base for the eight principal uprights. The long diagonal timbers which maintain its verticality, and at the same time transfer some of its weight to the walls, work as shown in **292**. The diagonals have their feet at points near the perimeter of the narthex ceiling, whence they reach across to the uprights of the opposite side. In doing so, the pairs of north and south diagonals can only barely be accommodated within the roof which they practically touch. All this refers only to the tower up to the bell chamber, whose ceiling forms the base of the tremendous spire. This has eight angles each formed by a long pole (presumably of fir) together with a vertical one in the centre with cross-rungs to form a ladder.

We can now approach the classic area of Maramureş, further north-east, via the Ţara Lăpuşului, that is the upper valley of the Lăpuş and its tributaries. Wooden churches here again exhibit a wide range of plans, with sanctuaries both of reduced and unreduced diameter, each providing examples of a rather unusual feature – the seven-faceted apse (**291** c). Gothic-type steeples occur throughout this group, many with and a few without corner turrets. Ornamental western porches may or may not be present. These churches differ from those of Maramureş proper in that their roofs are not divided into upper and lower sections, nor is the sanctuary roof differentiated. I show a tower and some carved detail from one of the two wooden churches at Rogoz (**306–307**).

From here it is only a step into Maramureş proper, just over the hills. In its narrower sense the district is defined as the valleys of the Viseu and Iza, with their tributaries, both minor affluents of the Tissa which now forms the Soviet border. (Beyond the river is northern Maramureş, long since cut off by political boundaries.) This is a comparatively isolated and scenically beautiful pocket of hilly and fertile ground, once shielded from marauders by the main Carpathian range and its outlying spurs. Rural traditions have lived on here and persist to this day. Nowhere else in

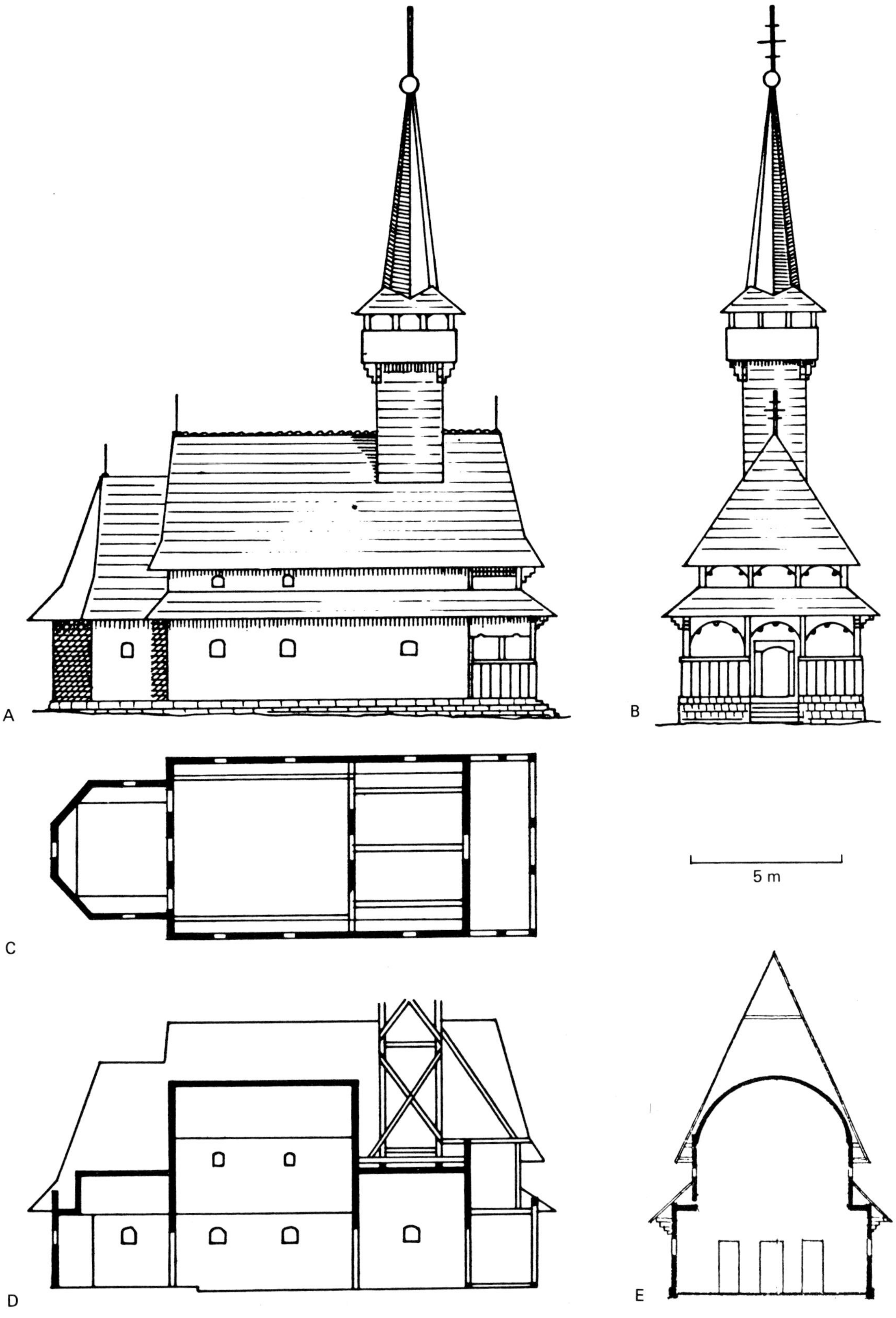

308 Characteristic features of major churches in Maramureş (A–D. Borşa; E. Sărbi). A. North elevation. B. West elevation. C. Plan. D. Longitudinal (east–west) section. E. Transverse section.

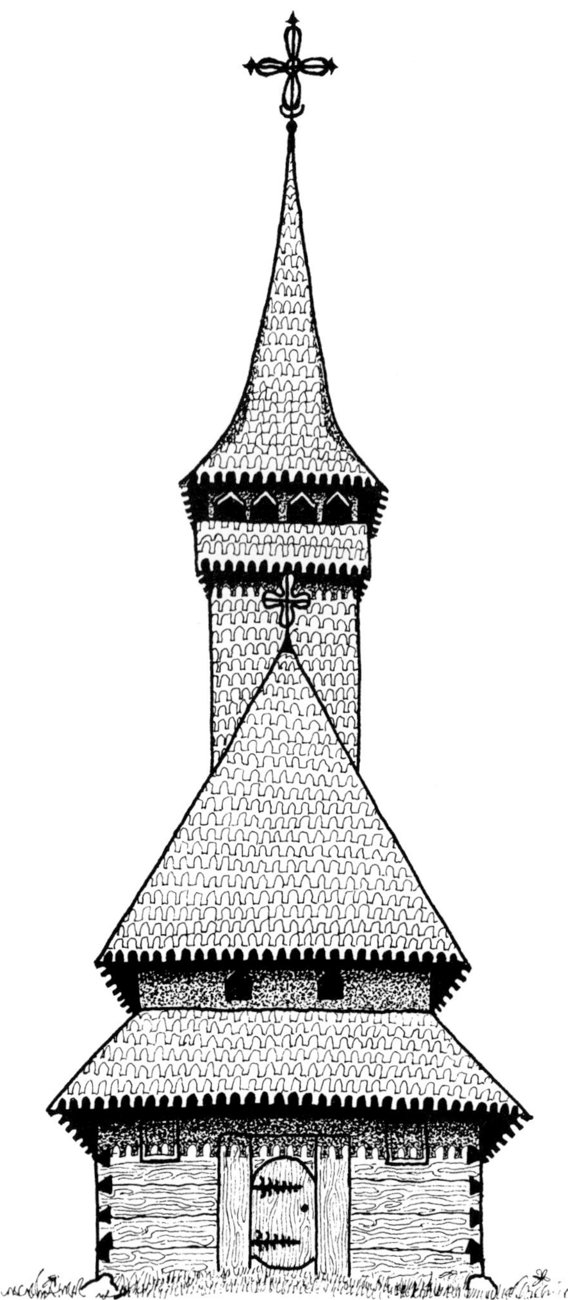

309 Ieud. Impression of the lower church, 1717.

Rumania (probably nowhere in Europe) do the country people use their national costumes – which vary from valley to valley – as a matter of course. The wooden village houses are as attractive as any in Rumania and one enters each compound through a monumental gateway of traditional design. Wooden church architecture flourished too and reached the climax of its development in the eighteenth century when the Gothic-inspired style of Transylvania was further elaborated and perfected here.

The plan, sections and elevations in **308** illustrate the salient features of a typical larger village church in Maramureş. The plan is the standard one with five-sided apse of reduced diameter and there is the usual western porch. The sections show a high naos ceiling which takes the form of a barrel vault. The sanctuary and narthex ceilings are low and the latter takes the main weight of the tower as shown in **292**. The tower itself, stabilised by diagonal timbers within the roof space, rises vertically to the bell chamber, whose overhang is supported on brackets.

The real novelty here is that the principal roof (but in this case not the sanctuary roof) is divided into two parts, the lower section being continuous with the roof of the porch. This comes about because the upper nave walls are set inwards, being carried on longitudinal beams (which may derive additional support from internal brackets). Thus the barrel vault of the naos, having a narrowed base, could be made appreciably smaller. As the transverse section (E) makes clear, the exposed link between lower and upper nave walls had to be either included under the main roof or provided, as here, with a roof of its own. This second roofing system had the advantage of leaving the upper nave walls exposed, so that the interior lighting could be improved by the insertion of high-level windows. Aesthetically, it offered the further advantage of diversifying the exterior. The western aspect of the church benefited most of all for the opportunity was taken to introduce a gallery over the porch, with arch-braced openings to match those of the porch itself below (B). All these arrangements remind one of Gothic masonry churches which were no doubt their source. Internally, the north and south sides of the naos (though not colonnaded) resemble narrow aisles, protected by their own lower roofs, while the windows above the aisle roofs resemble a clerestory.

Wooden churches are exceptionally numerous in Maramureş and many of them conform to this special local pattern, though there are also simpler ones as at Ieud where the porch is lacking (**309**). The more distinctive western aspect, with open porch and matching openings above, is here illustrated by Fereşti (**310**). The attractive small church at Bîrsana of which I give a drawing and a photograph (**311–312**) has a similar type of porch, but with only three arches above and below. There are also churches in the area, like Cuhea (Bogdan Vodă), where the system of reduplicated roofs extends to the sanctuary (**313**).

These and many other churches in the home valleys of Maramureş have the angled spire so widespread in Transylvania, but lack corner turrets. To find the most imposing of all churches of this category we

310 Fereşti. Fully developed western porch of Maramureş type, eighteenth century.

311 Bîrsana. Late-eighteenth-century church from the north-west. Drawn by Elizabeth Waterfield.

312 Bîrsana, viewed from the north-east.

313 Cuhea (formerly Bogdan Vodă). Church of 1718 showing reduplicated roofs round the east end.

have to re-cross the hills to the west, descending beyond them to the village of Şurdeşti (**314**). Basically, the church is nothing very extraordinary, judged by the high standards of this area, with the normal plan and an overall length of 18 m (**291** F). There are separate 'aisle' roofs, but no special one with lower ridge for the sanctuary. The western porch, while rather narrow, is decoratively treated, the wide openings which flank the entrance arch being each partially divided by a pendant (a Baroque touch). Above the porch roof a row of semi-circular arches, standing at the level of the narthex ceiling, complete the picture, and they turn the corners for a short distance along the south and north facades (compare **324**). Cantilevered brackets help to support both sets of overhanging eaves and a rope moulding runs all round.

Standing before the porch one looks up to the western gable-end of the roof with its curious projecting half-funnel which masks a ventilation opening for the roof spaces (**315**). Above this the tower is seen soaring skyward and it is this tower that really holds one's attention, at 54 m the tallest on record in the area, three times the length of the church. Unlike the arrangement at Fildu de Sus its square base here rises high above roof level to the bell chamber, a projecting course being introduced half way up to break the monotony. The bell chamber itself, with four arched openings on each side, is capped (as usual) by the splayed-out base of the spire, which here carries four very slender corner-pinnacles. The entire structure sits on the narthex ceiling, and one can find the feet of two diagonal buttressing timbers behind the open arcade above the porch. At close range, of course, it is not possible to appreciate the immense height of the tower: to do so one must stroll about the neighbourhood. For miles around it dominates this idyllic countryside, with its fields and woodlands and plum orchards, and hamlets with wooden houses and steep-roofed, thatched farm buildings. The church is rightly deemed a masterpiece and was restored in 1960 by the Historical Monuments Commission.

At the neighbouring village of Plopiş there is likewise an imposing wooden church, whose considerably later date probably accounts for the falling-off in its architectural standards (a common tendency in the outgoing eighteenth century). There is no lower tier of roofs (hence a rather high blank wall), perfunctory consoles, indifferent joints which are not dovetailed, and an unpleasing porch lacking the ornamental upper storey. All the same, its commanding position and high tower, modelled on Şurdeşti, make it another impressive landmark. It was restored in 1961 (**316**).

There is one more notable church-type found in small numbers in the area. This has a very large square porch which is treated as a separate entity and crowned with a belfry of its own. My example comes from Saliştea de Sus in the upper Iza valley and its plan resembles that of Văleni (**291** I and **317**). A similar porch may be attached on the south side of the narthex instead of the west. A charming church on this plan, said to have been built originally in Vişeu near Salişţea, now stands in alien territory at Techirghiol near the Black Sea coast.

Details of the external woodwork, whether in Maramureş or elsewhere in Transylvania, usually resemble what is found in Wallachia. Undoubtedly the most interesting features are the cantilevered brackets or consoles which support the eaves. The examples shown at Rogoz (**307**) and Harniceşti (**318**) are typical, the former showing also the church door, a large carved cross, and an incomplete rope moulding. One adjunct of many churches, especially in Maramureş, is so characteristic that it cannot be passed over: this is the monumental gateway to the church precincts (**319**). Unlike the gateways to private yards which have a large opening for carts and a small one to the side for people on foot, these church gates are triple and symmetrical. The craft of the carpenters and carvers who build and adorn them on traditional lines still flourishes, and this particular gate, photographed in 1974, had only just been completed.

Internally the iconostases are, of course, the principal objects of interest. They conform broadly to the universal Orthodox pattern and do not differ materially from the Moldavian specimens shown in **347** and **356**. It must be said, however, that in some smaller and earlier churches the iconostasis has only two doors – the 'royal' door and the one to its left (as seen from the naos). Also, the tiers of icons above the door may be reduced as in **320**, which does not possess (or possibly has lost) the usual series of Church festivals.

I must add some final paragraphs on the adjacent but now inaccessible country north of the Tissa where Rumanian villages presumably still exist and a number of churches of the Maramureş style still stand. This region belonged to Czechoslovakia between the wars and now forms part of Soviet Trans-Carpathia. It has already been mentioned in Chapter 3 as the meeting ground of Lemk and Rumanian influences and some wooden churches of intermediate type were illustrated there. The ones I wish to include here are, however, of almost pure Rumanian character. It is good to know, from published sources, that some of these churches have been restored and are now maintained as cultural monuments.

314 Şurdeşti. Church of the Holy Archangels, 1724. The tallest in Maramureş (54 m).

315 Șurdești. West face of the tower.

316 Plopiş. The church built between 1796 and 1811, seen from the south.

317 Saliştea de Sus, in the upper valley of the Iza. Church originally of 1650 (1680?).

318 Harnicești, church of 1770. Stepped consoles projecting from south nave wall.

The photographs reproduced here include the very similar and entirely typical pair, Aleksandrovka (Shandrovo) and Sokirnitsa, both some way down the Tissa valley in the vicinity of Khust (**321–322**). Others of the same group are Danilovo, Steblevka (Saldobosh) and Krainikovo. All have spires with corner-pinnacles, which are angled like the spire itself and suggest little ballet dancers. The spires are mounted in the usual manner (see **292**), the various diagonals being very long (up to 10 m) and sometimes duplicated for added strength. It is also interesting to note the slight convergence of the corner uprights, a factor which contributes to the gracefulness of the tower and eases the transition to the tapering spire above.

The church at Serednee Vodyanoye (Apșa de Mijloc), not far, as the crow flies, from Sighetu Marmației on the Rumanian side of the border, strikes a different note (**323**). Its tower, with high bell chamber and short pyramidal spire, is unusual and (like several churches in this area) it retains the archaic square sanctuary. My last illustration here shows the beautiful western porch at Maidan with its elaborately carved columns and upper range of nine arched openings (**324**). These are reminiscent of Șurdești, but the spire is without corner-pinnacles. Maidan lies in the main Carpathian range on the upper Rika, 50 km north of Khust. While this church accords with the style developed in Maramureș, one suspects that some other influence has crept in. It is interesting that Rumanian communities, or at least the strong influence they exerted, should have penetrated so far to the north, well away from the political boundaries of the country.

321 Sokirnitsa, Khust district, Soviet Trans-Carpathia. St Nicholas, 1709.

322 Aleksandrovka, Khust district. Church of St Paraskiva, basically seventeenth century.

320 Rona de Jos, Maramureş. Iconostasis.

323 Serednee Vodyanoye (Apşa de Mijloc), Soviet Trans-Carpathia. Upper church of St Nicholas.

WOODEN BELFRIES IN HUNGARY

The splendid wooden bell towers of northern Transylvania, inspired though they were by the Gothic of the neighbouring cities, belonged to Orthodox churches of the Rumanian villages and were the work of their own master carpenters. It was perhaps more natural that Hungarian communities should likewise have been influenced by the Gothic steeples of Transylvania, especially as that territory formed an integral part of the Hungarian State for centuries. Village carpenters in what is now the north-eastern corner of Hungary did in fact build magnificent wooden belfries – some with corner turrets, the ultimate proof of their descent from Gothic models. They differ, however, from Rumanian versions in being almost always free-standing: the churches themselves are in masonry, wooden ones being now rare in Hungary. It is interesting, too, that practically all such towers belong to the Reformed (i.e. the Calvinistic) Church. In the sixteenth and seventeenth centuries Calvinism enjoyed an enormous success among Hungarians, especially in the east and in Transylvania. Transylvania, in fact, became a great Protestant stronghold, but the Germans, led by Johannes Honterius of Braşov (Kronstadt) turned Lutheran while many of the Szekler element embraced Unitarianism. (These conversions, of course, did not affect the mass of the Rumanian rural population which remained faithful to Orthodoxy.)

The Calvinists in north-eastern Hungary today, together with their brethren now living within the Rumanian borders, form one of the largest Protestant communities in eastern Europe, numbering more than two million souls. Among the great figures of the movement immortalised in stone in the Monument of the Reformation at Geneva we find, alongside John Knox and Puritan and Huguenot leaders, Stephen Bocskay, 'the Protestant hero of the first Hungarian upheaval against autocratic rule'. Here Calvinism played a major role in the politico-religious struggle against the Habsburgs, and it proved resilient enough to withstand the Counter-Reformation. The main

319 Contemporary monumental gateway to a church precinct, Maramureş.

centre of the Hungarian Reformed Church is Debrecen, once called 'the Calvinist Rome', headquarters of the county of Hajdú-Bihar. The next county to the north is Szabolcs-Szatmár, also Reformed Church territory. All this area belongs to the upper basin of the Tisza (Theiss), several stretches of which form the Rumanian–Soviet or the Hungarian–Soviet border.

In the area so defined a number of imposing wooden bell towers can still be seen. They are not, of course, built in blockwork but in timber-framing which is usually based upon nine massive uprights: four at the corners of the main structure, four at the mid-points of the sides and one in the centre. As in Transylvania their spires are angled, for their base spreads out and carries the corner turrets if these are present. The shaft of the tower is vertical but in turn spreads out at the base to form a roof sheltering the open space at ground level. Again as in Transylvania the bell chamber – which may or may not overhang – has two to four arched openings, and a similar arcade surrounds the roofed space at the foot of the tower. The finest surviving belfries of this type date from the seventeenth century, others being no older than the eighteenth or early nineteenth.

Travelling north-eastward from Debrecen one can see a rather simplified late example, lacking corner turrets, at the village of Nyírmihálydi (**325**). Then we reach the small town of Nyírbátor which possesses one of the most impressive of all these towers, a tremendous thick-set structure with corner-pinnacles and four-fold openings to the overhanging bell chamber (**326**). The remaining examples depicted here stand close to the Tisza or between that river and the Soviet frontier. The neighbouring villages of Gemzse and Szabolcsbáka both have smaller towers differing in various details but each retaining corner turrets (**327–328**). At Vámosatya there stands a belfry of uncommonly tall and slender outline (**329**). It contrasts with Nyírbátor but resembles one brought from Nemesborzova in the same area and re-erected in the open-air museum at Szentendre, near Budapest. As a final example from this region I illustrate the very late but pleasing porch-belfry at Nagyszekeres (**330**). It shows that the traditions of the style were not yet extinct in the early nineteenth century.

While dealing with the north-eastern corner of Hungary it may be of interest to show the attractively primitive little Protestant church, with its all-wooden fittings, at Tákos (**331–332**). Such churches may once have been numerous but are now uncommon and this

324 Maidan, Mezhgorsk district. Eighteenth-century porch of the church of St Nicholas.

one is regarded as a museum piece. The altar – simply a table – stands on the north side, backed by a special panelled pew-pulpit for the pastor. There is a western gallery and ordinary pews in the nave, but those in the eastern end of the church face back westward towards the table and the pastor's pew. The woodwork is painted in rustic motifs of Renaissance origin, the ceiling panels being dated 1766. The basic structure of the church cannot be seen, owing to plastering both inside and out, but it is probably of framed timber.

I must now return to belfries, these being as a rule the only timbered structures belonging to Hungarian churches. Some of the great free-standing campaniles which are the most characteristic buildings of this category have already been seen. There are, however, in Hungary as in Rumania, many masonry towers with wooden caps which can themselves be impressive achievements of rural carpentry. Their bell chambers may have two, three or four arched openings, and some are completed by a set of corner-pinnacles. One such crowns the church at Fehérgyarmat which, as one might guess, stands not far from the Transylvanian border (**333**). The Romanesque church tower at Csaroda (near Tákos in the same area) is surmounted by a slightly over-sized cap like an extinguisher – a quaint combination (**334**). A little further to the west, between Miskolc and the Slovak border, the medieval churches at Bánhorváti and Boldva also have wooden

325 Nyírmihálydi, north-eastern Hungary. Bell tower of 1782.

327 Gemzse, near Kisvárda. Village bell tower.

tops (**335–336**). These examples, with their overhanging bell chambers, are still somewhat reminiscent of Transylvania, but that influence is now waning. There is hardly a trace of it at Miskolc itself (**337**), still less in the all-wooden belfries at Radostyán or at Szalonna near the Slovak border (**338–339**). Their upper storeys, far from overhanging, are of reduced diameter.

All the above bell towers belong to Protestant churches. Even in the extreme west of Hungary, where a few more wooden belfries exist, this is still generally true, but here there can no longer be any question of a link with Rumania. A typical one, capped by a small bell chamber, stands in the village of Pankasz west of Zalaegerszeg, whose open-air museum contains a simplified version from the adjoining village of Csöde (**340–341**). It will be noticed that the belfry from Schallendorf in nearby Burgenland (**342**), now in the Austrian open-air museum at Stübing, is of exactly the same type, and comparable ones exist over the southern border in Yugoslavia (**279**). Although it takes us outside the domain of architecture proper, and no link with Transylvania survives, I conclude with a charming one-piece bell-cot from Budafa, now preserved at Zalaegerszeg (**343**).

326 Nyírbátor. One of the mightiest of the free-standing belfries in Hungary, built 1640.

328 Szabolcsbáka. Village bell tower.

329 Vámosatya near the border with Soviet Trans-Carpathia. A very tall specimen dated 1691.

330 Nagyszekeres, east of Mátészalka. Porch-belfry built 1819 and 1836.

331 Tákos. Eighteenth-century Calvinist church, probably timber-framed with infilling of wattle and daub. The interior, looking west.

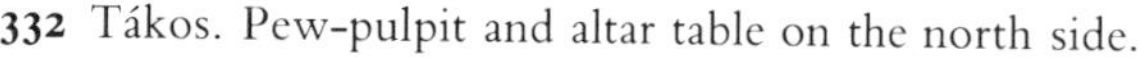

332 Tákos. Pew-pulpit and altar table on the north side.

333 Fehérgyarmat. Transylvanian-type wooden crown to medieval church tower.

334 Csaroda. Late Romanesque (thirteenth century) tower with wooden cap.

335 Bánhorváti. Wooden crown to fortress-like church tower of the fourteenth century.

336 Boldva, near Miskolc. Medieval brick-built church tower with wooden crown of Transylvanian type.

337 Miskolc. Belfry of Calvinist church (1557) with wooden upper storeys.

338 Radostyán, near Miskolc. All-wooden belfry of 1762.

339 Szalonna, near the border with Slovakia. Free-standing church belfry of 1765.

THE MOLDAVIAN STYLE

The former principality of Moldavia is equivalent to eastern Rumania of today (excluding the low-lying province of Dobrudja between the lower Danube and the Black Sea). Moldavia always had a relatively stable western border with Transylvania, formed by the heights of the Carpathians traversed by only a limited number of easy passes. On the other hand its eastern boundary has fluctuated considerably between the alternative river frontiers of the Dniester and the Pruth, for Bessarabia, the country between these rivers, has changed hands again and again. Roman Dacia, theoretically at least, included it. Kievan Russia probably claimed most of it between the tenth and twelfth centuries, but after the great disruption of the Mongol invasion (1241) the Tartars were left in control. In the fourteenth century the Wallachians (from whose

340 Pankasz, in the extreme west of Hungary. Free-standing belfry of Calvinist church, 1730.

Basarab dynasty Bessarabia derived its name) extended their sway over some part of the territory, but Moldavia, in view of its geographical position, was in a stronger position to colonise and to hold it.

The Moldavia of Stephen the Great (1457–1504) certainly included Bessarabia. But after his death, though native princes continued to rule on sufferance, Moldavia became an Ottoman vassal State (as Wallachia had done some years earlier). For about three centuries thereafter Turkey controlled the area and Moldavia – including Bessarabia – became the scene of perennial conflict in the long succession of Russo-Turkish wars, besides suffering incursions from time to time by Hungarians, Poles and Ukrainians. In the eighteenth century the Austro-Hungarian empire became involved in the territorial rivalries of the area. Transylvania, of course, already formed part of it. In the 1770s Austria extended its sway to Galicia, north of the Carpathians, at the expense of Poland, and then to northern Moldavia (or Bukovina) at the expense of the then tottering Ottoman empire. In 1812, following the last Russo-Turkish war, Moldavian territory suffered a further big loss: the Ottomans had to cede Bessarabia to Russia with the result that Russian and Ukrainian colonists began to arrive in considerable numbers. Russia held Bessarabia and Austria held

341 Belfry from Csöde now at Zalaegerszeg.

342 Belfry from Schallendorf (Burgenland, Austria) now in the open-air museum at Stübing.

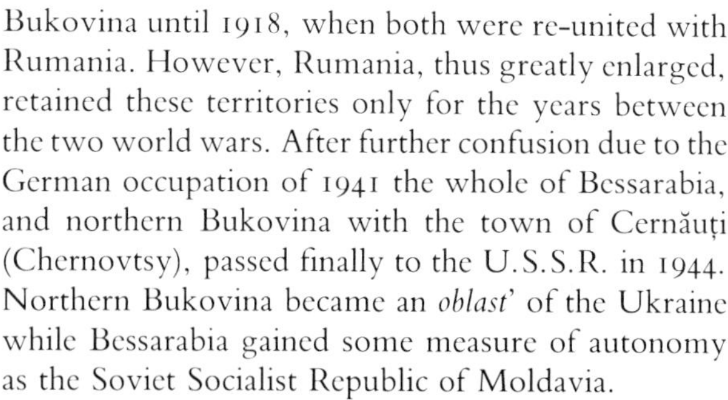

Bukovina until 1918, when both were re-united with Rumania. However, Rumania, thus greatly enlarged, retained these territories only for the years between the two world wars. After further confusion due to the German occupation of 1941 the whole of Bessarabia, and northern Bukovina with the town of Cernăuţi (Chernovtsy), passed finally to the U.S.S.R. in 1944. Northern Bukovina became an *oblast'* of the Ukraine while Bessarabia gained some measure of autonomy as the Soviet Socialist Republic of Moldavia.

It is remarkable that Moldavia's troubled and chaotic history proved not incompatible with cultural achievements of a high order. Both architecture and the subsidiary arts, all bearing a strong Byzantine imprint, flourished exceedingly. For this we have to thank the personality, and above all the piety, of some outstanding individual rulers, while leading nobles and ecclesiastics naturally played their part too. Stephen the Great is the best remembered of Moldavian princes, and his great equestrian statue overlooks Suceava, the capital city. Succeeding to the throne as a youth of twenty-one he divided his boundless energies and the many years of his reign between military and religious pursuits. In recognition of his determined (but ultimately fruitless) campaigns against the infidel Turks, confidently advancing after the capture of Constantinople, Pope Sixtus IV dubbed him the 'Athlete of Christ' – a signal honour for a non-Catholic. At other times Stephen had to repel the Hungarians encroaching from the west and the Crimean Tartars from the south-east. On the other hand he established satisfactory relations with Russia and with Poland (then a contiguous and often threatening power) and inaugurated diplomatic contacts with the Italian and other western States. An extremely pious ruler (though hardly blameless in private life), Stephen never doubted that God was on his side. Among his many religious foundations Putna and Neamţ are the best known. Moreover he generously supported some of the monasteries at Mount Athos, left orphaned, as he saw it, by the fall of the parent metropolis, Constantinople.

343 Village bell-cot from Budafa, now at Zalaegerszeg.

It was during the reign of Stephen the Great's illegitimate son, Petru Rareș (1527–46 with one interruption) that the Turks finally gained possession of Moldavia, though their policy at that time was simply to levy tribute through the local princes. During these years most of the now famous 'painted churches' of northern Moldavia received their marvellous clothing of late Byzantine frescoes, related to those of Athos – an immense undertaking carried through, surprisingly, without interference from the Turks. Artistic activity took other creative forms. Whoever visits the various monastic museums of the region – Putna and Dragomirna especially – cannot but be deeply impressed by the icons, the church furnishings, the embroidered vestments, the illuminated scriptures, displayed there. And the Moldavians, possibly even more than other Rumanians, seem to have an inborn artistic sense which still seeks expression in their daily lives. Their village houses, new or old, are invariably embellished with colour and carving while handsome monumental gateways stand before them. Nothing, in fact, is too utilitarian for adornment. The roofs of well-heads, and today even of bus-shelters, are often charming and ingenious examples of artistic craftsmanship.

The distinctive Byzantine architecture of Moldavia continued to evolve, producing original forms, well into the seventeenth and even the eighteenth centuries. It will be seen shortly that the wooden churches of the principality, unlike those of Wallachia, came to be much affected by the local Byzantine tradition. Whence comes this marked difference between the wooden churches of the sister principalities, whose masonry styles were equally Byzantine and continually influenced each other? Probably the explanation lies, at least in part, in Moldavia's geographical position in close proximity to the Ukraine. Over the centuries there were, of course, many political and military involvements between these neighbouring States, whether we think of the 'Polish' Ukraine of the seventeenth and eighteenth centuries or of the 'Cossack State' based, as a rule, on Kiev. There were also matrimonial links between their ruling families. In the religious sphere, the monastic movement based on Neamț (one of Stephen the Great's major foundations) was influential in the Ukraine. And close ecclesiastical links were proved again when a Moldavian nobleman and bishop, Peter Mogila, became Metropolitan of Kiev in 1633.

One's first impression of Moldavian wooden churches can be disappointing for the majority are of very subdued profile, with long house-like roofs and often no conspicuous external feature. This characteristic has been ascribed to the unwelcome presence of the Turks who, though surprisingly tolerant in religious matters, disapproved of any ostentation on the part of the Christians. It has been suggested, alternatively, that the domes and vaults to be described below demanded the protection of a conventional roof against the inclemencies of the weather. Whatever the true explanation, the Moldavian designers and carpenters certainly went to great lengths to compensate internally for the undue severity of the exterior.

Until the early eighteenth century the plans of these churches must have exhibited the same range of types as those of Transylvania and Wallachia (with which

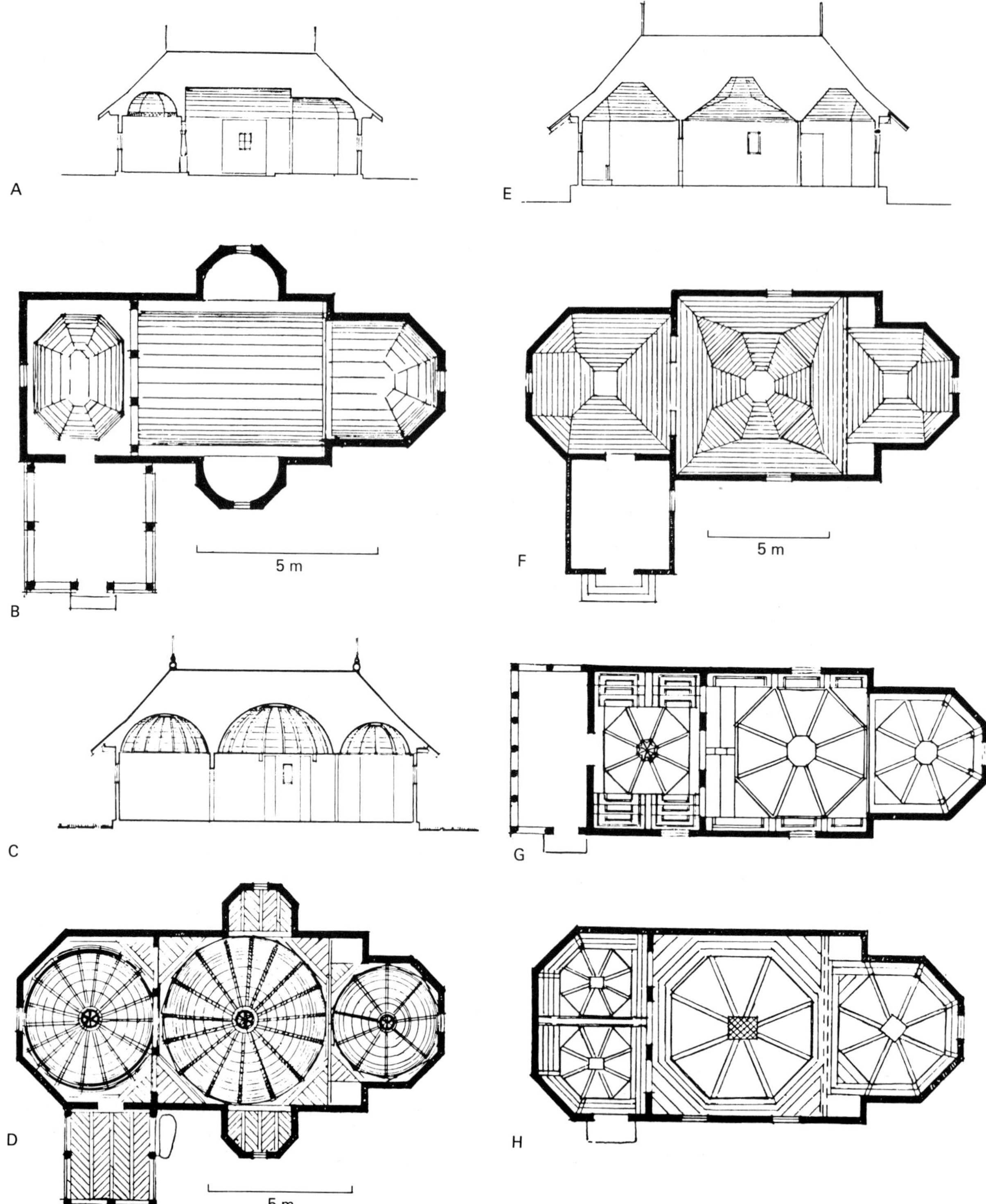

344 Moldavian plans and longitudinal (west-east) sections. A,B. Brăieşti. C,D. Cerviceşti. E,F. Dorohoi. G. Golgofta, Vaslui. H. Trestiana.

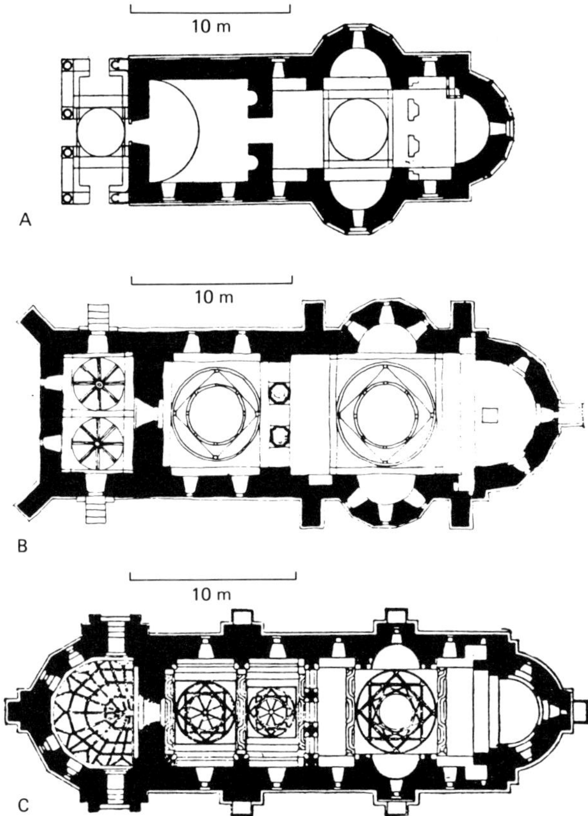

345 Masonry plans related to wooden types. A. Cozia: an early Wallachian trefoiled plan (1380). B. Church of the Three Hierarchs, Iaşi (1639): trefoiled with twin domes over pronaos. C. Dragomirna, monastic church (1608): internally trefoiled; polygonal west porch.

there are other links in points of decorative detail, especially the rope moulding). It is probable, however, that the plan with broadened naos, rare in other areas, early gained ground in Moldavia owing to the proximity of the Ukrainians, who used it continually. Several existing Moldavian plans, taken from the valuable paper by I. Cristache-Panait and T. Elian, are shown in **344**. Some are simple oblongs with narrowed, polygonal apse. But many of them possess, in addition to the eastern apse, lateral apses to north and south of the naos, each having three or five facets. It has been shown that these trefoiled plans, so characteristic of Moldavia, only came into use for wooden churches in the eighteenth century, in fact the majority date from the last quarter of that century or even later. Porches, which may or may not be present, are likewise an embellishment first seen in the late seventeenth or eighteenth century. As a general rule, where the west end of a church (that is, of its narthex) is square, the porch will be a western one, but where the narthex is polygonal the porch is transferred to its southern side. South porches are often large and square in plan, in which case they are usually surmounted by a bell turret and provide the main external accent of the church.

There has been some difference of opinion as to whether the Byzantine churches of Moldavia influenced, or were influenced by, contemporary wooden ones. The belief that brick architecture took over wooden forms was expressed by V. Vătăşianu, writing at the time under Strzygowski's influence. He quotes a source of 1791 describing how a masonry church was actually built around a small wooden one, every feature of which was duly copied. This could well have happened. Yet to my mind there can be no possible doubt that the wooden trefoiled plans were derived from local brick-built, late Byzantine models, and polygonal west ends (which are not uncommon) may have had the same origin (compare plans of masonry churches, **345**). The same must be true in some degree of domes, though they were difficult to construct in the unaccustomed medium of wood. The solutions adopted will be discussed below.

The ground plans in **344** are combined with ceiling plans and these, together with the longitudinal sections provided, give some idea of the rich variety which Moldavian interiors present. Normally, narthex, naos and sanctuary each have their separate ceiling unit. Simulated barrel vaults occur, either alone or in various combinations with domes (A, B), while many other churches have domes only. Barrel vaults have been convincingly attributed to the effect of the Transylvanian Gothic, a conspicuous element in the masonry architecture of Moldavia. But domes were most probably inspired by Ukrainian, and later by local Byzantine models. Some Ukrainian influence in this field was to be expected, and has been recognised by Rumanian scholars. In fact, the basic type of Ukrainian wooden cupola, built, like the walls, of solid horizontal timbers interlocking at the corners, was taken over in Moldavia where it generally forms a truncated, eight-sided pyramid only seen internally (**344** E, F; **354**, **359**). Such cupolas continued in use but were often supplanted by more realistic (if much less solid) domes resulting from direct Byzantine inspiration. These are based on a framework of curved ribs with infilling of boards (**344** C, D, G, H). In the case of Trestiana, a very late church, the narthex has paired domes of this type (**344** H and **355**). They were probably suggested by the famous church of the Three Hierarchs in Iaşi (Iassy) or some other similar Moldavian church, which themselves followed earlier Wallachian models (**345** B).

I can now comment briefly on the churches

346 Vama, Suceava county. St Nicholas, eighteenth century, from the south-east.

347 Church of Dragoş Vodă, Putna. Iconostasis seen from pronaos; northern apse visible on left.

348 Farcaşa. St Paraskiva, 1774. View from east showing large south porch.

349 Brăieşti. Church of the Assumption, 1790. South side.

350 Drăguşeni, Suceava county. St Spiridon, 1780, from the south-east.

351 Botuşana, Suceava county. St Dumitru (Demetrius), 1810. South side.

352 Bicaz Ardelean. St Dumitru, 1829, from south-west. A sounding-board hangs on the porch.

illustrated. At Vama there is an outwardly simple type without porch but with a free-standing belfry (**346**). The church is trefoiled, faceted at both ends, has a dome over the narthex and an amalgam of dome and barrel vault over the naos and sanctuary. The church at Putna, near Stephen the Great's famous monastery, is equally unobtrusive externally. It is known to have stood there in the fourteenth century but dates in its present trefoiled form (like most wooden churches in this area) from the eighteenth. It has a closed western lobby instead of an open porch and the church proper is covered by a continuous barrel vault with faceted extremities. The iconostasis, viewed from the pronaos in **347**, is typical of Moldavia and of Rumanian churches generally. The church at Farcaşa (Neamţ county) dedicated to that favourite female saint, Paraskiva, and the Assumption at Brăieşti (Botoşani county), are both good specimens of the plan with

353 Cozla-Draga, Neamţ county. Church of the Trinity, 1764. Details of western porch.

large, square southern porch-cum-belfry (**348–349** and plan **344** A, B). The same may be said of St Spiridon at Drăguşeni (Suceava county) whose porch is however enclosed. In **350** one can see the consoles supporting its eaves and the rope moulding round the apse, which continues along the oddly projecting wall beams at mid-height.

St Dumitru at Botuşana (Suceava county) has a big southern porch which wraps round the log-built base of a sizeable belfry (**351**). A smaller cupola projecting through the roof over the 'crossing' is supported by the solid old-fashioned pyramidal vault over the naos – something that could not be done by the frail 'fake' domes which were more popular at the time. Centrally placed, freely projecting cupolas like this are untypical of Moldavia and only appeared in modern times. The same applies to bell turrets rising, as they sometimes do, at the western end of the main roof – a non-Byzantine feature familiar, however, in other parts of Rumania. At Bicaz Ardelean (Neamţ county) such a turret is seen combined with a polygonal west end and a small southern porch (**352**). Cozla-Draga (also Neamţ) has a small turret in the same position. The west end of that church is square and preceded by an attractive porch, a detail of which is shown in **353**.

The interiors of these Moldavian wooden churches are made interesting by the complex ceiling patterns already shown diagrammatically (**344**). Photography is difficult in these cramped internal spaces but the 'Ukrainian' type of pyramidal cupola is shown in **354** and **359** and twin domes of Byzantine type in **355**. An iconostasis from one Moldavian church was shown in **347** and another, from Cerviceşti, is given in **356**. It conveys something of the glow of these wonderful gilded screens in the subdued light of the naos. These two examples may be compared with the iconostases

354 Cristești, Botoșani county. Naos ceiling.

355 Trestiana, Iași county, church of 1853. Twin ribbed domes of the pronaos.

356 Cerviceşti, Botoşani county. Iconostasis of the church of the Assumption, 1787.

357 Polyana, Soviet Bukovina. Church of St Nicholas, 1618, seen from the south.

358 Polyana. Eastern apse with consoles.

359 Lukovitsa, Soviet Bukovina. St Dmitri, 1757. Pyramidal naos ceiling with top of iconostasis.

from other Orthodox areas illustrated in Chapter 3 (**123**, **140**, **196**, **202**) and with the relevant text at pp. 141–7. Rumanian iconostases show the same general plan and the Royal Doors in the middle are, as usual, intricately carved. Above the doors come the icons devoted to festivals of the Church, above them again the extended *Deesis* with processions of Apostles. The fourth and final tier embraces medallions in various arrangements including prophets (bearing scrolls) or patriarchs. In most parts of the Orthodox world the middle of the festivals tier, immediately above the Royal Door, is devoted to the Last Supper. In Rumania however, as the photographs show, this is sometimes replaced by the Vernicle – St Veronica's legendary Kerchief bearing the imprint of Christ's face.

Both Bessarabia, now Soviet Moldavia, and the northern half of Bukovina, now part of the Ukraine, possess wooden churches of Moldavian type. Those of northern Bukovina tend to be as plain as possible externally, like one shown here from the village of Polyana, but on closer acquaintance they may reveal interesting detail, like the apse with its consoles (**357–358**). From the village of Lukovitsa in the same area I give an uncommon interior photograph showing the eight-sided pyramid, built of solid horizontal timbers, which crowns the naos (**359**). As suggested earlier the Moldavians seem to have borrowed this Ukrainian technique but they used it only for interior cupolas hidden under church roofs. Nonetheless, as I have shown in Chapter 4, the system here seen in miniature is identical to that once used in the eastern Ukraine on a grand scale.

6

Catholic churches in Poland and Czechoslovakia

The western Slavs, whose principal homes today are Poland and Czechoslovakia, have much in common. They have naturally had closer links with western Europe than the eastern Slavs, though the same can be said of the Croats and Slovenes of present-day Yugoslavia, that league of 'southern Slavs'. Geographically and historically both Poland and Czechoslovakia can be seen to form bridges between central and eastern Europe. The languages of the three principal peoples – Czechs, Slovaks and Poles – are closely related and all employ the Latin alphabet (though there is a wide difference between their spelling conventions). The rejection of Cyrillic and the adoption of the Latin script is to be associated with these peoples' westward orientation and, in particular, their adherence to the Church of Rome. From the point of view of the present survey this religious factor is, of course, of prime importance.

One of the great missionary enterprises of the Eastern Church (before its formal separation from the Church of Rome) was the Mission of Cyril and Methodius to the Slavs in the ninth century. It was directed in the first instance to Moravia, which is Czech territory. But the Byzantines failed to maintain the tie in the face of western competition. Bohemia, through most of history the more influential of the twin territories, and the one most exposed to German influences, opted early in the tenth century for the Latin Church. The Czechs therefore never formed part of the Byzantine Commonwealth. Nor did the Poles, who declared their allegiance to Rome later in the same century, in A.D. 966. This momentous decision, made under Mieszko I, the first king of a recognisable Polish State, may well have been prompted initially by political expediency. But the Poles never wavered in their devotion to the Roman Church and Poland has ever since remained the most staunchly Catholic country in the eastern half (if not the whole) of Europe.

This is my only chapter dealing with Catholic churches. It is mainly concerned with those of Poland where wooden churches lie thick on the ground, more particularly in the southern part of the country traditionally known as Little Poland. But the style extends without noticeable change of character beyond Poland's southern frontiers into Moravia and to a lesser extent into Moravia's neighbours – Slovakia to the east and Bohemia to the west. When some of these churches are described and illustrated in due course it will be made clear to which area each one belongs. However, before going on to architectural descriptions I must set out further aspects of the geographical and historical background of the style. The resulting picture is certainly confusing but it is relevant both to this and to other chapters.

The Polish State is unique in more ways than one. Unlike any other country in Europe its very location on the map seems to be in doubt and has continually changed. The Carpathians do indeed constitute a natural frontier in the south, though one by no means always respected. In the north too Poland can claim a natural frontier – the Baltic – even if she has managed to hold this seaboard only intermittently in the course of history. But to east and west there are no natural frontiers and Poland has pushed out and drawn in over the years like an amoeba, has been crushed and battered from east and west and even been obliterated as a political entity. Her great eastward expansion into non-Polish territory, which gained enormous strength from the historic union with Lithuania (1385), is remembered by Poles as one of the glories of their history, though the Ukrainians and others view it differently. It culminated, in the seventeenth century, in an empire which stretched from the Black Sea to the Baltic, and for a while embraced almost the whole Ukraine and much of western Russia. It led, inevitably, to a centuries-long and increasingly bitter conflict with the ever-growing power of Muscovy. Yet there was one recurrent menace common to both, that of invading hordes from the east: Mongols and Tartars in the thirteenth century, Tartars and Turks at intervals thereafter.

On the western side of the country we see a converse situation. Poland was not encroaching upon foreign territory but steadily suffering encroachment on the part of the Germanic States. This happened comparatively peacefully in Silesia, more violently in the north. As early as 1226 a Polish king unwittingly encouraged the process by inviting the Knights of the Cross – originally a Crusading Order – to help in subduing the pagan tribes of pre-German Prussia. His misguided action has been described as the most disastrous mistake in all Polish history. From the first these Teutonic Knights acted as the spear-head of Teutonic imperialism in northern Poland and far to the north-east along the Baltic coasts. Though defeated in 1410 at Grunwald (a battle commemorated by a street name in every Polish town) the Order remained a thorn in the flesh, retaining most of its vast northern conquests which blocked Polish access to the sea. The German *Drang nach Osten* did not abate. The Knights' great domains were later inherited by Prussia which had taken the name of the defeated tribe. Since the times of Frederick the Great, architect of the Prussian State, Prussian ambitions never ceased to grow. Their aggressiveness outdid that of the Tsars – with whom, moreover, they were liable to act in collusion against Poland.

Thus in the seventeenth and eighteenth centuries more and more Polish territory was engulfed on either side until the whole country, with Austrian connivance, disappeared from the map at the Third Partition of 1795. Ground down as they were, century after century, between the Russian and the German millstones, no wonder the Poles conceived for both peoples an inveterate loathing; and unhappily the events of subsequent history have done nothing to modify these traditional attitudes. Only the Austrian empire, though more than once a party to the partitions of Poland, and more than once (through its Habsburg House) a dynastic threat, seems to be spared some of the odium and profound mistrust which the Poles reserve for the other neighbouring powers.

Poland, set up again as a small Duchy by Napoleon but disappointed or ignored at every Peace Congress, had to wait for the First World War and the collapse of Tsarist Russia before achieving some recognition of her claims and resurrection as a major State. Between the wars she again held much of her old Ukrainian, White Russian and Lithuanian territory. She regained a short strip of Baltic coast where the city and port of Gdynia were built up out of nothing in record time. Danzig (Gdańsk) became a Free City while Germany smarted under the separation of East Prussia (not for the first time in history) from the parent State.

During the Second World War Nazi Germany launched a campaign, unprecedented in European history, to liquidate the entire Polish nation, besides the large Jewish minority living among them. In this unimaginable project they joined hands with Russia, as the Prussians had done in the eighteenth century, with a view to the total dismemberment of Polish territory. In the event, of course, these projects were carried out only in part, but Poland's experience after the war was nonetheless traumatic. The country was moved bodily westward, losing all the eastern territories to the Soviet Union while gaining, as a compensation, the long lost German-colonised areas to the west including the whole of Silesia, West Prussia to the Oder, and the long coastline of eastern Pomerania. These drastic changes in her boundaries were in some ways advantageous to Poland, but their cost in human distress to all the peoples involved was incalculable. Under chaotic conditions the German population, which predominated in the cities, fled or was forced westward towards the new Germanies. On the eastern side great numbers of Poles had to withdraw from the Ukrainian territory they had long since colonised, including the very Polish city of Lwów (L'vov). And the Ukrainians remaining within the new Polish boundaries (some of whom had been involved in anti-Polish activity during the war) were uprooted and dispersed, some finding a home in villages far to the west recently evacuated by the Germans.

These historical facts have a certain bearing on several chapters of this book. They explain how it came about that large sections of the hill-living Ukrainians or Ruthenians (Chapter 3) had to change their citizenship, from Polish to Austrian and (in 1918) back to Polish, while the latest frontiers have incorporated nearly all their homelands in the Soviet Union. On the opposite side of the country, centuries-long German colonisation in the north and west resulted in the appearance of Lutheran churches built in the western technique of framed timber (Chapter 7). Evidently the greater, multi-racial Poland of history eludes exact definition. But the heartland of the country, now united after centuries of division, and corresponding roughly to the kingdom in the days of its foundation, can more readily be defined. It is the river basin of the Vistula (Wisła) and its tributaries, besides the eastern affluents and upper reaches of the Oder (Odra). Such is the area with which this chapter deals. We are concerned with Polish Poland and its wooden Catholic churches, together with some that lie beyond its southern borders, in Czechoslovakia.

The main axis of the essential Poland is, then, the Vistula which connects Cracow, that beautiful ancient capital in the south, with Warsaw, capital since the beginning of the seventeenth century. Thence the river flows, partly through ex-German territory, to the Baltic coast east of Gdańsk. The Poles tend to be sentimental about their great river, about which much history and legend is woven. The national sentiment of the Poles is nourished too by their language, their religion, and the achievements of their great personalities in science, literature and music. Naturally enough, pride is taken in aspects of the country's political history, especially in the unique type of 'Royal Republic' or 'Republican Monarchy' they evolved – an elective monarchy whose powers were limited by the *Seym* or Diet through which the nobility (but not the *plebs*) could wield decisive power. Individual monarchs of both the older dynasties – the Piasts and the Yagellonians – have also, of course, earned lasting fame for their personal qualities, public spirit and leadership in war, but only very few of them can be mentioned in this chapter.

The nation's pride extends to all the cities of the country, however Polish or however Germanic their character. With the single exception of Cracow, mercifully spared, all the main towns were practically annihilated in the Second World War. The priority given, at a time of desperate housing shortage and financial disaster, to the restoration of Warsaw's old town centre was very significant. So too was the liberal use of strained resources for the restoration of historical and architectural monuments throughout the country. The same remarkable skill and meticulous care have gone into the rebuilding of brick Gothic churches in Germanic cities like Wrocław (Breslau) and Toruń (Thorn) as to any buildings of a more Polish tradition. At Gdańsk (Danzig) the vast Gothic cathedral of St Mary, whose vaults were smashed in, has long since been restored to its pristine state, but work still continues on the distinctive burghers' houses in the neighbouring narrow streets. Malbork (the Marienburg), the great fortified residence of the Grand Master of the Teutonic Knights, arch-enemies of the Poles, is the object of another loving long-term restoration scheme. Wooden churches, too, have had their fair share of attention in various parts of the country.

The wooden churches of Poland, as of Czechoslovakia, are a feature mainly of the countryside for very few have survived in the towns. They occur in many villages throughout the extensive plains of central and southern Poland and the hill country of the southern borders. Few foreign visitors ever see any for the churches are inconspicuous in themselves and often hidden among trees, nor is there much to attract the holiday maker to these regions. All the same, visitors to Cracow and the amazing salt mines at neighbouring Wieliczka, or those who make the pilgrimage to Częstochowa (possibly by way of that limestone wonderland, the Ojców National Park) could include some of these churches if they wished. But it is easiest of all for people staying at Zakopane, gateway to the Polish sector of the High Tatra and now a great summer and winter resort, for that area is rich in wooden churches.

Czechoslovakia contrasts with Poland, being predominantly mountainous. The hills with their extensive forests, their glades of vivid greenery, their charming villages, form ideal holiday country while many ancient towns and romantic castles attract the tourist. Bohemia as a whole is like a vast upland citadel and Prague one of the most beautiful cities in Europe. The Carpathians with their many subsidiary ranges follow on to the east, occupying much of old Moravia – still Czech country – and of Slovakia, where they culminate in the High Tatra on the Polish border. Compared with most of eastern Europe communications are excellent, industry (including rural industry) well developed and the standard of life high. The foundations of all this development were laid, no doubt, in the days of the empire. For centuries the Czechs belonged to the Austrian, the Slovaks to the Hungarian sphere, and Germanic influence, emanating from the towns, has been more long-lasting and more potent here than in Poland. So Czechoslovakia, and Bohemia in particular, became, materially, an advanced and very western country. From our own narrowly specialised point of view this has one drawback: modernisation has deprived Bohemia, over the last century, of most of its wooden churches. It will be seen, however, that Moravia provides some compensation.

In spite of the differences referred to, which attract the notice of travellers today, there has been no hard and fast historical frontier between the two countries, now Poland and Czechoslovakia, with which this chapter deals. The Austrian empire, besides possessing Bohemia and Moravia since 1526, incorporated Galicia too from the first Partition of 1772 until 1918, and it is now divided between Poland and the Ukraine. Silesia's history was even more chequered. Despite its basically Polish population it became, through most of the Middle Ages, a German-dominated Duchy, then a dependency of Bohemia and hence, for a time, of Austria, then (after 1740) part of the Prussian State. Germany was to hold most of Silesia until the Second World War when it reverted, after many centuries, to Poland. In view of the fluidity of these various frontiers it is not surprising that the rural architecture of the Catholic Western Slavs, whether Poles, Slovaks or Czechs, constitutes a single style.

I must now say something of stylistic origins, not only of wooden buildings (which cannot be viewed in isolation in these countries) but of the local architecture in general. As the result of long-continued contact with western Europe, especially through the Church, and the rise of purely Germanic cities, west European architecture became firmly established in Polish as well as Bohemian territory. The Romanesque, it is true, is only sparingly represented among surviving buildings. The Gothic, on the other hand, won increasing popularity and by the fourteenth century was established far and wide. In Poland it was under the last Piast king, Kazimierz or Casimir the Great (1333–70), a monarch in whom all royal virtues seem to have been united, that numerous churches and cities were first established – though the allegation that he 'found a Poland built of wood, and left it in stone' is wildly exaggerated. Sometimes, the Polish Gothic shows local or eastern ingredients, like the Byzantine frescoes found at Sandomierz, in the palace chapel at Lublin, and in the cathedral on the Wawel hill, Cracow. The impact of the style was re-inforced eventually by the late Gothic brick architecture of northern Germany (splendidly represented in towns like Wrocław, Toruń and Gdańsk) and in the south by the still more sophisticated late Gothic developed in Bohemia. But the wooden style seems to have been primarily a Polish product.

As the century of the Renaissance opened Poland found herself in a position of relative security and considerable influence. Members of the Yagellonian royal house also occupied the thrones of Hungary and Bohemia. The union with Lithuania was being consolidated – it became full and final in 1569. The accession of Livonia from a decadent knightly Order gave Poland again a Baltic coastline whence ships could operate against the supply lines of the Tsars, who needed to be kept in check (the most formidable was Ivan the Terrible). Nevertheless King Sigismund Augustus (1548–72), last of the Yagellonians, generally succeeded in maintaining the peace. He was followed, after two interregnums, by a notable elected monarch, Stephen Batory of Transylvania. During these reigns Renaissance learning penetrated freely. Copernicus was at the University of Cracow and many Poles studied at seats of learning abroad. Relations with Italy were close and a number of Italian architects who came to ply their trade in Poland disseminated their country's influence there. The Renaissance era was, however, short-lived and has left comparatively few monuments in Poland, the best being small-scale examples like the Sigismund chapel in the cathedral on the Wawel. There are also towns of predominantly late Renaissance or Mannerist character, notably the exquisite Zamość, only 50 km from the present Soviet frontier. As to wooden architecture, very little remains from the sixteenth century, and it was not obviously affected by the international style of the epoch.

The Baroque, on the other hand, is ubiquitous; it dominated the scene through most of the seventeenth and the whole eighteenth century and, as will be seen, had a marked influence upon wooden churches. This was especially true during the century 1680–1780, a period of intense building activity. It is interesting to note that this was also a century of political decline and disintegration. The country had recently been shaken by the great Ukrainian revolt under Bohdan Khmelnytsky who then proceeded to an alliance with Muscovy; Poland lost Kiev and all eastern Ukraine. Also, Muscovy had attacked in the north, even seizing the Lithuanian capital, Vilnius. The Swedes, at the summit of their imperialistic expansion, had invaded the greater part of Poland in 1655 and did so once more under Charles XII in 1700. His army was routed later at Poltava (1709) by Peter the Great, who was equally successful in his northern war against the Swedes, thus increasing the threat to Poland. During this period Polish morale found its best support in King John Sobieski's historic defence of Vienna against the Turks (1683). The eighteenth century saw further decay and disruption, leading up to the partitions. Yet through all these bad times for the nation the Church, far from showing signs of decline, must have maintained or even increased its activity and influence.

In the late eighteenth century, here as elsewhere, a phase of neo-classicism set in and tended to supersede the Baroque, which however lived on in the guise of folk art. In Poland there were neo-classical palaces and public buildings and some churches, often with mixed Baroque and classical features. Perhaps the most characteristic expression of the new style is found, however, in the rural manor house or *dwór*. These gracious but comparatively modest manors of the landed gentry, some of them wooden, continued to be built in considerable numbers during the early decades of the nineteenth century. They are basically single-storeyed with great roofs which may accommodate a few upper rooms, and there are often rectangular annexes or pavilions at the corners (**23**). Their classicism is usually limited to a pillared portico, which may rise high enough to form a frontispiece to the upper rooms as well. These manors are only marginally connected with the main subject of this chapter, but they will be referred to again in the Appendix on synagogues, which they evidently influenced. Again, it is noteworthy that many of these buildings date from a period when Poland was, politically, in continuing decline, or even completely eclipsed as an independent State.

In considering the wooden architecture of the area two general principles, already spoken of in earlier chapters, must be borne in mind. Firstly, the use of stylistic terms applicable to masonry buildings (usually 'Gothic' or 'Baroque') means little in the case of wooden buildings. Methods of construction depend on the capabilities of the timber itself more than on the period of construction, and have remained fundamentally the same from century to century. As a rule, stylistic descriptions can only relate to internal fittings such as altars and, externally, to towers and cupolas. For want of any better method I shall use the character of towers for a broad classification of the churches to be dealt with, but it would be rash to make deductions from this as to the order in which they were built.

This brings me to my second point, which is that it is impossible to deal with wooden churches on a strictly chronological basis. This is partly because the dates attributed to them, derived as a rule from parish records, only prove that a wooden church did exist on the site in question at the period stated. When records are more complete, as they are for instance for many Silesian churches, it becomes clear that extensive remodelling or even complete rebuilding took place at least every century. The other drawback of strict

360 Maniowy in the Pieniny hills, southern Poland. Cemetery chapel of 1723 from the north-east.

361 Veliny in Bohemia. Church of 1752, south side.

chronology – even if it could be achieved – would be its failure to correspond with the sort of evolutionary trends to be expected in masonry buildings. In wooden architecture complex forms were sometimes evolved at a very early date. On the other hand reversions to very primitive forms occur throughout the history of timber building, either because resources were lacking for anything more elaborate, or because only a simple structure was needed – as in the case of most cemetery chapels. Some good representatives of early types cited below were actually built in the eighteenth century.

In this chapter I am still concerned with churches built on the horizontal principle universal in eastern Europe – Strzygowski's *Blockbau*, the principle of the log cabin. It is true that towers of western origin, together with a method of construction equally western, were introduced in the sixteenth century. In the first place, however, I wish to deal with churches like those of the earlier Middle Ages when wooden towers, if they existed at all, would have been log-built and almost certainly free-standing. The churches to be discussed now have straight ridged roofs; there is no question of three separate elements, each with its own cupola, so popular in the Orthodox world. But there is often an independent roof, set at a lower level, for the sanctuary, which may be balanced by another lower roof over the western vestibule or the porch.

If these wooden churches of early type are compared with those built in stone or brick in the same areas, a close parallelism will be seen. These masonry buildings, which are very numerous throughout the region, must in fact be regarded as the prototypes of the wooden churches. The high degree of independence apparent in the wooden Orthodox styles further east is not echoed here. A comparison can only be made with Rumania, especially northern Transylvania, where Gothic architecture has been re-interpreted in timber with superb effect – for the purposes,

362 Veliny. Free-standing belfry.

363 Ustianowa, Rzeszów province. Seventeenth-century (?) church from the east.

surprisingly, of an Orthodox church (Chapter 5). The influence of the Gothic, followed eventually by that of the Baroque, is equally clear in the Catholic wooden churches of Poland and Czechoslovakia but it dates back to an earlier period and it takes a somewhat different form. In the remainder of this chapter attention will again be drawn to these close links between the architectures of masonry and wood. But they do not alter the fact that the wooden derivatives have attractive and important features not found in masonry, especially the surrounding galleries with their own roofs and the towers (to be described shortly) with their inclined walls and overhanging bell chambers.

A churchyard chapel like that at Maniowy (**360**) is the modern representative of an extremely simple, early type. Its eastern end is faceted (but not of reduced diameter), its western end square, with the only door, and the structural timbers are exposed. There is presumably one small window on the south side. A simple, undivided ridged roof covers the whole (but we have to ignore the Baroque spirelet). The roof is steep as it must be when destined to be clothed in traditional wooden shingles. The next stage of development is characterised by the narrowing of the chancel, which had in fact been standard practice in all larger churches for centuries. It no doubt recalls the influence – at least as early as Romanesque times – of masonry apses. My best example of this stage is another late church, at Veliny in eastern Bohemia (**361**). Again, a little Baroque lantern must be mentally excluded, and the windows visualised as much smaller. Subject to these reservations we have here a medieval church-type, its horizontal timbers exposed and nicely accentuated by the plastered interstices. A log-built fence around the precinct, with its own miniature ridged roof, completes the picture. There is a separate framed belfry too – a reminder that this complex is not really medieval at all (**362**).

364 Ustianowa. North side with projecting sacristy.

These two churches are too simple to show any very distinctive features. The next examples will be more typical of the style since they possess an external gallery with its own low roof jutting out from the church wall. The small church at Ustianowa in the south-east corner of Poland is an attractive example of purely Catholic type, though it has been used as an Orthodox church through part of its history (**363–364**). In this case the external gallery is confined to the narrowed, faceted chancel. Since the walls are nowhere boarded over, the basic structure of the building is plain to see. These two views also show the sacristy built on to the north side of the chancel – an almost invariable adjunct which gives these Catholic churches a characteristic element of asymmetry.

The cemetery chapel at Lipnica Murowana, embowered among great trees, is believed to be genuinely of late Gothic date though the external boarding and shingling have, of course, required renewal. It has the simplest possible plan and an open gallery encircling the whole chapel (**365**, **366** A). Another relatively simple plan, that of the much later but likewise towerless church at Gosprzydowa, is shown alongside, with its elevation (**366** B, C). The covered walk is here restricted to the west and north (where part of it is closed off as a storeroom). The proper attributes of a parish church are present here, namely, a western vestibule, a gallery (with two supporting columns) over the west end of the nave and a sacristy on the north side of the chancel. Part of the west end, together with the detached belfry nearby, are seen in **367**. Both these churches, and almost all those to be described hereafter, have their structural timbers exposed only where protected by the roof of the external ambulatory. Elsewhere the walls are boarded over (or occasionally shingled) for protection against the elements, which doubtless serves to prolong the life

365 Lipnica Murowana, south of Brzesko. Late-fifteenth-century cemetery chapel.

of these churches, but detracts somewhat from their beauty.

Among larger towerless churches, Tvrdošín in Slovakia has – perhaps because of heavy snowfall in the heights of the upper Orava – an ambulatory roof descending very low over the ground, and drawn up to a point over the western entry (**368**). In Poland again, the church from Syrynia (Upper Silesia), and its separate belfry, form a striking group: they were taken down and transported to Katowice in 1939 (**369**). At Poniszowice, also in Upper Silesia, there is another such group, the towerless church being seen here from the south-east (**370**). Other details are illustrated in the Introduction (**43**, **47**) while the interesting detached belfry is referred to below. All these churches may incorporate some work from the fifteenth or sixteenth century, though the last-named is known to have been reconstructed in the seventeenth century and again in 1775.

A sixteenth-century church from Kędzierzyn, moved in 1913 to Breslau (now Wrocław) and still standing in the Szczytnicki Park there, has a western tower whose base is of log construction (**371**). This tower has been attributed to eastern (presumably Ukrainian) influence. It may be the only survivor of its kind, for all earlier towers were displaced by the new type about to be described. It is claimed for Poniszowice that its free-standing early-sixteenth-century belfry is the oldest of this new sort in Silesia, or anywhere in Poland (**372**). It will serve to introduce the distinctive belfries which, throughout southern Poland and adjoining parts of Czechoslovakia, can be regarded as the hallmark of this style. Such towers are not built on the horizontal principle but have a timber frame or skeleton, a fact which by itself proves their western origin. The photograph shows how the walls slant inwards on account of the raking angle of the four corner uprights. Above, there is generally an overhanging bell chamber ultimately inspired (like those of Transylvania) by the machicolated defensive towers of medieval castles, and the bell chamber in turn has a short conical or pyramidal cap. Such towers came to be employed all over this area, sometimes standing alone, more usually combined with the body of the church. They must be regarded as an interpretation in wood of Gothic church towers, but a different interpretation from that seen in Transylvania (Chapter 5).

The towerless wooden churches described above all bear a general resemblance to similarly towerless examples built in masonry and their close relationship cannot be doubted. This is true of their plans, and

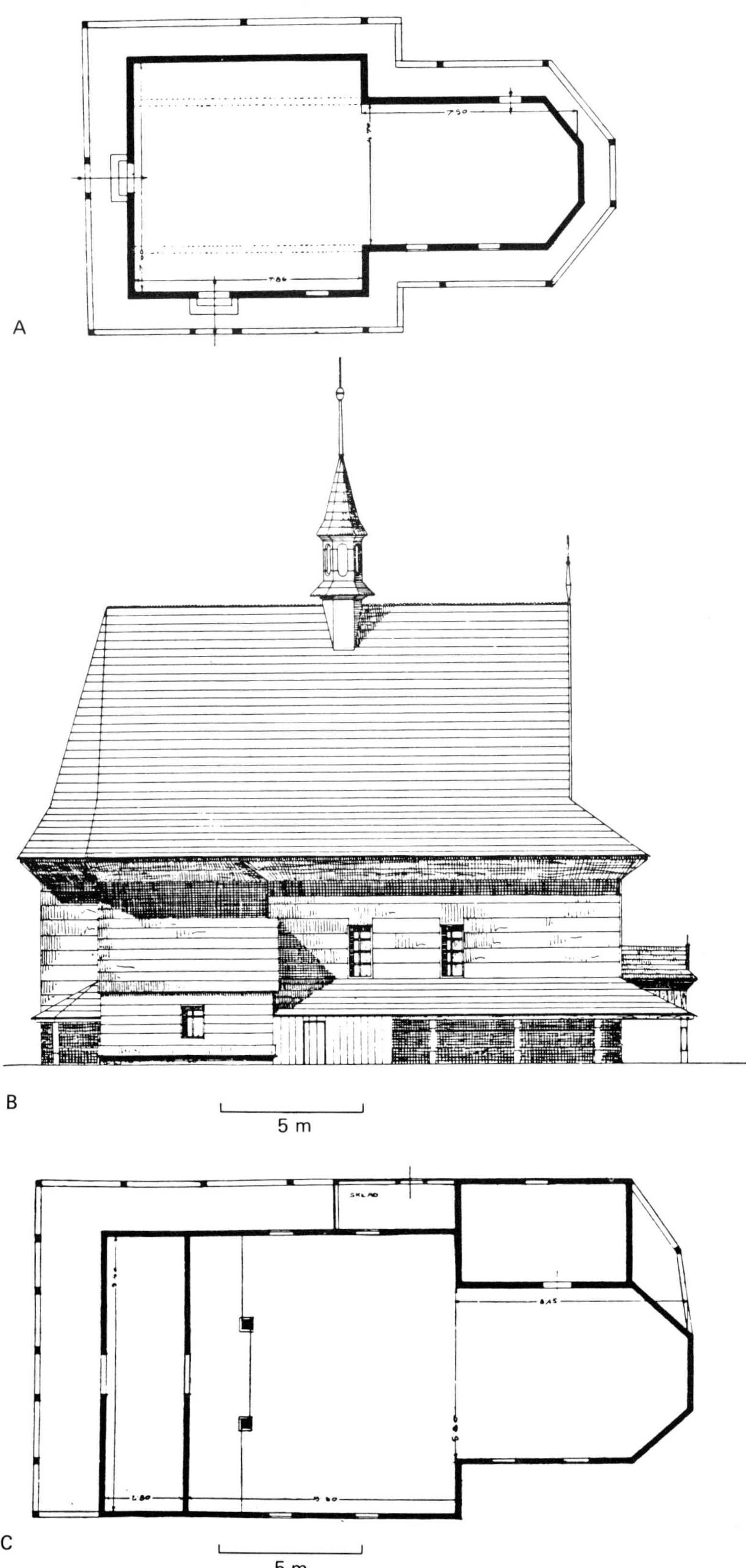

366 Polish towerless churches. A. Lipnica Murowana, plan. B,C. Gosprzydowa, north elevation and plan.

367 Gosprzydowa, south of Brzesko. North-west corner of the church built 1697, with its separate bell tower.

368 'Late Gothic' church at Tvrdošín in Slovakia.

369 Katowice, Upper Silesia. St Michael's church and belfry from Syrynia, possibly 1610.

370 Poniszowice, Upper Silesia. St John the Baptist, from the south-east. Mostly seventeenth and eighteenth centuries.

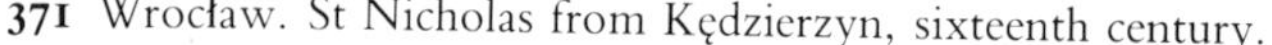

371 Wrocław. St Nicholas from Kędzierzyn, sixteenth century.

372 Poniszowice. Eastern end of the church with detached belfry of 1520.

373 Hrabová, Moravia, St Katharine's church. Second half of the sixteenth century (with later tower).

equally of their silhouette, including the disposition of roofs and the miniature cupolas or lanterns (appropriately called *Dachreiter* by the Germans) which sit, at points suitably reinforced, on their ridges. The parallelism of wood and masonry structures, initiated in Gothic times if not earlier, continued through the seventeenth and eighteenth centuries to which most of my examples belong, when Baroque detail assumed precedence over the Gothic. It is only to be expected, therefore, that the addition of a western tower to masonry churches of all periods – a tradition endemic in the western world – should likewise be reflected in their timber-built counterparts. This almost certainly happened from the late sixteenth century onwards. But it never became a general rule, for some wooden churches were still built with free-standing belfries in the seventeenth and eighteenth centuries (e.g. Gosprzydowa, **367**).

We have seen at Poniszowice a typical wooden belfry of basically Gothic inspiration and comparatively early date. From about the end of the sixteenth century attempts were made to attach such towers to

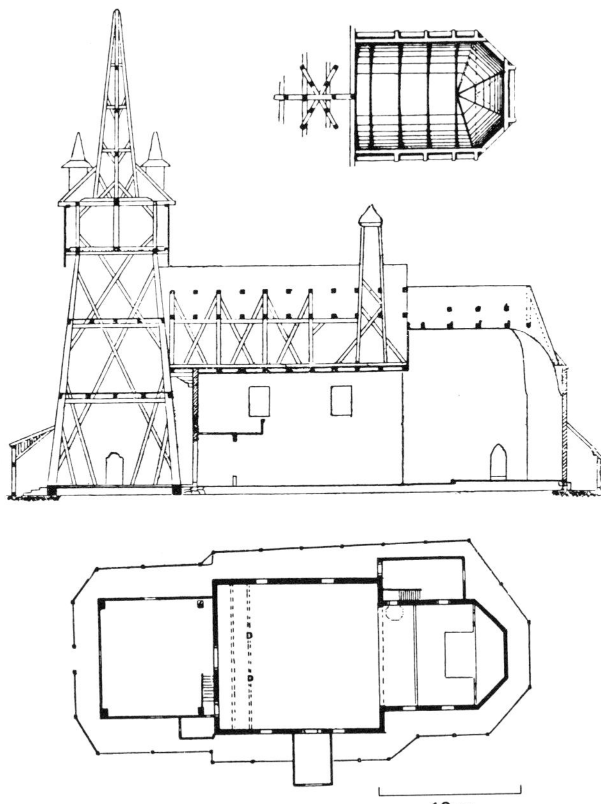

374 Komorowice (later Wola Justowska, Cracow). Longitudinal section, plan and ceiling diagram. Built sixteenth/seventeenth century with tower of 1712.

375 An aisled interior from southern Poland (Jeżowe).

the western end of wooden churches, a task complicated by the fact that church and tower were built in two different and indeed incompatible techniques. The solutions arrived at were not always the same. Close amalgamation was often attempted (e.g. **376–377**) but this could involve awkwardnesses like the intrusion of the two eastern corner-posts of the tower into the body of the church. In other cases the tower remained a virtually separate structure as at Mikulczyce in Silesia (since 1902 in the municipal park at Bytom), at Blizne south of Rzeszów, and at Hrabová in Moravia (**373**). Whatever the mode of attachment, the space under the tower, with its low ceiling, generally served as the vestibule of the church.

Many structural details are shown by the plan and longitudinal section of the church from Komorowice in Silesia (later moved to Cracow). They can stand for scores of wooden churches with combined belfries north and south of the Carpathians from Silesia to the eastern Polish frontier and from Bohemia to Slovakia (**374** and cf. **390–391**). It can be seen that the bell tower is a separate, framed structure, the feet of whose corner-posts are visible, in plan, in the corners of the western vestibule. The tower is applied to, rather than united with, the blockwork of the church itself. The

376 Osiek. Parish church attributed to the early sixteenth century.

nave has the usual western gallery or organ-loft supported, on its free side, by two short wooden columns. The small cupola on the main roof is seen to stand, in reality, on the tie-beams well below. As the section also shows, the chancel ceiling, which has wooden 'vaulting', is here higher than the flat ceiling of the nave (though in other churches it can be the same, or lower).

The chancel is narrower than the body of the church and terminates in a polygonal apse, as it almost always does. At the junction of nave and choir an arch-shaped opening is formed in the timber, representing, of course, the structural chancel-arch of masonry architecture. At this point a heavy beam spans the opening and, since this carries a large crucifix (generally with flanking figures of the Virgin Mary and St John), it may be termed the rood-beam. These last features, if not clear from the section, can be plainly seen in the drawing of a typical interior (**375**), though this particular church is aisled. On reverting to the plan, we see the sacristy occupying its usual position on the north side of the chancel. The broken line surround-

377 Grywałd. St Martin, fifteenth/sixteenth century, from the north-west.

ing the whole church shows the overhang of the lower eaves. This feature, however, is very variable. As pointed out earlier, the external ambulatory may or may not make the whole circuit of the church, it varies greatly in width and its roof may be supported in different ways. In this case it has its own small wooden columns at intervals, as seen in the corresponding external view (**390**) and in many other illustrations to this chapter.

Good specimens of wooden churches of this general type, and of comparatively early foundation, include Osiek near Oświęcim (Auschwitz) west of Cracow, and Grywald near the Czech border south-east of Cracow (**376–378**). In the latter case the square termination of the chancel is unusual, and regarded as an archaic feature. The village of Dębno in the same area possesses almost the only wooden church in Poland which has been widely publicised. Though not outwardly remarkable it has an attractive interior with patterned wall and ceiling painting of late Gothic date, a rather later altar triptych, and a decorative roodbeam (**379**). Other earlier churches shown here are Międzyrzecze (Pszczyna district) with tapering *flèche*

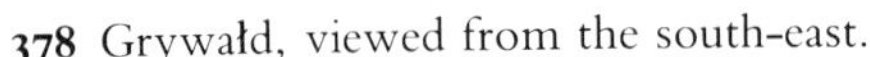

378 Grywałd, viewed from the south-east.

379 Dębno, church of St Michael the Archangel. Interior decoration of c. 1500 and later.

380 Międzyrzecze. St Martin, c. 1522, with tall later tower.

and Brzezinki (Kluczbork district) with exceptionally broad and tall western vestibule and a tower which appears to thrust through its roof (**380**, **381**). The two last-mentioned churches are in different parts of Silesia, while the interesting carved door at Wierzbie (**382**) comes from the neighbouring district of Wieluń.

Some good specimens of the style are found in the south-eastern province of Rzeszów. Sękowa – a church honoured by appearing on a postage stamp – has tremendous roofs, formed by the merging of the upper and lower tiers, and a much later tower (**383**). More imposing are churches that retain a massive western tower of Gothic type as at Nowosielce (**384**). Most characteristic of all are those that possess, in addition, an external gallery whose roof extends apron-like around the base of the tower itself, as shown in the section (**385**). A beautiful but anonymous example provided the subject for the etching in **386**. One of the largest and most impressive of these churches stands at Haczów on the borders of what used to be a Ukrainian area. It was swathed in scaffolding when I saw it but is well documented by the elevation, section and plan here reproduced (**387**). These show that the exceptional width of the church necessitated the introduction of aisles. On the north side, besides the usual sacristy, a chapel projects prominently from the nave and the space between these adjuncts is taken up by a storeroom. The external gallery which surrounds all these features is of ample width, and its roof is supported on a series of small wooden columns.

381 Brzezinki. Church of the Virgin's Nativity, 1550 and 1776.

382 Wierzbie. South door of St Leonard's church, first half of the sixteenth century.

383 Sękowa. Church of St Philip and St James, first half of the sixteenth century, with later tower.

384 Nowosielce. Church of 1595, rebuilt nineteenth century.

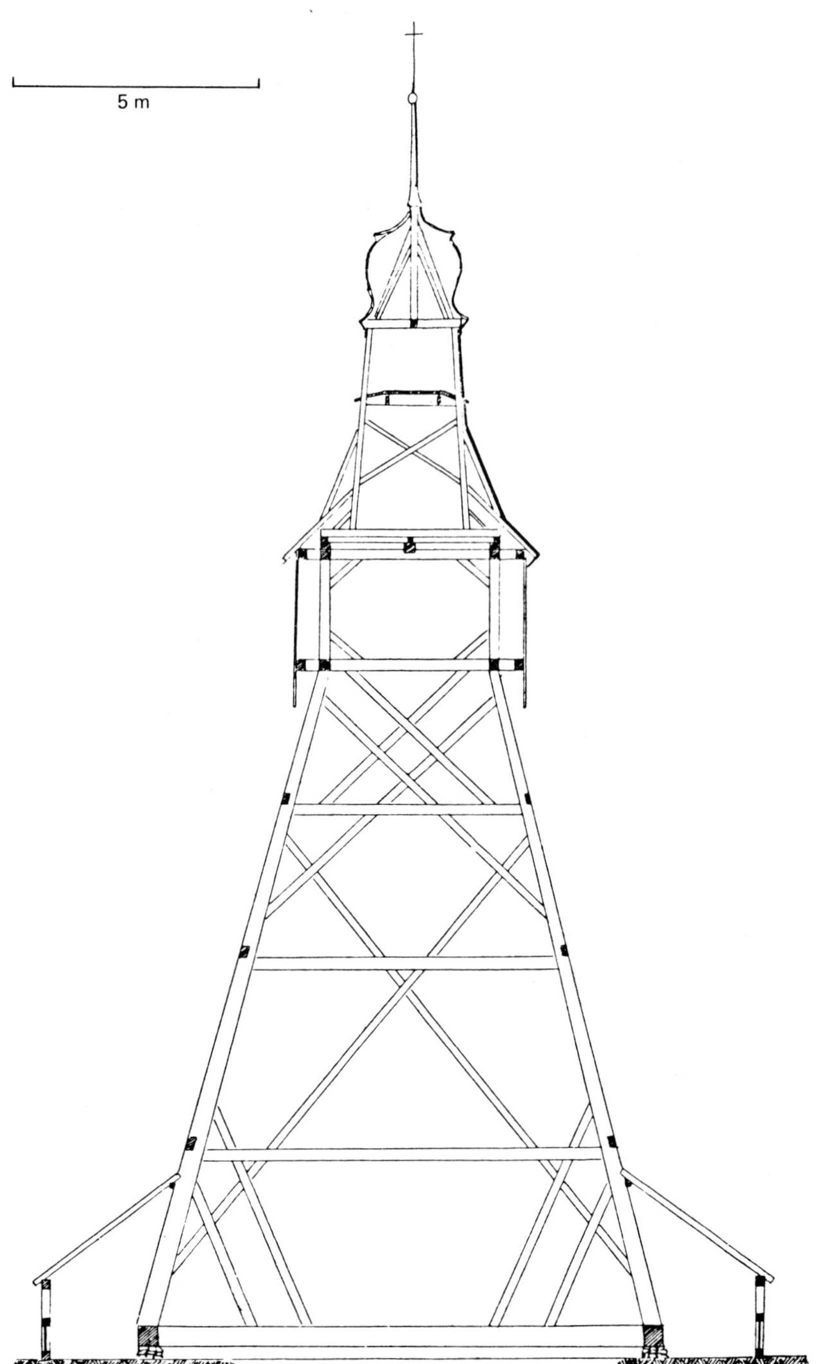

385 Jawiszowice, church of 1692. North–south section through the tower.

Returning westward we find the tradition of what I have called the Gothic tower, with its inclined walls, and with a gallery encircling its base, persisting into modern times. Towards the Czech border south-west of Cracow there are two wooden churches, both handsome specimens of their kind, which illustrate the point. One stands in the village of Gilowice (**388**). It was built originally about 1540 in the neighbouring village of Rychwałd; had a tower added in 1641; was dismantled and re-erected here in 1757; and has been expanded and modified since. This eventful life history has in no way impaired its architectural quality. Its most distinctive feature is the cap over the bell chamber, whose lines form a prolongation, at the same angle, of the corners of the tower below (the same happens also at Białka Tatrzańska and elsewhere).

386 Unidentified wooden church in southern Poland, from an etching.

The church of Lachowice in the vicinity, built as late as 1789, still maintains late Gothic traditions externally, but has an onion dome poised rather incongruously on top of its tower (**389**). The rustic carpenters responsible were certainly no architectural purists. Nonetheless, the church is a grand specimen of the traditional style and, like Sękowa, it has gained publicity and recognition by appearing on a postage stamp. As a last example I shall quote the fine church from Komorowice near Bielsko-Biała, brought to Wola Justowska on the outskirts of Cracow in 1951 (**390–391**). The two external views show the unsymmetrical north and south faces of the church and can be compared with the plan (**374**). Its tower was again of Gothic type but with corner-pinnacles – an alien element here, inspired no doubt by Transylvania. The

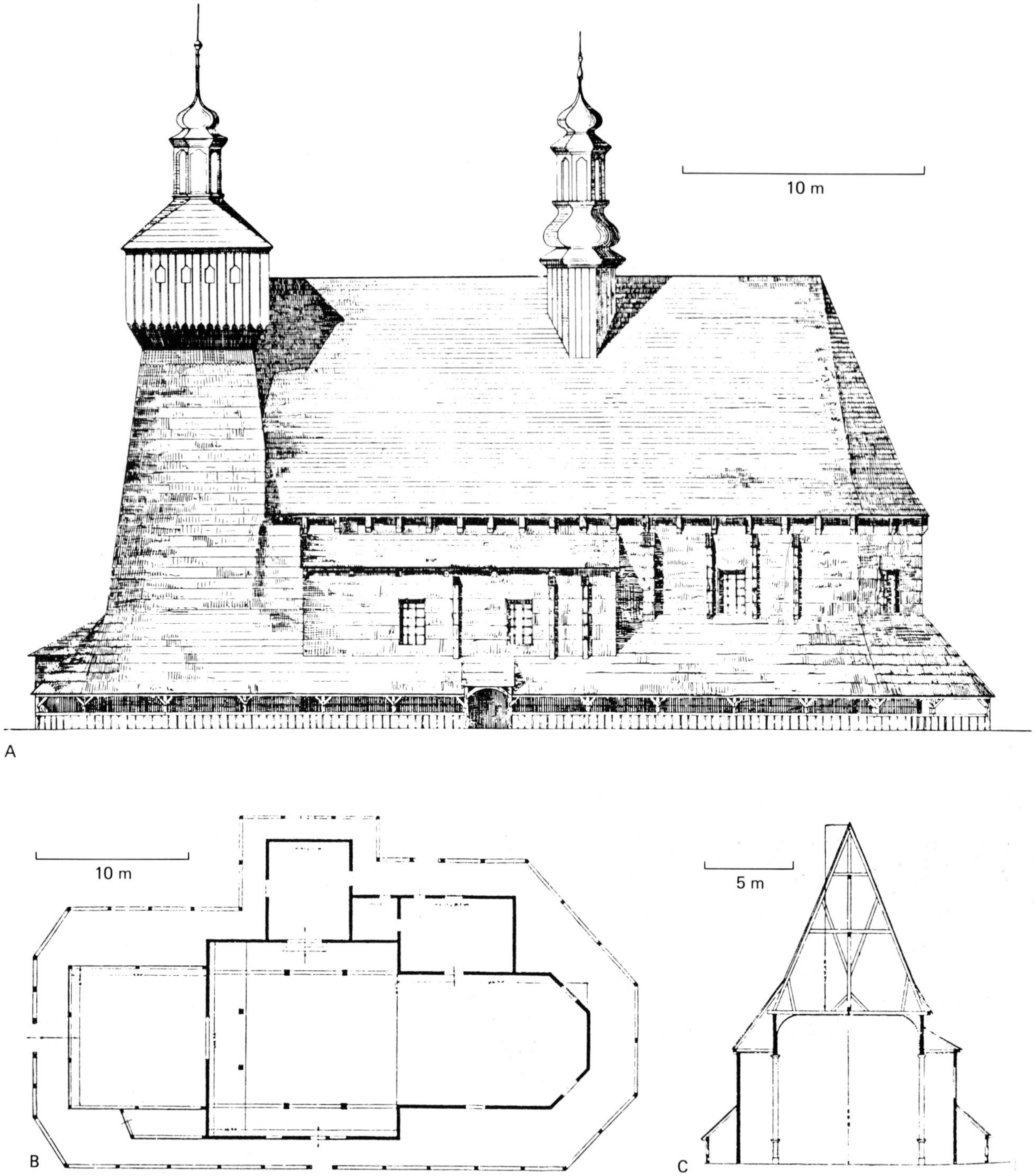

10 m

A

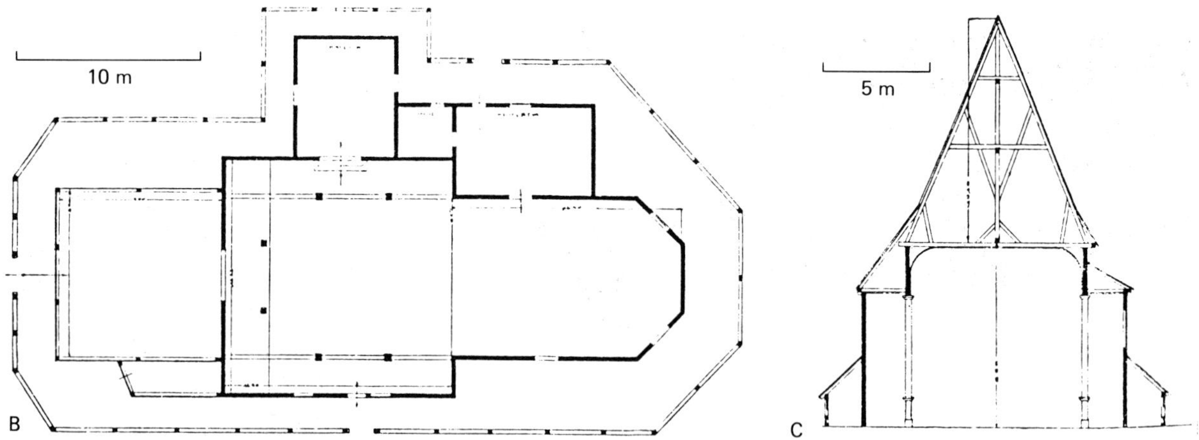

387 Haczów. Church of the Assumption. South elevation, transverse section and plan. Fifteenth and seventeenth centuries.

388 Gilowice, north-western view. Sixteenth and seventeenth centuries and later.

389 Lachowice, church of 1789 from the south-west.

390 Wola Justowska, Cracow. The church brought from Komorowice, Silesia, from the north-east. Built sixteenth/seventeenth century with tower of 1712.

391 Komorowice, the south side.

interior is shown later (**407**). The church was burnt down by some tragic accident in 1978.

All these churches illustrate another interesting point: the contrast between the styles of their exteriors, governed by the late Gothic tradition, and of their interiors, which are sure to be Baroque or Rococo or occasionally neo-classical. When Baroque taste began to sweep the country in the first half of the seventeenth century the traditional forms of wooden architecture could withstand the impact, but internal fittings could not, and all was soon changed. Among Polish wooden churches the only interior I have seen which can claim a decidedly Gothic character is that at Boguszyce, a village near Rawa Mazowiecka. It is an aisled church of 1558 described in Polish sources as late Gothic, with ceiling decorations of the same year described, on the contrary, as Renaissance (**392–393**). The altar and other fittings were, as usual, Baroque until deliberately substituted in recent years by Gothic pieces, of about the same date as the church or a little later. There is now a great sculptured polyptych at the east end and triptychs for the side altars, so one gains some idea of the original appearance of a richer wooden interior of the late Gothic.

I can now pass on to those wooden churches, very common in Poland and also in Moravia, which announce their Baroque character outwardly, at least in their most conspicuous feature – the western tower. It has been said already that these churches were not necessarily built or adapted any later than those which cling to the Gothic-type tower. All the same they form a convenient and easily recognised category, most of whose towers assumed their present form in the late seventeenth or eighteenth century. In a great many cases the churches as a whole date from that period, especially the years from the 1670s until the 1780s. Yet the main features of their layout – the narrowed and faceted apse, the surrounding covered gallery – are the inheritance of a much older tradition.

At Lachowice we saw a perfect western tower of the older fashion, but a superimposed bulbous dome gives it a Baroque flourish (**389**). At Łodygowice, near Żywiec (south-east of Bielsko-Biała), the same process is carried further (**394–395**). The originally seventeenth-century church which here dominates the countryside was modified in 1797. To the second date belong the side-chapels, which also make the plan cruciform (**396**). Also of the same date is the existing tower, where a fully developed Baroque spire, composed of two bulbs with an open lantern between, surmounts the essentially medieval, overhanging bell chamber. This odd arrangement is very common in the south of Poland. In Moravia there are further

392 Boguszyce, St Stanislaus (Stanisław). Aisled, 'Gothic' interior of 1558.

examples and a good one can be seen in the open-air museum at Rožnov pod Radhoštěm (**397**). Many churches of this group show a tendency to disguise the sloping corner timbers which were the traditional basis of the tower's construction, or to reduce their angle, eventually to the point where they no longer sloped, but stood vertically. These measures raised problems, since only well splayed-out corner-posts left enough space for the vestibule under the tower. The solution sometimes adopted was to mount the corner uprights of the towers on the ceiling beams of the vestibule below so that they did not come down to the ground – an expedient we have already seen in use in Transylvania. This is what happens at Łodygowice, as the section through the lower half of the tower shows (**396** A).

The vertical or near-vertical tower, from which the anachronistic overhanging bell chamber has been eliminated, would certainly seem more appropriate in Baroque churches. There are many of these, too, in southern Poland, often beautifully set among trees, like Przydonica north of Nowy Sącz and

393 Boguszyce. Ceiling decoration in the nave.

394 Łodygowice, the Baroque church seen from the west. 1634, 1797, though modifications probably continued throughout the period

395 Łodygowice. South side with projecting transept.

Mikuszowice in the country south of Bielsko-Biała in Silesia (**398–399**). The last-mentioned photograph gives an idea of the site as a whole with its surrounding wall, log-built and roofed, and principal gateway to the precinct. Similar to these is Sedliště near Frydek-Mistek in Moravia, one of the best specimens in Czechoslovakia (**400**, **401**).

The example of Bielowicko (a village west of Bielsko-Biała) shows how some churches of this class can absorb a perfectly vertical tower of moderate size (**402**). The building is here somewhat telescoped in the east–west line and the tower neither forms a separate element of the plan nor provides space for a vestibule between its feet. Instead, the tower surmounts the western bay of the nave itself immediately above the gallery, but it still has its own support system. The weight of the west side of the tower is taken by two uprights just outside the wall, short sections of them being visible in the photograph. The eastern uprights come down in the nave, very close to the small supporting columns of the organ gallery. Such vertical supports are of course more acceptable in a church interior than the slanting corner timbers of the old-fashioned tower would be. Three more minor churches, all from Moravia, are illustrated here (**403–405**). They are Lipná, with no western tower, but an elegant little lantern in the middle; Hodslavice, complicated by a two-storeyed transept on the north side; and Vyšni Lhoty, clothed all over with shingles, and romantically placed on the very summit of a high hill.

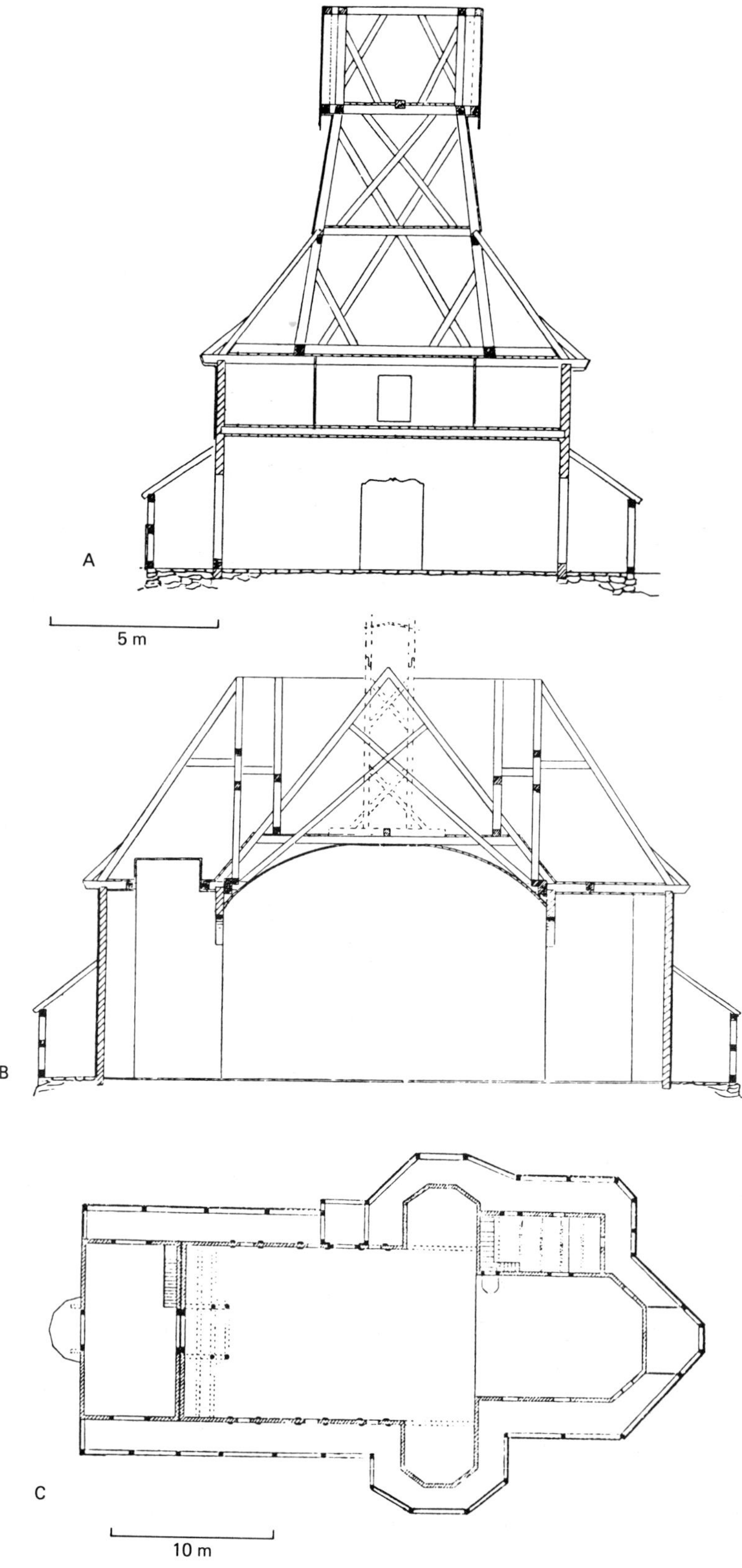

396 Łodygowice A,B. Transverse sections through western vestibule and tower, and through nave. C. Plan.

397 Rožnov pod Radhoštěm, Moravia. The church from Větřkovice, mid seventeenth century.

398 Przydonica. Church of 1527 and later. The west front.

399 Mikuszowice. Church of St Barbara, 1690, with its log-built surrounding wall.

400 Sedliště in Moravia. Church of 1634 and later, west front.

401 Sedliště, seen from the south-east.

As pointed out earlier, the overwhelming majority of these Catholic wooden churches are Baroque inside, whatever their external aspect may be. The three sample interiors shown here illustrate successive degrees of elaboration. At Binarowa (near Gorlice, Rzeszów province) there is ceiling decoration of the sixteenth century while both wall paintings and the relatively restrained furnishings belong to the seventeenth (**406**). The church from the Silesian borders which stood until 1978 at Wola Justowska afforded a good example of contrasted exterior and interior styles. It showed no outward trace of the Baroque, except for a miniature cupola on the nave roof, but things were very different inside, as the photograph shows (**407**). Here, among the gilded garlands and pilasters and broken pediments, archangels dance, bishops gesticulate and winged cherubs romp. In the interior of Jurgów near Nowy Targ, with its strangely contorted rood-beam (combined however with a Gothic altar-rail), Rococo exuberance reigns (**408**).

In the eighteenth century, wooden churches of two new types make their first appearance: those with two western towers and those of cruciform, centralised plan, with four short arms. In view of the dependence

402 Bielowicko in Silesia. St Laurence, 1701.

of Polish wooden architecture on masonry prototypes it is surprising that the twin-towered church did not appear earlier, for there were potential models in every part of Poland, including early medieval ones in the south. On the other hand local sources of inspiration for the centralised, cruciform church are less obvious and probably none ante-date the Baroque period. One can point, however, to some chapels at the Bernardine monastery of Kalwaria Zebrzydowska, to Święta Anna near Częstochowa, and to Protestant churches at Jelenia Góra (Hirschberg) and elsewhere. There is also the church of the Sisters of the Blessed Sacrament in Warsaw, one of those that figure in Canaletto's well known paintings of the city.

Churches of twin-towered plan are widely scattered and not confined to the south which is the real home of Polish wooden architecture. They naturally tend to be broad in plan and therefore often have aisles. Their towers generally project somewhat from the western facade, the main entrance lying between them. The church of Tomaszów Lubelski, its towers crowned with bulbous domes, has interesting internal features including a type of hollow buttress-pier between the bays such as I have otherwise met with only in Finland (**409** A, **410**). Kampinos, west of Warsaw, has its towers terminating in obelisk-like pinnacles instead of bulbs (**411**). At Porzecze Mariańskie, near the Vistula south-east of the capital, there stands one of the most successful churches of this class with western turrets and intervening gable of typical Baroque forms; it also

403 Lipná in Moravia, south side.

404 Hodslavice, 1551, with two-storeyed north transept.

405 Hill-top church of Vyšni Lhoty, 1673.

406 Binarowa, Rzeszów province. Interior of sixteenth/seventeenth century

407 Komorowice, later Wola Justowska. Interior with mostly eighteenth-century adornment.

408 Jurgów. St Sebastian's church, 1670 and later. The mainly Rococo interior.

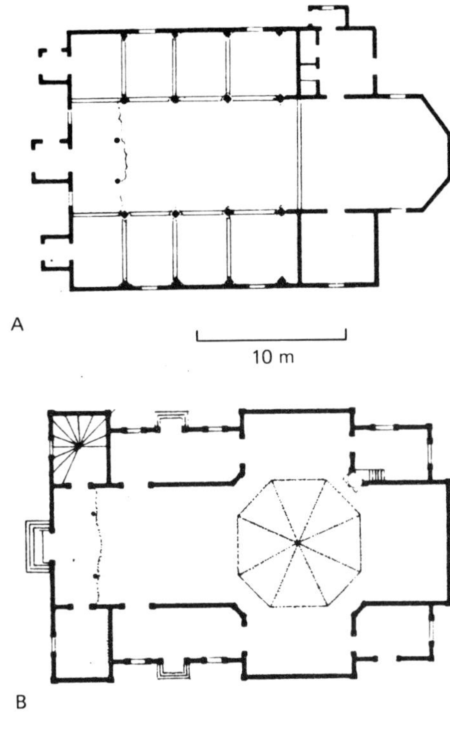

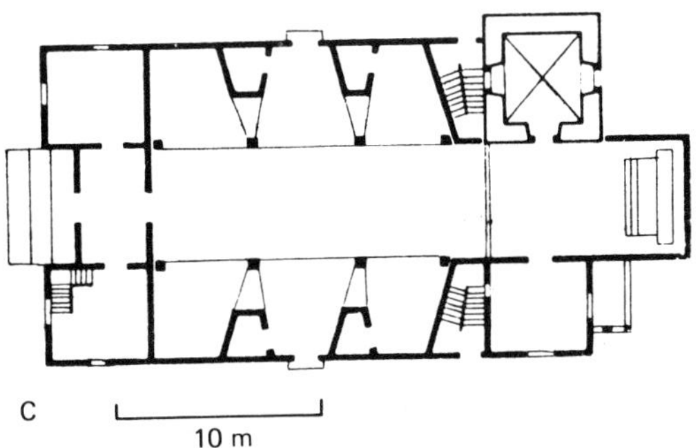

409 Plans of twin-towered churches. A. Tomaszów Lubelski. B. Mnichów. C. Szalowa.

has fully developed transepts (**412**). At Mnichów north of Cracow the church likewise has twin towers and a spacious transeptal east end. It has a mixed character and could have been included among centralised churches (**409** B). At Szalowa in the district of Gorlice such a perfect late Baroque interior has been achieved with paint and stucco that the underlying timber structure disappears from view: this is a minor masterpiece of architectural make-believe (**409** C). The church is also a popular religious centre. At Whitsun, 1972, despite dismal weather, the whole population of the area, possibly a thousand strong, seemed to have gathered from far and near for the festival, on foot or by country cart. The village at that time was virtually inaccessible to motorised traffic.

410 Tomaszów Lubelski, province of Lublin. Church of the Annunciation, 1727.

Centralised churches with their four short arms offer no long internal vista; the central space dominates and the eye is led upwards to the cupola in the middle. At Bralin in the district of Kępno there is a pilgrimage church of this character standing isolated in the fields, with a subsidiary building, for the shelter of pilgrims, wrapping round the western side. Its plan shows a plain cross with tapering arms, and a central altar (**413** A and **414**). Two cruciform churches from the country west of Poznań – which was ceded to Prussia under the First Partition soon after they were built – are illustrated here. They are Buk and Łomnica, both with Baroque gable-ends and both having a central cupola which is the main source of light (**413** B, **415–417**). Far away in the Moravian hills, at Velké Karlovice, there is a 'twenty-four-sided' parish church, this plan being known also from such widely separated areas as the Ukraine and Finland (**413** D, **418**; cf. **215** E and **478** F). An architectural curiosity that may be mentioned at this point is the church at Olesno (Rosenberg) in Upper Silesia. It is like a six-pointed star, there being five radiating chapels while the sixth arm forms a passage linking the whole complex to a traditional church. The unique radial symmetry of the building is difficult to appreciate externally; only a bird's eye view would do it justice and the plan must suffice (**413** C).

I shall conclude this section with two notable but

411 Kampinos, province of Warsaw. 1773–82.

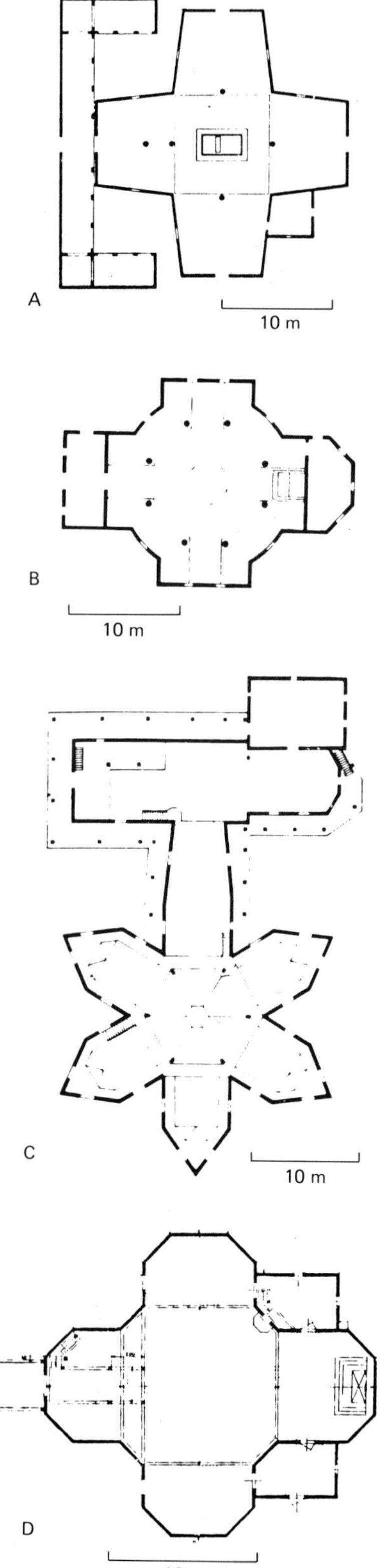

413 Plans of centralised churches.
A. Bralin. B. Buk.
C. Olesno. D. Velké Karlovice.

very different buildings, both from the region of Hradec Králové in north-eastern Bohemia. Being probably unique they defy classification. The church at Loučná Hora (**419**), unfortunately abandoned and neglected at the time of my visit in 1976, is unusual for its exact east–west symmetry: the vestibule and porch to the west are the mirror-image of the chancel and sacristy to the east. They form steps leading up to the higher, mansard roof of the nave, which culminates in a graceful Baroque lantern. The structural timbers are exposed to view so enhancing the beauty of the building, which seems untrammelled by tradition and could be a modern caprice. Still less traditional is the extraordinary structure at Koči u Chrudimě (**420**). The huge irregular pyramid, incorporating a bell chamber, has been added as a western vestibule to a late-fourteenth-century stone church. The covered bridge (over what seem to have been fish-ponds) forms part of this most original composition, which dates from 1721. It is well enough known and prized to have been featured in the current standard issue of Czechoslovak postage stamps.

I hope I have now characterised the Catholic wooden churches of the western Slavs. A few paragraphs must be added, however, on their free-

412 Porzecze Mariańskie (Gożlin), Warsaw province. Church of 1776, south-western view.

414 Bralin, pilgrimage church of 1711.

415 Buk, near Poznań. Church of the Holy Cross, c. 1760. North face.

416 Buk, the centralised interior.

standing belfries, whose oldest surviving specimen at Poniszowice was illustrated earlier (**372**). Separate belfries are almost always present when the church itself does not incorporate a western tower, and there are many instances where a church built in masonry is accompanied by a wooden bell tower, standing on its own somewhere in the precinct. Some have an additional function, being adapted as gate towers. Two are pictured here: a gate tower at Rybnica Leśna in the Silesian hills which is Gothic (**421**) and one from Mogiła near Cracow which is typically Baroque (**422**).

For the rest, nearly all these towers incorporate the inward-sloping corner timbers which are a favourite expedient in the wooden architecture of the area, and a very distinctive one, since there is no corresponding form in masonry. This is true of many attached towers already shown (e.g. Hrabová, Grywałd, Gilowice, Lachowice) and free-standing ones can be just the same. Some have an overhanging bell chamber as at Tomaszów Lubelski (**423**). Others, conversely, have an upper storey of reduced diameter (e.g. Mnichów and Zubrzyca Górna, **424–425**). A curious belfry at Trstné, near Liptovský Mikuláš in Slovakia,

417 Łomnica. The centralised, cruciform church of 1770, from the north-west.

418 Velké Karlovice, Moravia. St Mary of the Snows, mid eighteenth century.

419 Loučná Hora, Bohemia. Church and part of belfry from the south-west.

420 Koči u Chrudimě, Bohemia. Timber vestibule of 1721 to church of St Bartholomew.

421 Rybnica Leśna, Silesia. Gate-belfry to St Hedwig's church, sixteenth/seventeenth century.

422 Mogiła (Nowa Huta), Cracow. Gate-belfry of 1752.

423 Tomaszów Lubelski. Free-standing belfry.

424 Mnichów, south-west of Kielce. Bell tower of 1768 by the church of St Stephen.

425 Zubrzyca Górna, west of Nowy Targ. Eighteenth-century bell tower.

426 Trstné in Slovakia. Seventeenth-century bell tower.

427 Ticha in Moravia. Belfry in St Nicholas's churchyard.

428 Village bell-cot from Vrbětic now at Rožnov pod Radhoštěm.

has an open lower storey so that the whole timber framework can readily be seen (**426**), and a very similar one is prefixed to the church at Brežany near Prešov, further east. At Ticha in Moravia the bottom of the churchyard belfry forms a miniature chapel, with overhang and spirelet above (**427**): this is all that remains from a big wooden church destroyed by fire in 1964. The same basic idea is expressed in a tiny rustic belfry now in the museum at Rožnov pod Radhoštěm (**428**).

Although relinquished in the attached belfries of many later churches, one must concede that the old system based on inclined timbers, which was nearly always retained for free-standing towers, produced by far the most interesting results, and it was also mechanically more stable. For both reasons, presumably, this method of construction retained its popularity right through the eighteenth century, both among the Poles and among the Lemks (as was seen in Chapter 3). One of many striking examples in southern Poland stands at Spytkowice north-west of Nowy Targ. Placed on the axis of the church, opposite its west door, it is distinguished by its broad base, rapidly tapering outline, prominent projecting roof at mid-height, and an apex which is unmistakably Baroque (**429**).

429 Spytkowice, north-west of Nowy Targ, Poland. Free-standing belfry of 1758.

430 Starý Halič, Slovakia. Detached bell tower of 1673 adjoining fourteenth-century Gothic church.

A still more impressive tower stands next to a masonry church at Starý Halič in southern Slovakia (**430**). It harks back to that ancient feature, the overhanging bell chamber, which is here exceptionally spacious with four arch-braced openings on each of the four faces. A tower of such proportions needs massive support and the complex framing is based on twelve principal upright timbers. Only two of these are actually vertical while the remainder, set peripherally, are inclined inwards and determine the slope of the tower walls immediately under the bell chamber. Below this the walls, nicely shingled all over, splay out further on a subsidiary framework. This is certainly one of the most memorable wooden towers in eastern Europe, as impressive in its different way as the Hungarian ones described in Chapter 5.

7

Protestant churches of the margins

This last chapter brings together the Protestant or Evangelical wooden churches of widely separated areas. They are brought together, not so much because of the close bond of a shared faith, Lutheran in this case, as because that faith expressed itself distinctively in church architecture, on which the plan of this book is based. It is true that certain church buildings of the Hungarian Protestants are included in Chapter 5. Needless to say this is not because that community professes Calvinism as opposed to Lutheranism, but simply because the great wooden bell towers there dealt with are closely related to those of Transylvania.

The typical medieval church with its long nave and colonnaded aisles proved unsuitable for Protestant worship, in view of the particular emphasis now laid on the spoken word. Nor did the separation of the choir from the body of the church, or the traditional sanctity of the altar, tally with the new doctrines of Luther and Calvin. Probably the late Gothic hall church, with broad aisles as high as the nave, was the best available model for early purpose-built Protestant churches in central and western Europe. The Dominicans, themselves a preaching order, had contributed to the development of this design which the Protestants improved by building galleries (sometimes in two tiers) into the aisles. These enabled a far bigger congregation to sit within earshot of the preacher and, with the same end in view, the pulpit was usually positioned against a pillar well down the nave. The church conceived as a preaching hall became the basis of Protestant as also of Anglican architecture, the rectangular plan being that usually favoured in western Europe. Among the earliest churches built specially for worship under the new dispensations were those designed in the 1670s and 1680s by Christopher Wren, mostly in the City of London just devastated by the Great Fire (1666). Their plans are very various and ingenious but it is those with galleried aisles and west end, like St Clement Danes and St James, Piccadilly, that are most characteristic of the new architecture and even reminiscent of some wooden churches described in this chapter.

After the conclusion of the Thirty Years War (1648) experiments were made in various European centres in building or adapting churches for the Protestant communities, now at last enjoying some sense of security. In Germany, where L. C. Sturm was the great theoretician of the movement, the cruciform, centralised church with short arms (*Zentralbau*) generally gained recognition as the plan best suited to the new form of worship. This had repercussions not only in the eastern marches of the Germanic world (since the Second World War incorporated for the most part in Poland) but also in Sweden and Finland as will be seen below. Purity, not to say severity, of form was deemed (at least in earlier days) the ideal to be aimed at. Conversely, exuberance of detail was at first frowned upon by the Protestants. It was left to the artists of the Counter-Reformation to exploit it in full measure, though their monopoly did not always remain unchallenged.

Bearing in mind the background thus briefly sketched, we can now pass on to the first of the main areas where Protestant wooden churches form one element in the architectural scene.

POLAND AND SLOVAKIA

The long German presence in the north and west of what is now Poland resulted in the introduction of wooden buildings of western origin – those based on a timber frame or skeleton and often described as half-timbered. It was in western Europe, of course, that this method of construction was first evolved and is most at home. It is best represented in the German countries where some superb half-timbered houses and civic buildings still stand, despite appalling war-time destruction. Even churches of framed construction are numerous there, and a recent publication revealed that no less than 270 still exist in the old province of Hessen alone. A few are to be found also in France and in the English west country.

One might have omitted all reference to timber-framed churches in this book as being alien to the traditions of eastern Europe where blockwork based on horizontal logs is the norm.* I was reluctant, however, to leave out a whole class of timber-built churches which occur commonly in parts of Poland and are in themselves objects of great interest and beauty. The great majority are – or rather originally were – Protestant churches, though a few mentioned in these pages may have been intended for Catholic use from the beginning. Protestant ones appeared after the great tide of Lutheranism had swept all northern Germany in the sixteenth and seventeenth centuries. Bohemia and the Slav and Magyar countries further east were likewise engulfed by the Protestant tide (here often expressed as Calvinism) which however was swept back in the Counter-Reformation. Nonetheless, Protestant outposts survive in present-day Czechoslovakia as they do (more extensively) in Hungary. In this chapter I include several notable wooden churches of the Slovak Protestants, at least one of which is timber-framed like those of Poland.

The eighteenth-century church and its detached belfry at Nowe Dwory, in the countryside north of Poznań, can serve to introduce timber-framing (**431–432**). The church is unusual in having an external skeleton of timbers completed by internal boarding, while the reverse applies to the tall attached tower. The free-standing belfry close by was stripped for restoration when I passed that way in 1975, with the result that its timber-framing was nicely displayed. The principal timbers are seen to be sturdy uprights, eight in number, joined together by horizontal members; together they form a pattern of rectangular panels. To ensure the rigidity of this framework a system of diagonal timbers is superimposed: short struts across the upper corners and long diagonals below, which cut through two or more of the basic rectangles. The tower is surmounted by a raftered, pyramidal roof, which was due for re-shingling. All the wall timbers lie in the same plane since their points

* Another school of timber-framing used to flourish and is still well represented in the south-eastern corner of Europe, especially Bulgaria and Greece, and extends to Turkey. That technique is, however, not represented in this book, since I have not discovered any churches so built.

431 Nowe Dwory near Czarnków, north-western Poland. Timber-framed church of 1792.

432 Nowe Dwory. The detached belfry under restoration.

433 Dzierżąźno Wielkie, near Czarnków. South side of church built 1595.

of attachment, and all their overlaps, are treated as 'lap joints'. The open panels enclosed by the main timbers of the tower would normally have been covered in by boarding like the church except for openings left on each face of the bell chamber. The finished tower, a simple and practical example of timber-framing, presents a pattern of squares and St Andrew's crosses probably not intended for show. But other examples of framed buildings will show how the patterning of the timbers was often carefully thought out with a view to their decorative effect (cf. **445**).

The great majority of framed buildings have their timbered panels filled in with another material, usually white-washed to contrast with the dark wooden framework. This infilling or 'nogging' is generally of brick in northern Poland and walls so built are sometimes referred to as 'Prussian' since their distribution coincides with the old areas of German colonisation. In these first examples the vertical and horizontal timbers form a close-meshed network of small squares, interrupted only by doors and windows. Such buildings attain stability without the use of diagonals and this is probably an archaic arrangement. Some of the examples are in fact relatively early, e.g. Dzierżąźno Wielkie (**433**), but the system was still sometimes used in the seventeenth century as at Golce further north (**434**). Both these churches have a partially detached western tower, though at Golce its base exactly matches the church proper. Both are black and white in the manner of west European half-timbered buildings, and the infilling appears to be brick.

As can be seen from the photograph, the plan of

434 Golce near Wałcz. Church of 1669 from south-east.

Golce is rather broad in relation to its length, the east end is square and the chancel is not narrowed down to demarcate it from the nave. These are common characteristics of the churches in question, governed by the Protestants' requirement of a preaching hall, in which the importance of the altar was reduced so that the chancel no longer needed to be emphasised as an area of special sanctity. The result was a reversion to simpler plans than those favoured by the Catholics, though the polygonal eastern extremity was often retained. The specimen plan and section of a (now lost) church in West Prussia is given in **435** A–C. It shows the features just mentioned. In addition, one notices that galleries are provided (in this case round three sides only) so that the maximum number of worshippers could sit within range of the pulpit, which occupies a focal position against the north wall. The figure also gives the pattern of wall timbers, where diagonals pass through five panels of the rectangular framework, and the position of the roof rafters above. The transverse section shows one of the arch-braced roof-trusses complete with tie-beam, and there was boarding from truss to truss to make a ceiling of barrel vaulted form. The two other specimen plans are from Brandenburg, whence they tended to penetrate into Prussia. That shown in **435** D retains, like many framed churches of the region, a three-faceted eastern end, while E is polygonal at both ends. This curiosity among plans approaches the form of a centralised church, similar results being more usually achieved by the short-armed cruciform plan widely adopted in the eighteenth century.

Two more churches from the Poznań area are shown here, both having typical, unremarkable framing infilled with brick. To the north-west on the Warta there is Sieraków, a late-eighteenth-century specimen, in which the western facade and squat tower have a unified design (**436**). Klępsk, south-west of the city, belongs to the second half of the sixteenth century, though the Gothic-type tower is much later (**437–438**). In an area rather poor in interesting detail, the lovely wrought-iron hinges of its south door cannot fail to catch the eye. Further south of Poznań, near the small town of Leszno, there stands a charming timber-framed church at Dąbcze (**439**). Here the wall timbering has been deliberately exploited for its decorative qualities, the main motif being that sometimes known in Germany as the 'Swabian housewife'

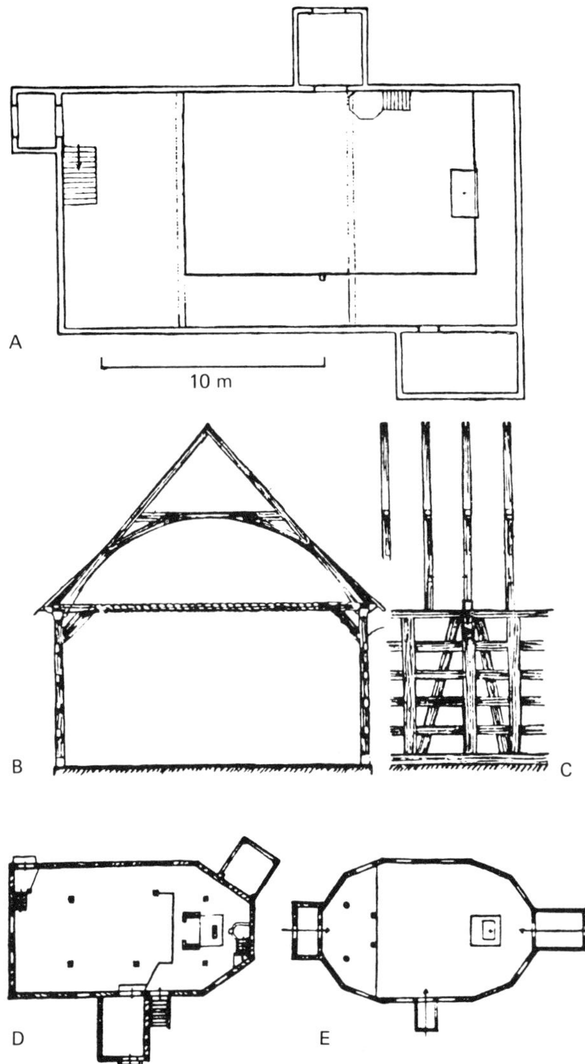

435 Plans of framed Protestant churches. A–C. Katznase (church no longer standing) near Malbork (Marienburg): plan, transverse section and diagram of timbering. D,E. Churches at Hermswalde and Storbeck in Brandenburg.

436 Sieraków on the Warta. Framed church of 1782–5.

(**445** B). The narrowed chancel of these last two churches suggests Catholic origin as well as present-day use. This may also apply to Kaczkowo in the same area which is cruciform, with faceted east end and squared arms (**440**). Timber-framed buildings extend some distance eastward from here. The easternmost I have seen is the church at Jedlec north-west of Kalisz, a point corresponding almost exactly with the old German border up to 1914.

Journeying northwards from Poznań to the Baltic coast, one reaches an area largely dominated by Germans since the days of the Teutonic Knights. As might be expected, churches and other timber-framed buildings are fairly common here, their range extending indeed right up the coast to the Baltic States (now U.S.S.R.). In the area of Gdańsk (Danzig) there are still some beautiful timber-framed domestic buildings, often with their upper storeys 'jettied' or overhanging, and some with an open, arcaded ground floor. In the big ports of Gdańsk itself and Königsberg (now Kaliningrad) in former East Prussia, there were splendid multi-storeyed warehouses and granaries, often with amply projecting dormer at the very top for suspension of the pulley. All these were destroyed in the Second World War, but some minor examples may survive inland.

Two framed churches from the country east and south-east of Gdańsk are illustrated here. Both have steeples which stand well forward from the body of

437 Klępsk. Second half of the sixteenth century, with tower built c. 1657.

438 Klępsk. The south door.

439 Dąbcze near Leszno. Church of 1667–8, south-eastern aspect.

440 Kaczkowo. Cruciform framed church of 1729.

441 Stegna near the Baltic coast. Timber-framed church of 1681–3 from the west.

442 Stegna. The interior looking north-westward.

the church and which carry the characteristic clocks of the area, with double-ended hour hand but no minute hand. Church and belfry are here built in a matching technique with timbers used decoratively, often in the patterns shown in **445** E, F. Stegna (Steegen), the earlier of these two churches, has its pleasing pink 'nogging' exposed to view (**441**). At Kieżmark (Herzberg) it is plastered over as shown in **443–444**. One sees also how well the large round-headed windows fit into their allotted spaces, specially arch-braced to receive them. Each church has a porch at the foot of the tower but Stegna possesses in addition a two-storeyed extension on the south side, representing a second entry to the church apparently combined with the sacristy. Its interior (**442**) gives an impression of the wide open, unencumbered space always aimed at in Evangelical churches, with galleries extending from the Baroque organ at the west end along the south and north walls. The ceiling is coved but flat in the middle, conforming to the pattern of the roof trusses, and painted with biblical figures and parables. Suspended from the ceil-

443 Kieżmark, south-east of Gdańsk. Church of 1727.

444 Kieżmark. South side of the western tower

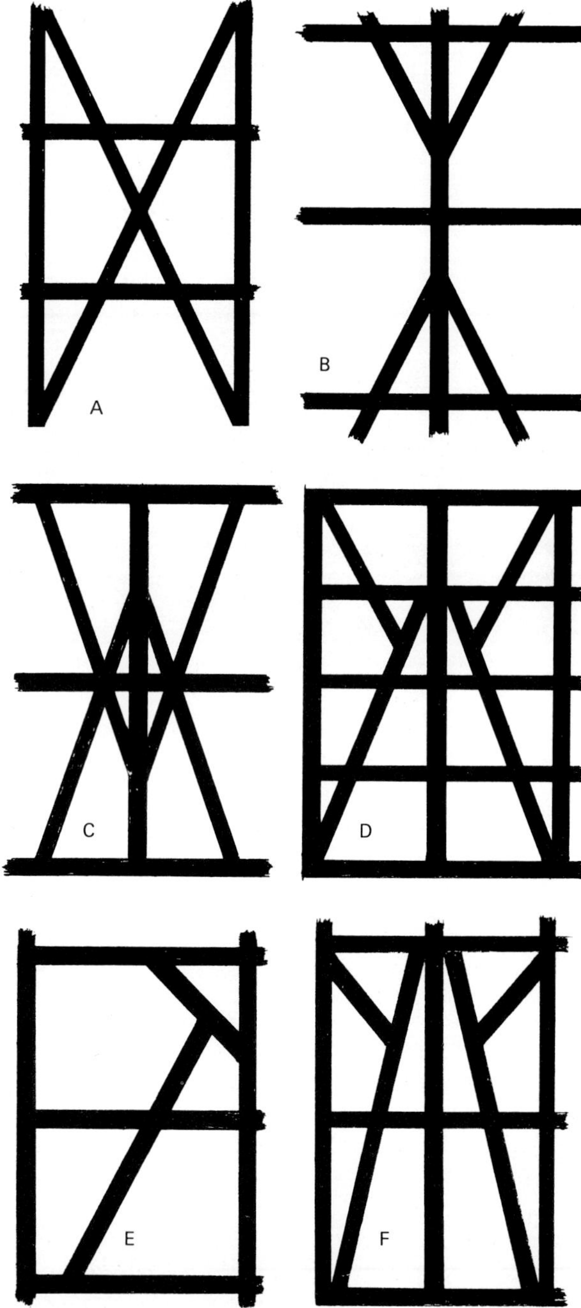

445 Common patterns in exposed timbering of framed churches in Poland and Slovakia. A. St Andrew's cross. B. 'Swabian housewife'. C,D. 'Wild man'. E,F. Arrangements seen in the Baltic area.

ing are candelabra, as well as a beautiful model ship, symbolising the voyage of the Christian life.

Interesting and arresting though some of these churches are, scattered between western Poland and the Baltic seaboard, one must visit Silesia to see the most remarkable timber-framed church in the country, or indeed anywhere in Europe. It stands at Świdnica (Schweidnitz) south-west of Wrocław (Breslau) and should be an obligatory place of pilgrimage for those interested in this sort of architecture, or in the troubled history of the Silesian Lutherans.

The Reformation had a tremendous impact among the German States and in much of the Austrian empire of which Silesia then formed a part. By 1570 the northern Germanic world had turned solidly Lutheran. The Austrian emperors, however, would not tolerate this threat, as they saw it, to the established order. It was Ferdinand of Styria, afterwards the Emperor Ferdinand II, who launched the Counter-Reformation and pursued it with ruthless ferocity throughout his dominions. During the Thirty Years War then intermittently raging many Silesians, exposed to constant persecution and an occupation by grievously undisciplined troops, reverted to the Catholic fold while the surviving Lutherans clung to their convictions under extreme difficulties. Even after the Peace of Westphalia (1648) which brought the long-drawn-out conflict to an end, Lutherans had no churches in which to worship until the Austrian authorities reluctantly granted permission for three to be built: in Glogau (Głogów), Jauer (Jawor) and Schweidnitz (Świdnica). These were the so-called churches of the Peace (*Friedenskirchen*), permitted however only under severe restrictions. They were to be built outside the town walls, bell towers were not allowed, and the material used was to be wood and clay only: stone and brick were banned.

This last stipulation led to the building of the existing, enormous timber-frame church at Świdnica (and of a similar one at Jawor), whereby the letter of the authorities' ban was observed but its spirit obviously defied (**446–450**). The ambitious projects were entrusted to an architect from Breslau, Albrecht von Säbisch, evidently a person of outstanding imagination and audacity. So expensive an undertaking was too much for the resources of the Lutheran *Gemeinde* in these small Silesian towns, but support was sought – successfully – from other Protestant communities both at home and abroad. Once construction had commenced at Schweidnitz in August 1656 it proceeded at surprising speed so that by November of the following year the church could be

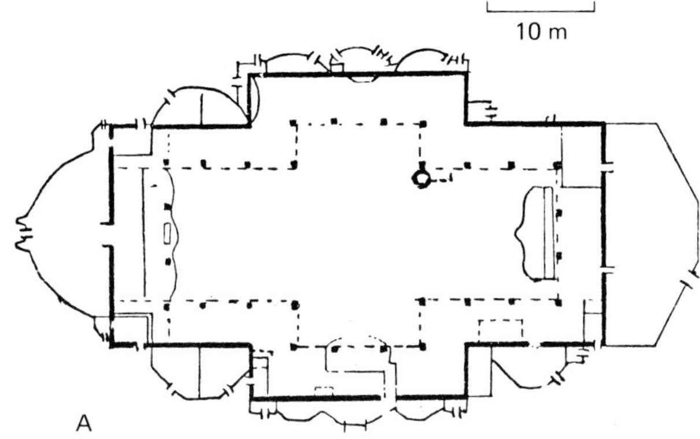

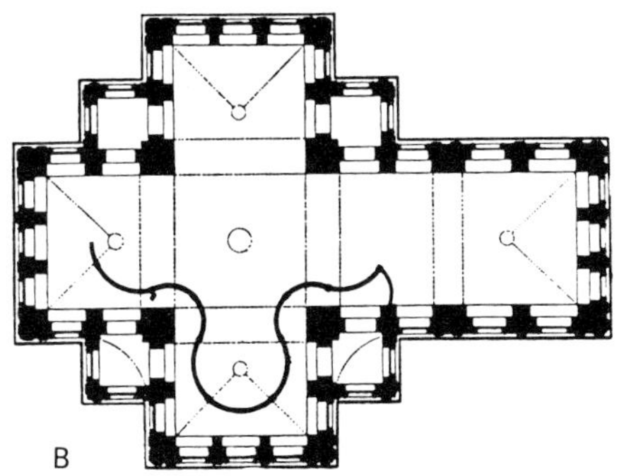

446 Plans of Protestant churches. A. Świdnica, timber-framed (diagrammatic). B. Jelenia Góra, masonry church.

handed over in usable condition to the parish.

The fundamental shape, corresponding to the original layout of the church, is shown by the heavy outline in the plan (**446** A) which however does not claim exactitude. Though cruciform, the plan is far from equal-armed: the east–west axis measures 44 m, the north–south axis 30 m, while the arms are 20 m wide (vast dimensions for a wooden church, even without the later extensions). The plan can be visualised as transeptal, the transepts cutting across the middle of the longer east–west axis. As seen from outside, the building is reminiscent of a Gothic cathedral whose nave, choir and transepts all have aisles, with their roofs lying at a lower level than the main roof. Here the ends of all four arms, closely corresponding to their vertical sections, likewise have roofs in two ranges like a basilica, and the wall between them is furnished with what look like clerestory windows. One is not deceived: the spaces occupied by the galleries inside are in reality aisles. They lie exactly under those lower, lateral roofs, so conspicuous externally, while the clerestory windows above them help to illumine the main nave. Von Säbisch was surely influenced by Gothic models when he conceived this great church which, apart from Jauer, remained unique.

Inside, one finds a vast uninterrupted space surrounded by tier upon tier of wide galleries (**450**). Their inner faces are supported by the same stout posts which, higher up, form the mainstay of the 'clerestory' walls: these vertical timbers thus correspond to the colonnades which separate nave from aisles in any Early Christian basilica or medieval church. At the western end a special gallery supports the mighty Baroque organ. On the north and south sides, including recessed portions filling the greater part of the transepts, the galleries are suspended in two tiers. At the east end, behind the tall free-standing altar canopy, there are no less than three superimposed galleries (with a small second organ perched at the top). It is said that all told three thousand people could be seated in the church, and four thousand more find standing room. Most of them would have been in full view, and all within easy earshot, of the preacher thundering from the high pulpit on the north side.

It is worth having a second look at the outer walls, since their structural woodwork is so conveniently exposed and perfectly reflects the internal planning. The end facades of all four arms are basically identical. They are divided by six principal vertical timbers into five sections, the two outer ones corresponding to the 'aisles'. The remaining three in the centre rise, between the 'clerestory' walls, as high as the springing of the gable. Each section is itself divided by more slender vertical timbers into three strips, the middle spaces being occupied by long windows. Massive horizontal beams divide these facades into four storeys and one can easily see the original fenestration, now somewhat obscured: the first upper floor had five long windows, the second three, the third (within the gable) small ones only in a different pattern. Since bricks, the normal infilling in this area, were not allowed, all the panels not occupied by windows were closed with the local equivalent of 'wattle and daub'. The lower walls of the original structure are no longer visible because of later accretions, which however do not detract from the interest of the church but rather add to it.

As we see it today, the church differs considerably from von Säbisch's imposing but austere original. In the eighteenth century the Baroque – identified though it might well have been with the Counter-Reformation – gained entry to the interior, appearing in pulpit, font, the great altar reredos and the two organs. Outside, as seen in **448–449**, a large vestibule was added at the west and a baptistery at the east end, both crowned with half-cupolas applied to the original facades (incidentally, the pattern of wall-timbering

447 Świdnica, Silesia. The timber-framed Lutheran church seen from the south. 1656–8 and later.

known in Germany as the 'wild man' is visible here, compare **445** C, D). Along the north and south sides we find a succession of chapels and projecting porches, some of the latter being entries to the ornate private balconies or 'boxes' (*Ranglogen*) allotted to eminent citizens. Against the outer walls of these chapels and porches are many family monuments, memorials of wealth, privilege and piety, in the florid fashion of the Baroque and Rococo. How could all these signs of ebullient confidence have succeeded the era of persecution? Political events in fact conspired to ease the lot and support the morale of the Protestant community. In 1740 Frederick II of Prussia – unprovoked but unashamedly ambitious – seized Silesia from Austria and added it to his wholly Protestant kingdom. After this the Lutherans of Schweidnitz could embellish their church without risk of incurring the displeasure of the Austrian civil authority, whose relentless opprobrium they had suffered for a century.

448 Świdnica. The east end with projecting baptistery.

449 Świdnica. South-western view with vestibule built onto the west arm.

About two hundred miles south-east of the Wrocław–Świdnica area, in the region of the High and the Low Tatra mountains, one of the residual Evangelical communities of Slovakia has its home. What is now Czechoslovakia has harboured a number of reformers and Protestant sects, but the wooden churches I deal with here are Lutheran and the three larger ones, all of cruciform plan, were almost certainly influenced by those at Świdnica and Jawor. It is interesting to note, however, that the influence of western timber-framing, so splendidly exemplified in Silesia, found itself in sharp conflict, among the Slovaks, with the traditional log construction of eastern Europe. In fact, only one of the four churches I shall mention can be described as timber-framed, though there is some mixture of techniques among the others.

Near Dolný Kubín in the Orava valley, lower down than the archaic Catholic church at Tvrdošín, there is the Lutheran church of Istebné (**451**). It is a comparatively small, broadly oblong church in solid log construction, which is concealed, however, by vertical boarding. A bell tower, wooden only above, stands separately. There is little to distinguish the building, externally, from any other simple wooden church and I was myself attracted to the spot, on a Sunday morning in 1973, by the unaccustomed sound of hymn singing. The interior is unexpectedly colourful, its walls and flat ceiling being adorned with paintings in a rustic style. Both altar and pulpit are Baroque, the latter being adorned with sculptured biblical figures standing in deep, arched niches. There are galleries, including that diagnostic feature of a Lutheran church – an eastern gallery behind the altar.

The other churches under this heading are much larger and cruciform, and were all apparently built in the first third of the eighteenth century, even if modified later. One of them is Hronsek on the River Hron just south of Banská Bystrica (**452–454**). Its main east–

450 Świdnica. Interior looking eastward.

west axis is bisected by a transept with shorter arms. The church is notable for its framed construction which however produces nothing of the black-and-white effect that might be expected. As at Nowe Dwory in Poland (**431**), the panels of the main framework are boarded over internally, and wood against wood produces little contrast. An attractive feature, on the other hand, are the special little roofs which shield all the exposed horizontal timbers from the rain; they are repeated on the adjoining free-standing belfry. Another point of interest is the pattern of diagonals to the left of the west door; this is the 'wild man' again. The interior has single galleries practically filling the four arms, with seats in sloping banks reminiscent of a theatre. The supporting posts of these galleries also support the semi-cylindrical 'vaults' over the arms, but these do not extend into the square central space, which has a flat ceiling. This roomy interior is said to seat 1100 people.

Further north again, at Paludza near Liptovský Mikuláš in the Váh valley, there stands another of these big Evangelical wooden churches which I found sadly dilapidated but not quite abandoned in 1973 (**455**, **456** A). The outside is very plain except for a striking detached belfry, on a masonry base, which stands (exceptionally) at the east end. The roof behind the tower is gabled, while the extremities of the other

451 Istebné, Slovakia. Lutheran church of 1686. Interior with altar and eastern gallery.

452 Hronsek, Slovakia, 1725–6. Timber-framing at the west end.

three arms are hipped. These shorter arms each have two dormer windows on either side and two more at their ends (see below). The wall construction is not framed as at Hronsek but of horizontal blockwork, clothed in vertical boarding both inside and out. Despite this basic difference in the method of construction, these two churches are closely related. Both are cruciform, though at Paludza only the eastern arm is lengthened. Both have galleries in all four arms though at Paludza these are in two superimposed tiers and differently laid out, and there is an additional single gallery on the north side. The plan (**456** A) shows all these arrangements as well as the freestanding altar in the eastern arm, the pulpit at the junction of the east and south arms and the organ at the west end (positioned as at Kežmarok, **456** B).

The shallow 'barrel vaults', unlike those at Hronsek, fly over the upper galleries to abut against the outer walls, the consequent spreading strain being taken by iron ties spanning all four arms. These simulated vaults are sliced off at an angle at the ends of the arms to fit under the hipped roofs, and at their inner ends they run on into the central space to form a cross vault. Finally, there is provision (again unlike Hron-

453 Hronsek, the detached bell tower.

455 Paludza. Lutheran church, probably 1773–81. Bell tower at the eastern extremity.

sek) for light to penetrate the ceiling vaults. It comes from the above-mentioned dormer windows (six to each of the three western arms) and reaches holes in the vaults through short boarded tunnels. All this adds up to an interesting if rather clumsy design. The interior is enormous and must have seated thousands.

Further east, on the River Poprad and not far from the modern town of the same name, one more major Protestant church claims attention. Along with various Gothic and Renaissance monuments and ancient houses it is one of the sights of Kežmarok (Käsmark), a medieval royal town. The master carpenter responsible was a certain Georg Muttermann of Poprad, from his name presumably a German. The fact that the church is wooden is not obvious outside, since its typical east European blockwork is rendered with cement which in turn is plastered over (**457**). Additionally there are uprights (against the inner walls) which help to support the principal rafters of the roof. Once again the church is cruciform, but here it forms a true equal-armed Greek cross, and the roofs of the arms are half-hipped at their free ends. The low-roofed chambers in the angles between the arms provide a clue to the special character of the interior which

454 Hronsek. Interior viewed from south to north.

457 Kežmarok. Lutheran church dated 1717.

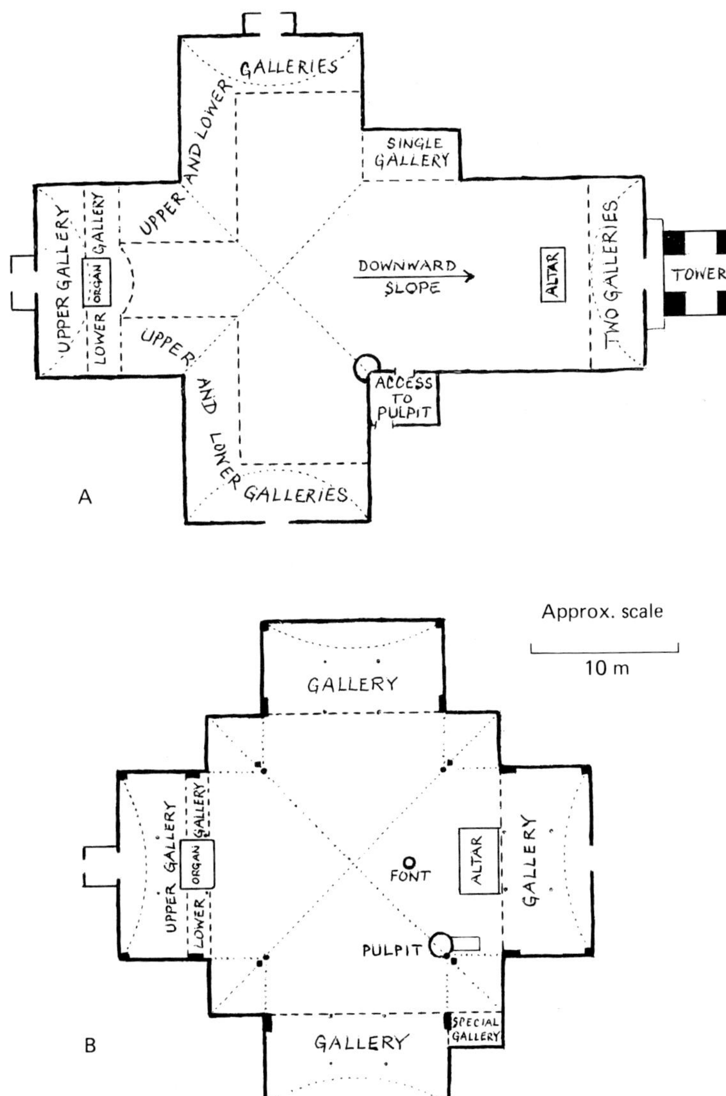

456 Sketch plans of cruciform Protestant churches in Slovakia. A. Paludza. B. Kežmarok.

distinguishes this church from others of the group, though it can be matched in Finland.

The plan and interior views (**456** B, **458–459**) show up the distinctive features in question. Apart from the absence of a long eastern arm the main dimensions are almost identical to those at Paludza, a sure sign that the two buildings are related. But at Kežmarok we find the interior transformed by the suppression of the inward-pointing corners between the arms – in effect these have been turned inside out. At the same time the galleries (single, except to the west) have been pushed back into the ends of the arms. The combined effect of these operations has been to create an enormous open space in the middle of the church. The points at which the arms would normally have met still require supports and these are provided in the form of slender spiral columns of yew (reinforced subsequently by a second stout post behind). One interior photograph (**458**) shows the south-west corner with its spiral column, the south gallery with one of its own (also spiral) columns, the font (which stands in the middle line) and portions of the 'barrel vaults' complete with iron ties as at Paludza. The other inside view (**459**) shows the elaborate Baroque organ which, resting on the lower western gallery, rises high above the upper one. To the east, the organ is balanced by a lofty and even more sumptuous Baroque altar-piece or reredos, again with twisted

458 Kežmarok. Interior, view into the south and west arms.

459 Kežmarok, west end with double galleries and organ.

columns. This is placed against the eastern gallery, the space below which is screened off. This interior, capable of seating 1460 people, is something of a masterpiece and almost unique among surviving wooden buildings, though some synagogues could have matched it. The church is now under protection as a national monument.

These last three churches have cross-shaped plans, very similar dimensions, galleries in all the arms and other shared features. They cannot be placed in a logical order of progression – indeed Kežmarok, the most sophisticated of the three, is the earliest in date – but they must be regarded as siblings, of common parentage. One parent whose inspiration they doubtless shared was the great timber-framed church at Świdnica described above. It must have been renowned in Lutheran circles ever since its completion in 1658, and it appears to have set a fashion for the centralised plan so well adapted to the needs of Protestant worship. Moreover, Slovakia and Silesia both still belonged to the Austrian empire so that communications between the two areas cannot have been unduly difficult. More importantly, both were subject to the onerous restrictions imposed on Protestant church-building after the Thirty Years War. As pointed out above, these relegated churches to the outskirts of certain towns and disallowed the use of masonry even for foundations. Clearly, ways and means devised for overcoming these limitations in one area must have greatly interested the brethren elsewhere.

Though none of the derivative churches (if such they are) equalled the size or capacity of Świdnica, they shared its cruciform layout, the characteristic arrangement of the galleries and the free-standing altar. At Hronsek the builders did their best to emulate the timber-framing of the model in an area ignorant of this technique. If this is enough to mark down Świdnica as one parent of the big Slovak wooden churches, one still needs to identify another, and another can be tentatively suggested. In 1706 the Emperor, under pressure from Charles XII of Sweden, allowed several new Protestant churches in Silesia to be erected in masonry – these were known as the churches of Grace (*Gnadenkirchen*). Two of them, at Hirschberg (Jelenia Góra) and Landeshut (Kamienna Góra), were designed by Martin Frantz, an architect born of German parents in Estonia, then part of the Swedish empire. The Hirschberg plan is shown in **446** B. Both churches are cruciform and are known to have been modelled on that interesting building, the Katarina Kyrka in Stockholm (**493**). These Silesian derivatives were in construction between 1709 and 1718 and their influence could well have been brought to bear on the big Slovakian wooden churches which were built a little later, so reinforcing or modifying the inspiration of Świdnica. The cruciform plan and two-tiered, rather obtrusive galleries are close to those in Slovakia, while the barrel vaults could have inspired copies there. Paludza also seems to follow Jelenia Góra in its long eastern arm, Kežmarok in its projecting angle-chambers between the arms.

Summing the matter up, I interpret these three big wooden churches in Slovakia as a valiant attempt by the local Protestants to build as well, under conditions of adversity, as their co-religionists in Silesia had done. It seems likely that both von Säbisch's great church at Świdnica, and the later brick-built ones by Frantz – churches which they certainly knew at least by repute – served in some sense as their models. If the same quality was not achieved in Slovakia, the attempt did at least produce a few memorable buildings, of dimensions which dwarf all neighbouring wooden churches, whether of the Catholics or the Uniate Ukrainians.

FINLAND

Having admitted the Protestant wooden churches of Poland and Slovakia to this book, I must include some account of the Finnish ones as well. These widely separated communities are (or were) united by the powerful bond of Lutheranism which finds expression, as we have seen, even in architecture. Whether Finland can rightly be included in any work on eastern Europe is another question, and this dilemma was referred to in the Introduction. Geographically there can be no doubt about it: Finland lies in the longitude of Rumania and Bulgaria and shares a very long frontier with Russia. Yet Finland today forms an integral part of the Scandinavian bloc, is decidedly western in outlook and, since the sixteenth century, has been solidly Lutheran in faith. Finland formed part of Sweden for more than six hundred years until, between the early eighteenth and the early nineteenth centuries, the Russians took progressive advantage of Sweden's dwindling power to appropriate the country. But Finland's 110 years as an autonomous Grand Duchy under the Tsars have left little trace, and no great legacy of love. The Finns' sentiments about the oppressive policies of Nicholas II are best expressed in a famous picture by Edvard Isto now in the National Museum. It shows Finland – a blonde maiden on a rocky shore – being threatened by a sinister and rapacious double-headed eagle, which tries to wrest from her grasp the book of Finnish laws and liberties.

Finland is very rich in Lutheran churches, a great many of them timber-built, and since their architectural links are with Sweden the line drawn between the two countries in this chapter can only be arbitrary. But it must be stressed that however western in appearance these churches may be, and whichever side of the frontier they stand, they remain faithful to the horizontal principle of construction which was never challenged (except in the case of belfries) by the timber-framed technique of western Europe. However, Finland, from the point of view of this study, has a still more fundamental eastern link. As mentioned in the Introduction the Finnish family of peoples, widely distributed today in northern Russia as well as Finland itself, apparently took a major share in the early development of log construction, which was to be adopted universally by the Slavs and the Scandinavian peoples. The Finns always remained leading exponents of this building technique. In modern times they were instrumental in introducing the 'log cabin' to the early American colonists, so making a notable contribution to the settlement of that continent (see Appendix 1). And it has been seen already in Chapter 1 that the most pure and primitive of all log constructions, descended unchanged from the ancestors of those log cabins, still survive as serviceable field barns and stores in northern Finland and Karelia.

This strangely beautiful country, so different from any other in Europe, was ground down almost flat by the ice sheets of the Ice Age. On withdrawing after many thousands of years the ice sheets left behind countless mounds and ridges of morainic material which dammed back the waters, frustrating their natural outflow towards the sea. The result was a maze of lakes and rivers of inconceivable complexity, providing, however, limitless possibilities of communication by water. Except in the farthest north forests were the natural, and on rockier ground the only possible, vegetation while cultivation, even of hay, could only occur patchily. The abundance of forest land, especially of conifers which provide the straight timber required for blockwork, has encouraged the survival of that traditional technique until now. Another effect of the ice sheet, due to its immense weight, was to press down all northern Scandinavia into the viscous magma underlying the earth's crust. It is still recovering by up to a centimetre a year. At some points on the arctic seaboard of Norway a succession of raised beaches records the gradual upheaving of the land. Along the Finnish coasts, and

460 Log-built boathouse and a church boat, in the Seurasaari open-air museum, Helsinki.

among the countless off-shore islands, the configuration of the water's edge can alter appreciably even in the individual life-time. And there are cases where churches, built by the water's edge, now stand some distance from it.

Many of the Protestant churches described in the first part of this chapter – especially those in Silesia and Slovakia – were very large by wooden church standards. In both Orthodox and Catholic regions one commonly finds that every village, even every hamlet has (or had) its own church and there was seldom any need for them to exceed modest dimensions. The Protestants, on the other hand, generally thought in terms of much larger churches at strategic points, with correspondingly extensive catchment areas. This is certainly true of the Lutheran churches in Finland, and their problem was to assemble their congregations from the intricate network of rivers, lakes and islands which make up the average Finnish parish. Special church boats were the usual solution: beautiful clinker-built rowing boats with up to fourteen pairs of oars in which the parishioners used to row themselves to church on a Sunday morning. Some have been preserved in their original log-built boathouses or in replicas of them, as in the open-air museum on Seurasaari island near Helsinki (**460**). The old photograph shows a fleet of church boats in operation, probably in the 1920s or early 1930s when many were still in use (**461**).

The earlier surviving wooden churches of Finland and Swedish Norrland follow the general pattern of masonry churches in the same area. The available models were late Gothic or followed in that tradition and could not well have been earlier, since there was little colonisation in these sub-arctic regions until the mid fourteenth century at earliest. The great majority of the early settlements, Finnish or Swedish, stood in the coastal strip. Since the waters of the Gulf of Bothnia formed a link rather than a barrier between its western and eastern shores, and since the two were so long united under the Swedish crown, intermingling of populations took place freely and it is not surprising that the whole area forms a single architectural province. In preparing this study I was obliged to set a westward limit to my travels, which did not extend to northern Sweden. It remains true, however, that the Finnish wooden churches cannot be fully understood without frequent references to their Swedish links.

461 A flotilla of church boats on Finnish inland waters, from an old photograph.

It follows from what has been said that the earlier wooden churches to be dealt with here are mainly concentrated along the seaboard of the Gulf. As far as Finland is concerned this means coastal Ostrobothnia (an area otherwise noted for its ancient trade in timber and tar). Though they certainly existed previously, the surviving wooden churches date at earliest from the early seventeenth century. All are Protestant – though less distinctively so in their architectural features than the cruciform types developed later. On the Finnish side they stand (or stood until recently) at many points from the northern extremity of the Gulf to the area of Turku (Åbo) in the south. Among these are some of the earliest specimens known on either side of the Gulf, which suggests that Finland took the lead in this particular development. These are 'long' churches whose plans, following from the above-mentioned masonry prototypes, are simple oblongs, variegated only by small rectangular adjuncts – a porch, a sacristy, the occasional superimposed or semi-detached steeple. But, in contrast to the very small wooden churches which are the general rule in eastern Europe, these Finno-Swedish Lutheran churches are large – up to 30 × 10 m. This fact alone necessitated the development of special techniques of timber construction. It is noticeable, too, that windows are now increasingly taken into consideration not merely as a practical necessity but as an essential element in wooden church design.

A particularly fine church of the type in question existed, until it was destroyed in a disastrous fire in 1968, at Hailuoto on the island of the same name near the northern end of the Gulf of Bothnia. It owed its final form to extensions carried out after 1656, but this extended structure incorporated the original church of about 1620, of which a restored perspective view is shown in **462** and the plan in **463** A. It was a very plain building but several features were of special interest. One was the consistent use of the horizontal principle, not only for the walls up to roof level but for the

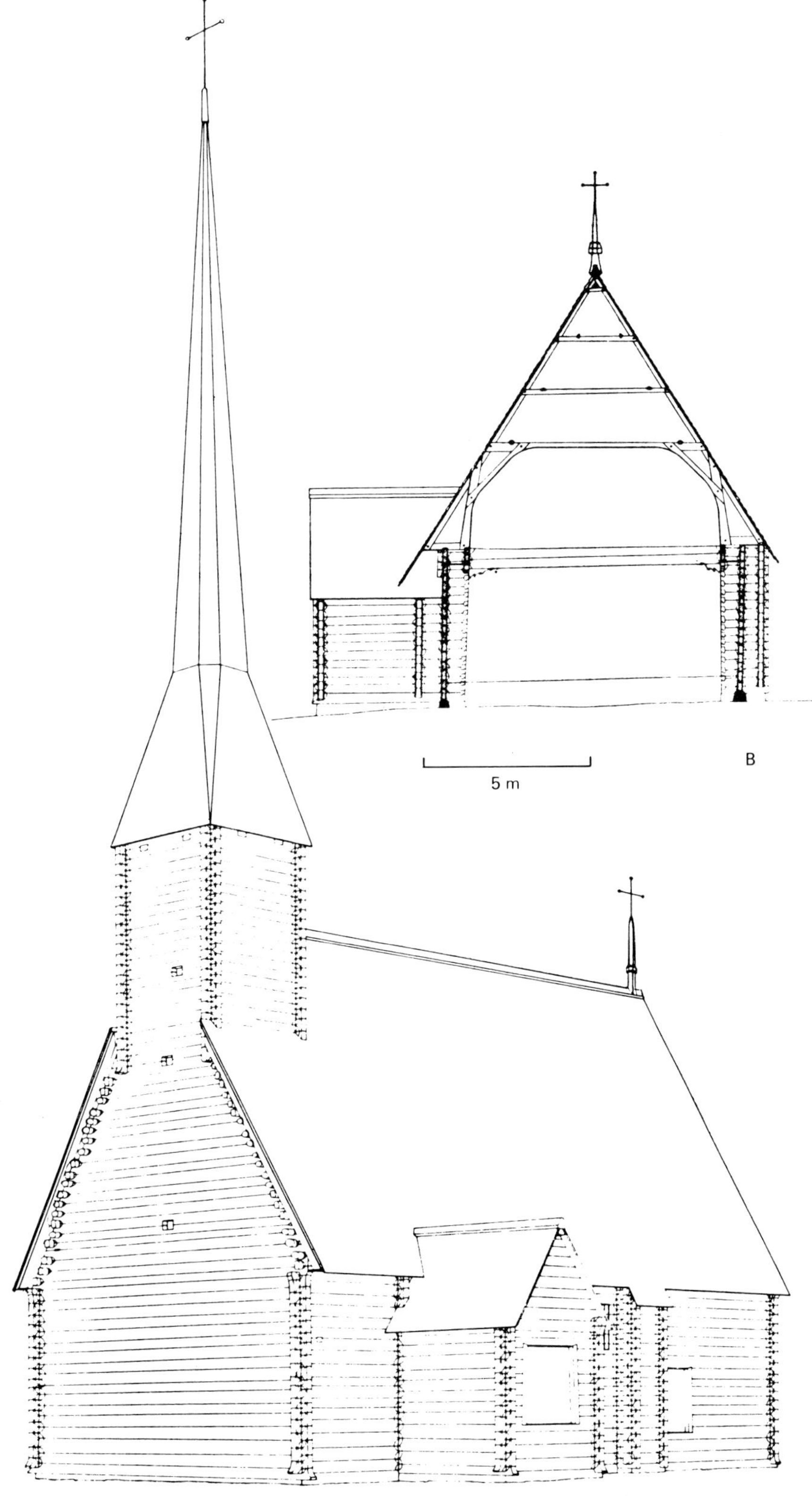

462 Hailuoto island. A. Reconstruction of the original church of 1620. B. The transverse section which remained unaltered.

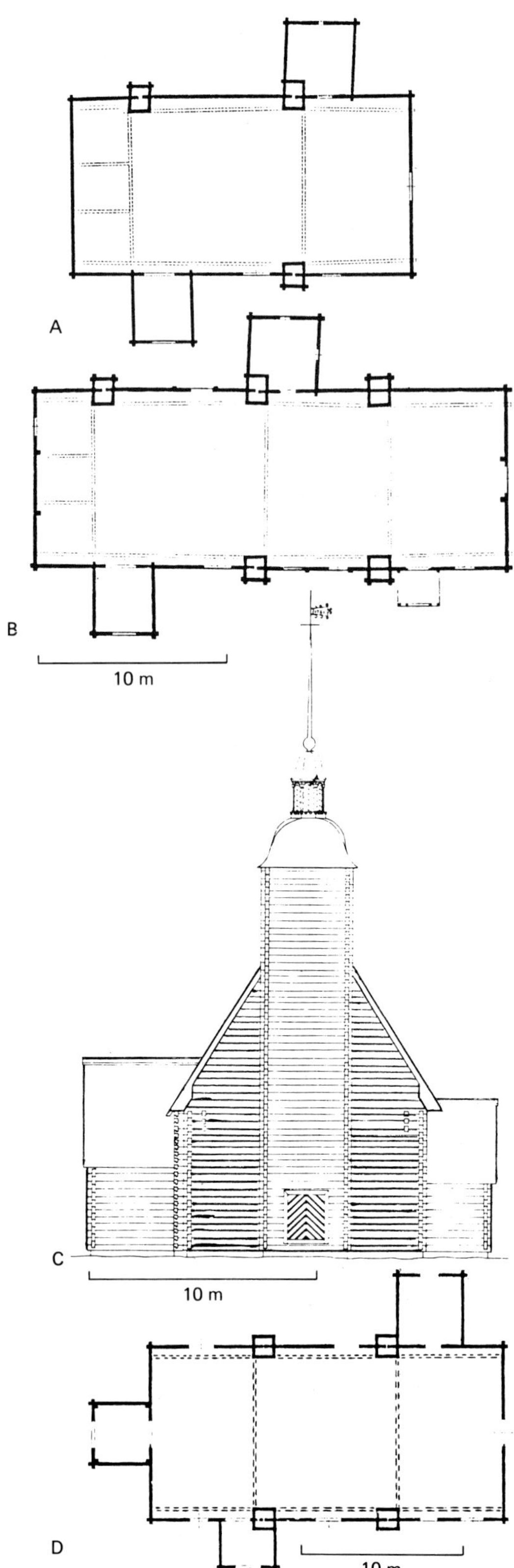

463 Finnish 'long' churches. A. Hailuoto, state in 1620. B. Hailuoto, state after 1656. C,D. Utajärvi, 1762, west elevation and plan.

gable-ends and, at the west end, for the tower up to the base of the spire. Moreover the western section of the roof itself showed the archaic structure described in the Introduction (cf. **1**, **2**). Its main supports were horizontal logs or purlins resting on the timbers of the west gable at one end (they are seen projecting in **462**) and, at the other end, on the corresponding timbers of the transverse wall, level with the inner face of the tower. (Strzygowski, who identified such a roof at Sodankylä from photographs, would have been delighted with this feature at Hailuoto, but he seems never to have visited either place.) Possibly the whole church was so roofed originally. But the available records show a normal raftered roof between the tower and the east end, the pattern of whose sixteen trusses determined, in turn, the form of the ceiling (**462** B).

Both plan and perspective drawing show another interesting characteristic of this church, shared with several similar ones on both sides of the Gulf, namely the use of tall, hollow, pier-like log structures to re-inforce the walls. These are termed by Strzygowski *Hohlpfeiler* or *Blockpfeiler*, but since they both resemble and act like the buttresses of masonry churches, I prefer to call them buttress-piers. They are square in section and constructed of short horizontal pieces most carefully jointed at the corners (**41** F, **472**). The walls pass through them so that each buttress-pier projects both internally and externally, though they may be boarded over outside (**464**). The hollow internal space generally disguises junctions in the wall timbers, so these buttress-piers, besides strengthening the whole wall and roof structure, facilitate the use of shorter timbers than would otherwise be needed. It will be noticed from the plan that the north wall of the original Hailuoto church had two buttress-piers, the south wall only one. The reason is that the log-built porch on the south side, with its timbers correctly jointed into those of the wall, served the same purpose as a second buttress-pier, which it thus replaced.

These buttress-piers, when occurring (as they normally do) in pairs, have the top timbers either of their eastern or western faces extended right across the church to form tie-beams, at the level of the springing of the roof. Like other tie-beams, these serve to counteract the outward thrust of the roof. Details of the ingenious carpentry involved are well seen in two internal views from the later church at Utajärvi, south-east of Oulu (**465–466**). The church as a whole is built on virtually the same principles as the seventeenth-century examples, though in this case the tower stands forward from the west front (**463** C, D). Internally, two of the topmost timbers of the buttress-

464 Muhos on the Oulujoki. Church of 1634 showing external projection of the buttress-piers.

piers together make up the tie-beam, forming one piece with their fellows on the opposite side, and the next timber below forms a kind of supporting bracket. The tops of the buttress-piers are also drawn out to east and west at right angles to the ties, and likewise have supporting brackets, formed in this case from two timbers sliced off at an angle. Such longitudinal beams, running parallel and almost in contact with the walls, form the basis of the ceiling. Ceilings have a vaulted appearance, their commonest pattern being that shown in the Hailuoto section (**462** B). As the figure shows, the timbers of the principal roof trusses determine the profile of the ceiling, which is fully boarded from truss to truss, its flat median portion being at the level of the collar-beam. The interiors of Kristiinankaupunki (Kristinestad) with its decorative tie-beams and of Vöyri (Vörå) have ceilings built in exactly the same way (**467**, **477**).

The plan of Hailuoto in its later phase shows how the church was lengthened to four bays with the addition of a third pair of buttress-piers (**463** B), but the tall spire was found to be unstable and stood only in a truncated form until the whole building, including a fine free-standing belfry (**500**), was lost in the fire of 1968. Some other longer churches of this type likewise have three pairs of buttress-piers and four bays. An example stands at Tornio at the top of the Gulf, just on the Finnish side of the border, though it was modified by the subsequent addition of transepts (**468**). Its tall spire, while plainly in the Gothic tradition like the early one at Hailuoto, has non-Gothic convolutions at its base. The tower it surmounts is sunk in the west front from which approximately one-third of its diameter projects: compare the Kristiinankaupunki interior where the inward projection of a similar tower can be seen (**467**). Standing just west of the Tornio church is an interesting gate-belfry with little intersecting gabled roofs of Gothic derivation (**469**). The octagonal basement storey is log-built, but above this the construction is trestled. Similar belfries exist, or have existed, in northern Sweden as at Piteå across the bays to the south-west, where a stone prototype may have suggested the wooden form. Nearly all the separate belfries in the Bothnian region

465 Utajärvi on the Oulujoki, 1762. South-east corner of the interior to show structural details.

466 Utajärvi. North-western buttress-pier (touched up to clarify jointing system).

467 Kristiinankaupunki on the Gulf of Bothnia, 1698. The interior looking west.

468 Tornio, on the Bothnian Gulf. Church built 1684–6, from the south-east.

469 Tornio. The free-standing belfry, c. 1686–8.

are, however, of Renaissance or Baroque character, and will be spoken of later.

The four-bayed plan is exceptional. The majority of these 'long' churches are of only three bays separated by two pairs of buttress-piers with their tie-beams. Examples in northern Sweden were Råneå, Umeå and Luleå on the Gulf of Bothnia (all seventeenth century) and there is Jukkasjärvi (1726) far away in the Arctic near the modern mining town of Kiruna. In some smaller churches, however, only a single pair of buttress-piers provided re-inforcement midway along the walls, as at Överkalix (1690) north of Kalix at the head of the Gulf. Northern Finland provides parallel examples of both types, and one of each is met with on the journey from Tornio into Finnish Lapland – a journey offering many delights whether the traveller's main interests are geographical, botanical, faunistic or architectural.

At Tervola on the Kemijoki, not far from Tornio and on the borders of Lapland, we come to a small wooden church of 1687–9 (**470**). The boarded exterior is painted a dull red as most of these churches are

470 Tervola on the Kemijoki, church of 1687–9.

believed to have been originally. It looks rather uninteresting though two of the buttress-piers show up clearly, the other two being disguised respectively by the porch on the south side and the sacristy on the north. Inside, however, the church most attractively displays its timber work in various finishes: it is left plain for the walls, the coved ceiling, the buttress-piers and heavy compound tie-beams; painted green and white for the pews and the western gallery; elaborately carved and coloured for the pulpit (a professional work).

Some way beyond Tervola the road reaches Rovaniemi, administrative headquarters of Finnish Lapland and the only real town in this far-northern area. On crossing the Arctic Circle a little further on the motorist, hitherto warned by road signs against stray elk on the road, is now warned against reindeer. Odd reindeer can now be seen from time to time, though in summer the big herds are all driven away by the Lapp herdsmen to higher and remoter feeding grounds. This was at one time purely Lapp country and the wooden church at Sodankylä, about a hundred kilometres north of the Arctic Circle, was built in 1689 for the Lapps from several neighbouring villages who were converts to Lutheranism. In the course of the eighteenth century, however, many Finnish immigrants settled in the area and a new stone church was built here in 1859. Fortunately the old wooden one still stands and is well cared for. When I stayed in the village in June, 1975, the sun could not set, though it seemed to try; and it was a novel experience to wander around the church in the midnight hours while mists rose from the river and a ruddy sunset merged insensibly into sunrise.

This church is a degree simpler than Tervola, possessing (like Överkalix) only a single pair of buttress-piers, and outwardly it is more attractive to the eye since the constructional timbers, with their elementary style of corner-jointing, are everywhere visible. The main door, giving access to the church through the western porch, measures only 5 ft (1.5 m), a fact possibly explained (it has been suggested) by the short stature of the average Lapp (**471**). The ceiling, coved on either side and flat in the middle, is typical of the

472 Sodankylä. Buttress-pier in the south wall.

style but its relationship to the roof structure (probably based on purlins) is not clear. In contrast to the rough execution of the walls the two buttress-piers are most carefully constructed with sophisticated joints and are evidently of great strength (**472**). They are joined by a system of superimposed tie-beams which form a complete transverse partition across the ceiling space (**473**). The pulpit, built against the northern buttress-pier, is a home-carpentered variety and an appropriate match to the other internal woodwork, all plain and unpainted. East of it, a low transverse beam supported in the middle by two uprights braced to form an arch, roughly demarcates the chancel. All the main timbers have been trimmed with the axe, not sawn, a fact which accounts for the pleasing unevenness of their texture.

I must now proceed to consider the adoption in Finland of the cruciform plan which, in the eighteenth century, was found to provide the ideal setting for Lutheran worship, and at the same time to simplify construction. There were, in the first place, 'long' or linear churches provided with transepts which were

471 Sodankylä. Lapp church of 1689. The western porch.

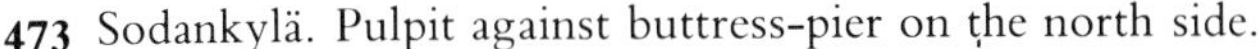

473 Sodankylä. Pulpit against buttress-pier on the north side.

474 Pihlajavesi. 'Pseudo-cruciform' church of 1780–2.

lower than, and subsidiary to the main axis – a plan for which there are possible masonry prototypes in Sweden. Such churches have been described as 'pseudo-cruciform' and, whenever actually built, can be regarded as representing an intermediate stage on the way to the fully centralised church with four short and equal arms. Examples are Pihlajavesi, Keuruu and Kuru, places in the lake complex west of Jyväskylä and north of Tampere (**474–475**). In these and similar cases the north and south transepts, projecting at right angles, provide the same re-inforcement to the principal walls as did the buttress-piers of the 'long' church, which are therefore no longer required. Pihlajavesi and Keuruu possess incorporated western towers in the Gothic tradition, though their form is Renaissance rather than medieval. Kuru is similar in layout, having a continuous barrel vault from west to east which is not interrupted by the low ceilings of the transepts, but its Baroque belfry is virtually free-standing (**499**). Like so many of these churches it stands close to a waterway, and an old church boat survives.

475 Keuruu, 1756–9. Another pseudo-cruciform church, with patterned shingling of the roofs.

476 Vöyri. Church built 1626, transformed 1777. Western aspect.

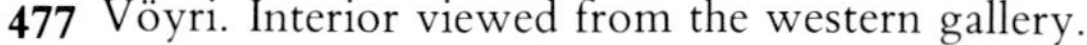

477 Vöyri. Interior viewed from the western gallery.

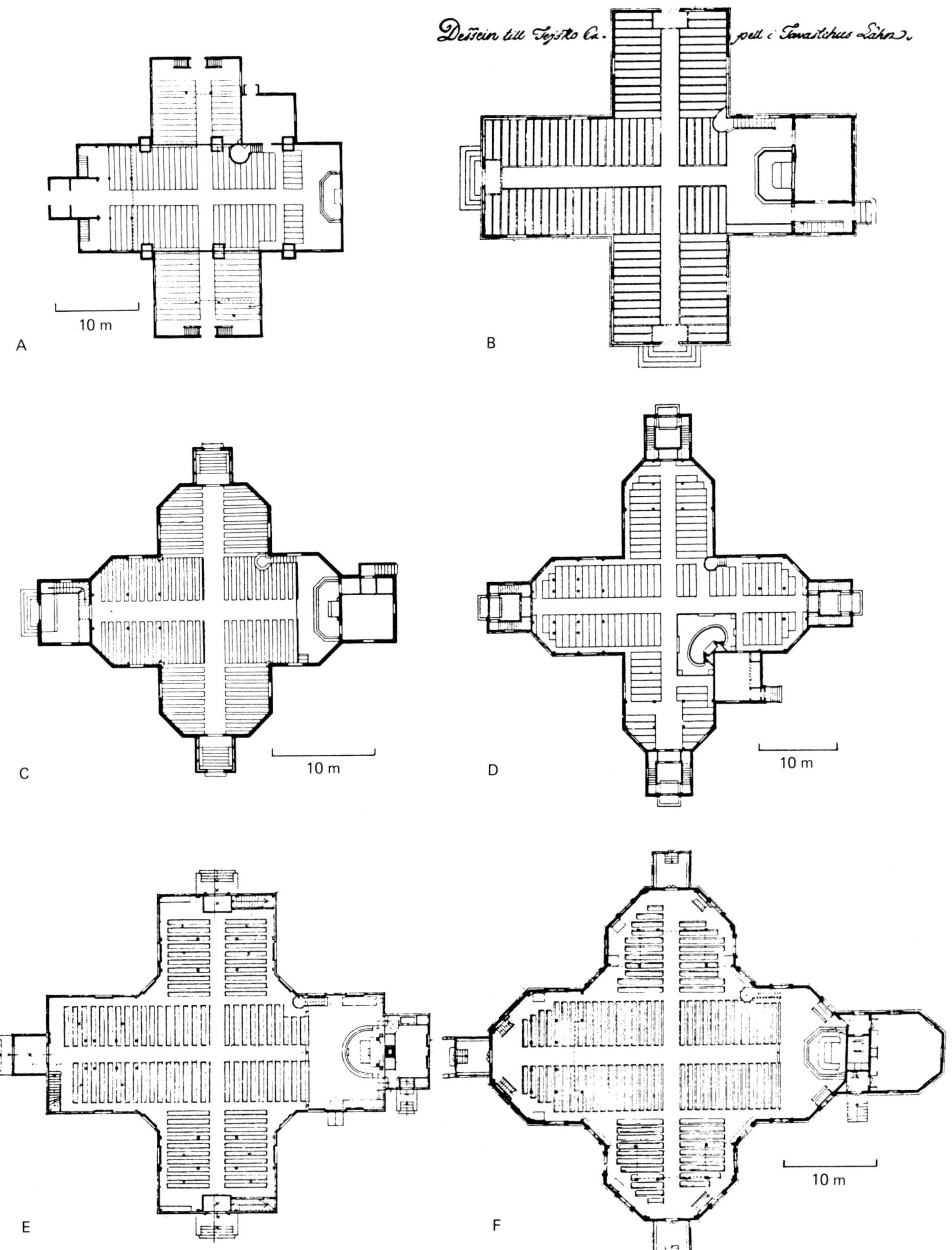

478 Finnish fully cruciform plans. A. Vöyri, 1777. B. Teisko, 1788. C. Oulainen, 1753. D. Ilmajoki, 1764–5. E. Orivesi, 1781. F. Ruovesi, 1777–8.

479 Petäjävesi. The 'Bothnian' belfry, 1821.

480 Petäjävesi. Simple cruciform church of 1763–4, south side. Note sacristy built on to eastern arm, and polygonal doorway to south arm.

In the interesting case of Vöyri (Swedish Vörå), near the port of Vaasa, there is still a Gothic-type steeple set into the west front exactly as at Tornio. This was a typical early 'long' church with three pairs of buttress-piers (**476**, **478** A). Then in 1777 it was resolved to convert it to the cruciform plan then in vogue, thereby increasing its capacity to one thousand seats (thanks to galleries provided in both the new arms). In the process two now superfluous buttress-piers had to be eliminated. The elaborate polychrome pulpit, the work of a specialist carver, is typical of many. The interior is otherwise austere (**477**).

We come, then, to those wooden churches which were planned from the beginning as equal-armed crosses, churches where the central space dominates. Such plans offered the over-riding advantage, in an era of rapid population growth, that a greatly increased number of worshippers could be accommodated within easy range of the preacher. Moreover, the new plan had structural advantages. As was stated earlier, the various angles of the building themselves served to strengthen the walls so that buttress-piers were no longer needed. On the other hand massive tie-beams (often compounded of two or three separate pieces) were retained and usually thrown across the opening of each arm (**477**, **496** etc.).

Plans of this type can arise by the natural process of adding one rectangular element to another, as already described in relation to Ukrainian churches (Chapters 3 and 4). Strzygowski wished to believe that this had happened spontaneously, in early times, in all the regions where wooden churches evolved, including Finland. The idea is attractive but unfortunately, in the case of Finland at least, untenable. There is no evidence of wooden cruciform churches existing in northern Scandinavia before the late seventeenth cen-

481 Maksamaa. Church of 1824 with neo-classic features and traditional belfry.

tury and (surprisingly perhaps) no evidence of influence from the neighbouring Russian territories to the east, where cruciform plans (if for a very different style of church) had existed since the late Middle Ages. When centralised churches first appear in Sweden and Finland, they must be seen as reflecting the international vogue for this architectural form which, first launched in the Italian Renaissance, was gaining popularity throughout Europe in the late seventeenth and eighteenth centuries. It must be admitted, however, that the immediate source of inspiration for the earliest centralised churches in Finland, built in the 1660s and 1670s, is not clear. Apparently they were all wooden, and all have disappeared, but if masonry models were responsible for their appearance few were available at that time. Throughout the seventeenth and eighteenth centuries the development of Finnish church architecture was strongly influenced by Sweden. However, the only major centralised church in construction there around 1660 was Jean de la Vallée's Katarina Kyrka in Stockholm (**493**), followed by the Kungsholm church about 1673. The former's specific role will be mentioned below, but possibly these two churches exerted from the beginning a more widespread influence on architectural ideas both in Finland and in Sweden. In Stockholm itself, for instance, a chapel of St Olaf, of timbered construction and cruciform in plan, was built in 1673–4.

A range of Finnish cruciform plans is reproduced in **478**. The simplest ones present four squared-off arms meeting at right angles, the end of the eastern arm often being partitioned off to form the sacristy. One of the earliest of these in Norrland was the town church of Piteå on the north-west coast of the Gulf of Bothnia, built in 1684–6. In Finland the type was perpetuated in a plainer form – i.e. with the central cupola reduced or suppressed – alongside more elaborate versions. One of these simplified Finnish churches, particularly attractive because its constituent

482 Maksamaa. Wooden figure by the belfry door.

timbers are not covered over, stands at Petäjävesi among the lakes west of Jyväskylä (**479–480**). A domed ceiling over the crossing no doubt represents an ancestral cupola, no longer visible outside (compare **496**). Attached at the west, but not forming part of the main structure, is one of those beautiful 'Bothnian' belfries which will be referred to again later. Among the numerous churches scattered along the Bothnian coast some retain (despite their often very late dates) this simplest of cruciform plans. At Maksamaa (Maxmo) for instance the ends of the arms have been given neo-classic pediments instead of the normal hipped roofs (**481–482**). The traditional belfry has a rather wide lower storey, and beside its door we find, sculpted in wood, a poor man with collecting box begging for alms. Many of these appealing figures are met with up and down the country.

My third example of the same elementary cruciform plan comes from a very different environment a long way away. It is the Lapp church near Inari, nearly 300 km beyond the Arctic Circle and by far the northernmost building to find a place in these pages (**483–484**). It is said to have been built by carpenters from neighbouring Norwegian Finnmark, but its character is Finnish and the whole structure, including the stumpy attached belfry, is in blockwork. The axes of the church (without the tower) measure 15 m, the width of the arms being about one-third of this. The 'barrel vaulted' ceilings are kept low, so that the tie-beams penetrate and help to support them, being surmounted by an arched framework for this purpose. There are galleries in the west and north arms supported on paired baluster-shaped columns and a pulpit of home-made character. This unpretentious church stands among birches not far from the shores of a small, lonely lake. To reach it from Inari takes about two hours, the rough path leading through woodlands of stunted birch and pine and past patches of desolate swamp. This is a walk for lovers of solitude only.

Reference to **478** will show how these cruciform churches could be further centralised, by progressive shortening of the arms and by the cutting off (as it would appear in the plan) of their various right angles. Each eliminated right angle was thus replaced by two angles of 135°. By this process the ends of the arms could be rendered elegantly polygonal, while 'cutting off' the internal corners enabled the best use to be made of the interior space. So architectural effectiveness was enhanced, while larger congregations could be seated within sight and hearing of the pastor. There was another advantage in these new-style plans with their sixteen, twenty or twenty-four angles: though

483 Lapp church near Inari, arctic Finland, with log-built western tower. Built in 1760s.

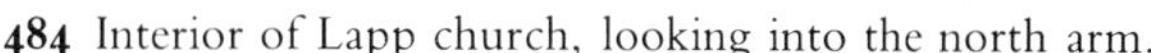

484 Interior of Lapp church, looking into the north arm.

485 Kiiminki. Church with twenty corners, 1760.

they demanded greater skill and labour in the building, shorter logs could be used for some or all of their sides. This meant less destruction of timber and accorded with the Swedish Government's edicts, issued in the early eighteenth century, regarding the conservation of forest resources.

It was the polygonal *arms* that first made their appearance, being introduced by a well known Ostrobothnian architect named Hans Biskop whose earlier work was carried out in Sweden proper. He experimented also with faceted extremities in non-cruciform churches, a few of which exist in both countries, but they enjoyed greater popularity as an adornment to the cross-shaped plan (**478** C, D). An example is Biskop's church at Övertorneå (1736) on the Swedish side of the boundary river. This twenty-cornered plan, first seen in Finland in the 1750s, became familiar there in the following decade. There is an example at Kiiminki (Oulu district) where it is accompanied by the usual Bothnian belfry (**485–486**). At Haukipudas in the same area a similar plan is complicated by extensions projecting from three of the arms, and this results in a fascinating play of roof surfaces (**487**). Inside, this church has the regulation massive tie-beams at the opening of each arm but it is unusual in lacking galleries, so that the organ stands at ground level. Round the walls, biblical scenes by Toppelius are painted in a realistic and dramatic style (**488**).

An alternative, sixteen-cornered plan has the extremities of the arms left square but the *internal* right angles eliminated, as in St Olaf's, Stockholm and the town church at Umeå (Swedish Bothnia) of 1724. In Finland churches of this plan (**478** E) came to be preferred to the twenty-cornered variety and the majority were built later, between 1780 and the end of the century. The most interesting of all cruciform plans are, however, those which combine the characteristics of both the categories just mentioned. In these churches no right angles remain but there are no fewer than twenty-four angles of 135° (**478** F). Though several others were planned only three of these remarkable churches were completed according to the original design: Kuortane (1777), Ruovesi (1777–8)

486 Kiiminki. The adjoining 'Bothnian' belfry.

487 Haukipudas. Church of 1762 with an elaborated version of the same plan.

488 Haukipudas. The Expulsion from Paradise by Mikael Toppelius, 1770s.

489 Ruovesi. Church with twenty-four corners, 1778, from the south-west.

and Ylihärmä (1785–7). Ruovesi, in the western lake region north of Tampere, is offered here as an example. I must not omit to mention, at this point, the existence of the very same plan in the rather earlier wooden church at Velké Karlovice in Moravia (**418**), a coincidence to which I shall revert at the end of the chapter.

The large and impressive church at Ruovesi, by the master builder Matti Åkerblom, has steep hipped roofs leading up to the central lantern so often lost in Finland, though it does not here connect with the interior space (**489**). The four arms were originally equal, but a sacristy was added as an eastern extension in 1852 and porches project to the north, south and west. The facets of the arms have long windows (divided into upper and lower sections where there are galleries inside) encased between wooden pilaster-strips. The layout is completed by a simple free-

490 Ruovesi. The free-standing belfry.

standing belfry with octagonal upper storey (**490**). But it is the well lit and exceptionally spacious interior that reveals the real genius of this wholly centralised design (**491–492**). The internal space seems all the vaster as no sharp corners impinge upon it between the arms. The arms themselves, short, apsed and barrel vaulted, do not look like separate parts of the building but merely form exedrae extending the central space. Neither tie-beams (two to each arm) nor the galleries (whose middle portions are deeply recessed in the north and south arms) seem to obtrude, as happens in many centralised churches of less accomplished design. The 'vaults' of the four arms join the great central saucer-dome, flat in its centre, which appears to be mainly supported on simulated vaulting arising from the corners. This saucer-dome is wisely kept low (c. 14 m) leaving a big empty roof space above. The ribbing seen in **491**, though by no means ill-designed, only dated from 1904–5 and was removed in 1978. I have therefore included a recent photograph to show the ceiling as now restored to its original condition (**492**). This grand interior, 35 m across, seats 1500 people without a sign of congestion.

These three plan types with the 'cut corners' were well known in Sweden from the 1720s onwards, though all existing examples in Finland belong to the second half of the eighteenth century or the beginning of the nineteenth. They could have developed, through the ingenuity of local master builders, from the simpler pre-existing cruciform plans. But since the earliest examples were in Sweden, the Swedish connection, at this period, cannot be ignored. There were now several Stockholm architects busy with cruciform stone churches, including C. F. Adelcrantz who was responsible for the Adolf Fredrik Kyrka and for radical alterations to the Katarina Kyrka, both major landmarks of the city. It is also true that a curious character of some Finnish wooden churches – the placing of the altar *between* the south and east arms (**478** D) – can only have originated in the original floor plan (later abandoned) of the Katarina Kyrka.

A further proof of the Swedish link is the fact that royal decrees issued in 1759 and (more explicitly) in 1776 required that all projected church plans should be submitted to the Superintendent of Public Architecture in Stockholm for scrutiny. However, the control thus intended appears to have been largely ineffective and was quite often ignored by the Finnish master builders who evidently had minds of their own. In the end it was they who led the way in these ultimate developments of the cruciform wooden church and the Swedes who lagged behind. Interesting evidence of this is provided by the case of an advanced 'sixteen-angled' plan proposed in 1781 for the church in Haapavesi by Simon Silvén, a native of the place. The plan was disallowed by the Swedish authorities and a very ordinary cruciform church, with some neo-classical features, substituted.

One last category of wooden cruciform churches must be described. In south-east Finland a number of 'double cruciform' churches were built during the eighteenth century, so called because arms were added to a plan already of cruciform character. L. Pettersson has traced their origin and evolution in a paper distinguished by masterstrokes of detection and deduction from which, however, I can here draw only a few salient points (see Pettersson 1959). The story begins at Hamina (Fredrikshamm), formerly a garrison town which, like Viipuri (Vyborg) further east, has frequently changed hands between Sweden–Finland and Russia. At Hamina two successive wooden churches

491 Ruovesi. View into the south arm, with ribbing dating from 1904–5.

492 Ruovesi, as restored in 1978: the central space with east and south arms.

493 The Katarina Kyrka of Stockholm in its original form, built between 1656 and the 1690s.

were built on the same site, the second or church of Elizabeth (1748–51) under a newly established Russian regime. Pettersson describes their design as 'a simplified and up-dated modification, adapted to the technique of blockwork' of the already famous church of Katharine (Katarina Kyrka) in Stockholm, built between 1656 and 1690 (**493**). As pointed out earlier the church in question exerted its influence as far afield as Silesia. It is a very large and (for its period) very original cruciform structure by Jean de la Vallée, a French architect employed, like his father before him, at the Swedish court. The plan shows angle-chambers, and the cupola was originally of double construction, the external one being wooden. Pettersson's ingeniously reconstructed plan of the second wooden version in Hamina, with elevation derived from earlier sources, is given in **494** A, B. He found strong evidence for the tapering arms, apparently an exercise in false perspective which could only have been conceived in Stockholm. The theory is that the Katarina Kyrka, either directly or through the wooden versions at Hamina, set a fashion for 'doubly cruciform' churches which radiated in all directions. Its influence spread to the coasts and off-shore islands of the Gulf of Finland and to the lake region further north, while to the east it reached the shores of Lake Ladoga and the gates of St Petersburg (Ingermanland, as this area was called when it belonged to the Swedish empire).

Attempts to follow the trend set by Hamina during the remainder of the eighteenth century, and the early nineteenth, involved some simplification. The double ranges of windows were, indeed, generally retained, whereas the elegant mansard roofs of the model were replaced by steep hipped roofs (sometimes described as 'Dutch'). But when the roofs of the angle-chambers between the arms were drawn right up to form a pyramid supporting the high cupola, the effect was no loss but unquestionably a gain. Though it is difficult to be sure about Soviet territory, I believe the only surviving example in this category is Juhana Salonen's late church of Lappee (as the medieval parish was

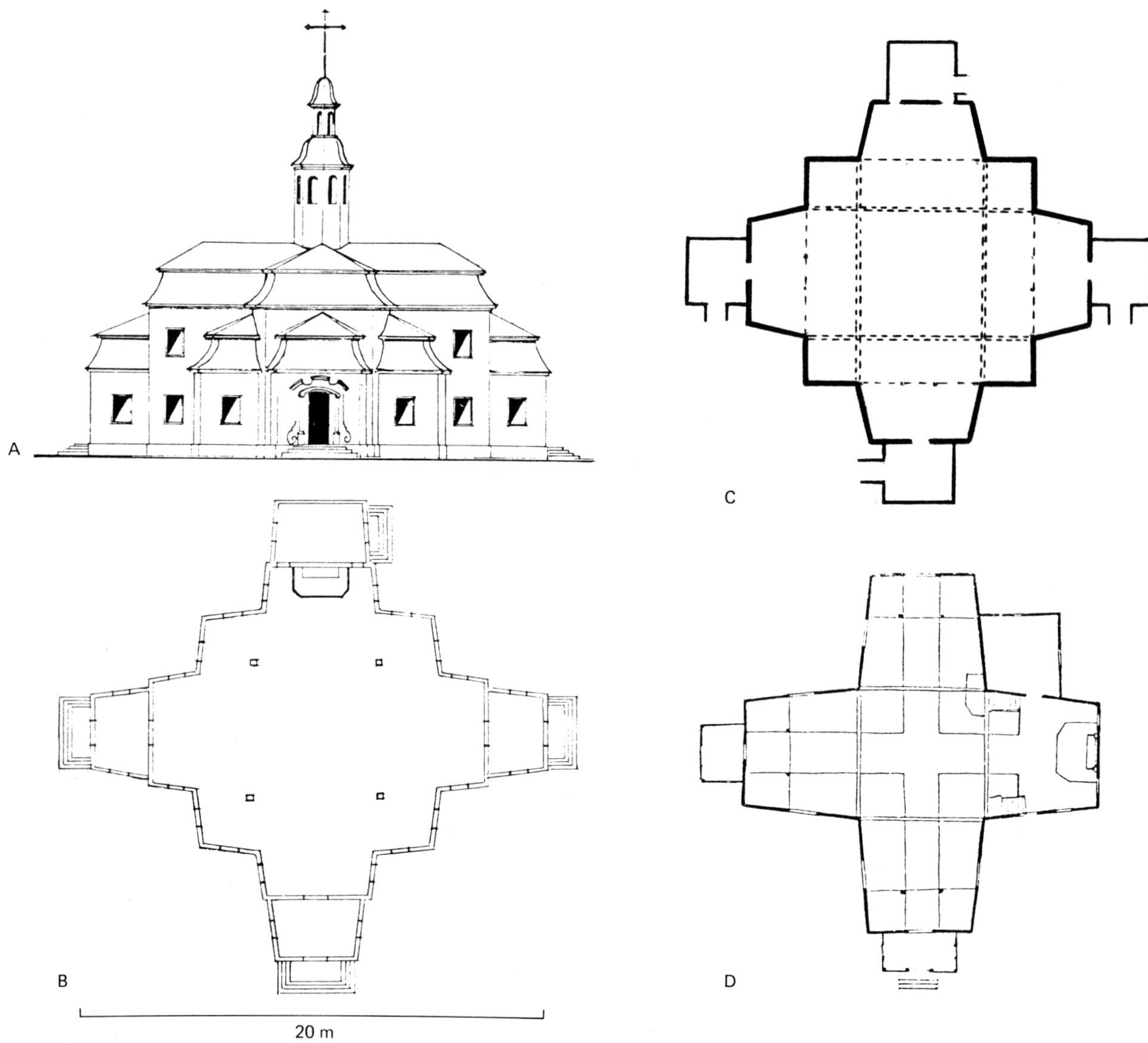

494 The tradition of Hamina (Fredrikshamm). A, B. The second 'Elizabeth' church of Hamina, western elevation and restored plan. C. Church of Lappee, old plan. D. The church on Lavansaari island.

called) at Lappeenranta, the Finnish port on the vast lake complex of Saimaa (**494** C, **495**). It is a splendid building, though visually impaired by the external pine boarding of 1837 and the loss of the shingles in 1881. The great internal space now has no uprights apart from pairs of short ones supporting the galleries in the south, north and west arms. There are, however, abnormally long intersecting tie-beams which tend to obstruct one's view of the broad, flattish dome, at present painted a deep blue with golden stars. The barrel vaulted arms narrow down towards their extremities and thus probably enhance one's impression of their length. In any case, this is one of the finest and most spacious interiors in Finland. The watercolour (**496**) shows the inside of a smaller and simpler wooden church (now lost) whose dome and vaults are likewise thought to be inspired indirectly by the Katarina Kyrka. The same could be said of many other churches, such as Petäjävesi, already cited as an example of the simplest cruciform plan. I would add that this interior, with its quadrangle of massive tie-beams and simulated vaults, is typical of Finnish cruciform churches in general.

Pettersson suggests that ambitious churches like Lappee, derived from Stockholm via Hamina yet rooted at the same time in popular craftsmanship, acted as a challenge and a counterblast to the neo-classicism being disseminated, at the same time, from near-by St Petersburg. This may be true. No such claim could be made, however, for the minor deriva-

495 Lappeenranta. The church of Lappee, 1792–4.

tives of the Hamina School, the fruit of far-reaching compromises with the modest local traditions in timber architecture. What they do show is how new features, amalgamated with traditional ones, can be absorbed into a common stock to be drawn upon at will. Some of these lesser derivatives retained the basic essentials of the Hamina plan (e.g. Antrea, **497**), others lost the angle-chambers. Some renounced the tapering arms, others retained them but ceased to be planned as a 'double' cross (**494** D). The latter subtype achieved, in fact, a wide distribution – from Jyväskylä in the north-west (1775) to the islands, now Russian, in the Gulf of Finland: Suursaari (1768) and Lavansaari (1783).

On both sides of the Gulf of Bothnia, whether on the coasts or inland, the 'Bothnian' type of free-standing belfry is common and, as much as the churches themselves, seems to belong to the landscape. These belfries began to supersede those of Gothic type, of which Tornio retains an almost unique example (**469**), about the end of the seventeenth century. The Bothnian belfries are 'stepped', consisting normally of three storeys of diminishing diameter, the lower two being square and the uppermost octagonal. Since they were generally intended as gate-belfries to churchyards, they have a through passage at ground level. The upper storeys bear delicate blind arcades with flat pilasters and classic capitals, between which are shutters (some of them openable for bell ringing) of patterned and painted woodwork. Stylistically,

496 Kärkölä, near Lahti. A church of 1754 no longer standing. Watercolour of the interior by Armas Lindgren.

497 Antrea. Church of 1767, a reduced version of the 'Hamina' type.

498 Free-standing 'Bothnian' belfry at Utajärvi, c. 1762.

these belfries seem to derive from the French late Renaissance, transmitted via Stockholm as a consequence of Jean de la Vallée's building activities. During the 'Great Northern War' of 1700–21, when Sweden–Finland, weakened by the various overseas adventures of Charles XII, was worsted by Russia, most architectural projects were set aside. But after the Peace Treaty in 1721 these new-style belfries enjoyed enormous popularity and were built everywhere. Moreover, though first developed on the Finnish side of the Gulf, they were now introduced into Swedish Norrland, the Ostrobothnian-born church builder Hans Biskop being responsible for many.

Typical Bothnian belfries are shown in **486** and **498**. The very late one at Petäjävesi (**479**) proves the unabated strength of local wood-building traditions early in the nineteenth century. Other Finnish belfries, similarly of late Renaissance derivation but not strictly 'Bothnian', also occur. A fine example stands at Kuru where both upper storeys are octagonal and the bulbous roof forms give a pronounced Baroque character to the whole (**499**). Nearly all these towers have a base of solid blockwork which may be concealed by exterior boarding but is easily seen, for instance, in **479** and **499**. However, the upper storeys usually depend for support on a 'trestle' of converging oblique timbers rising from near the base of the tower (**500**). This ancient system of construction, also possessed by the

499 Attached belfry at Kuru, 1781.

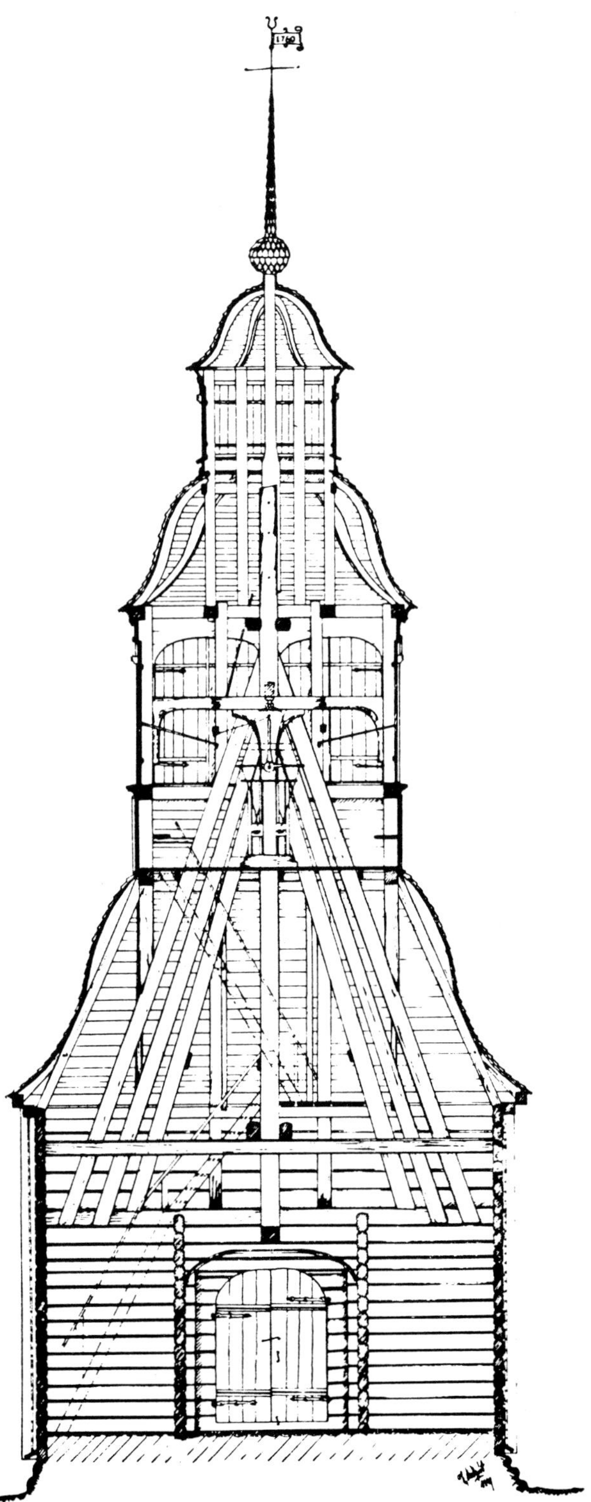

500 Section of the Bothnian belfry on Hailuoto island, burnt down in 1968.

Gothic Tornio belfry illustrated earlier (**469**), is obviously related to that used in some imposing wooden towers in southern and central Sweden. There, the massive timbers of the trestle may be permanently exposed to view, though protected by scale-like shingles. These magnificent belfries, like the one from Hallestad re-erected at Skansen, do not extend to Finland (or to the far north of Sweden) and so unfortunately fall outside our area.

Earlier in this chapter I mentioned the belief cherished by Strzygowski that the cruciform plans so frequent among Finnish wooden churches had evolved in early times and could have become the common property of widely separated peoples. Also he was the first, I believe, to draw attention to the identity of Finnish plans like Ruovesi to that of Velké Karlovice in Czechoslovakia – certainly a surprising coincidence if nothing more – besides which there are Ukrainian parallels. But there is nothing to show that the 'twenty-four-angled' plan, the special object of his interest, appeared earlier than the eighteenth century in these or other areas. My own belief is that it could have arisen independently in each country, for this particular plan is the logical consummation of the endeavour to perfect the layout of the cruciform church. At the same time I would not rule out the supporting influence of Baroque models in any of the countries concerned.

Unfortunately (I am bound to say) Strzygowski's Finnish speculations did not end there. He persuaded himself that the false barrel vaults of some Finnish wooden churches (to me merely imitative of masonry vaults), and even their occasional choir screens carved by eighteenth-century craftsmen, indicated a significant relationship with the proto-Romanesque churches of the Croatians away south in Dalmatia. Such far-fetched notions, thrown out as a challenge, may broaden the mind and stimulate discussion, but I can only regard them as preposterous, and their author as wholly misguided. I feel that Strzygowski, in turning his attention to Finland towards the end of his life, was no longer in full possession of his critical faculties. But the fact will remain that his work and his personality were a valid and welcome stimulus to generations of scholars over many years, in wooden architecture as in other fields of research.

This chapter concludes my survey of the wooden world of eastern Europe, with the churches and belfries which seem to me the finest expression of its rural architecture. We have completed a roughly clockwise circuit moving first of all from north Russia to the

Ukrainian homeland in the south, then south-westward into Rumania, thence north-westward to Poland, and finally north again to Finland next door to the original country of departure. Four chapters were devoted to the huge areas inhabited by Orthodox (including Uniate) believers, one each to those of the Catholic and Protestant communities further west. This arrangement has underlined the dependence of church architecture, and of wooden architecture in particular, upon religious affiliation. Yet most of Rumania makes an exception to the rule, having western-influenced wooden churches despite its ancient tradition of Orthodoxy. So from that fifth chapter onwards we begin to see clear links with western Christendom and the architectural scene becomes more easily intelligible to the western traveller.

All the same, it is the very unfamiliarity of these churches, and their exoticism due to the qualities of the timber itself, that are most likely to appeal to lovers of architecture who travel in eastern Europe. My own reaction, only partly foreseen when I took up the study, has been one of amazement at the variety of designs and structural solutions of which a single material was found capable. Of course, this variety can be attributed in part to liturgical differences and to some variation in the skills handed down in particular areas. But one is always aware of another factor, and that is the inborn artistic sense of the villagers and the rural craftsmen themselves who, generation after generation, have added their quota of individual genius to the local tradition. Among the satisfactions of travel which I have experienced in these countries I would number the enjoyment of this craftsmanship, especially where it represents a live and continuing tradition. Let us not forget, however, the still more intimate and enduring bonds between each village community and its church. In some at least of the countries surveyed village churches can still play that part in the spiritual life of the people for which they were created and evolved. Museum sites are useful, but I hope the day will never come when every surviving wooden church is a museum piece and nothing more.

APPENDIX I

The log cabin in North America

The early habitations of northern and eastern Europe, transplanted to a new continent, enjoyed an extraordinary new lease of life at a time when, in their home countries, they were already being reduced to subsidiary roles. For the log cabin of America, the very symbol of pioneering days and the object almost of a cult in the present age, was nothing more nor less than the primitive log dwelling discussed in the Introduction. C. A. Weslager has written a history of the log cabin incorporating the findings of previous writers on the subject, and I owe most of the facts here quoted to his comprehensive study.

The English settlers who, in the early seventeenth century, were the first colonists on the Atlantic seaboard of America did not – unfortunately for them – know anything of this method of construction. It formed no part of their heritage, so the Pilgrim Fathers and other early immigrants attempted to build in the more difficult technique of timber-framing with which they were familiar at home. The Dutch and French who were early on the scene were likewise ignorant of the blockwork principle. So too were the American Indians – surprisingly, in view of their unlimited timber resources. (However, they later acquired this skill from the European community, as did the Negro slaves on the southern plantations.)

At the time of the early white colonisation of America the techniques of log building, though scarcely known in western Europe, were widely employed in the forested areas of central Europe – where they have since almost died out, except in the Alps and the uplands of Bohemia. Log building was also widespread in Scandinavia where it survives in considerable vigour to this day. It is therefore not surprising to learn that the log cabin made its *début* in America (to use Weslager's phrase) in the Swedish settlement on Delaware Bay, south of New York, about 1638. Some 50% of the 'Swedes' settled here were in fact Finns either from Finland itself, which then formed part of the Swedish kingdom, or from northern Sweden, where many Finns had been settled since the sixteenth century. The Finns above all were experts in the blockwork technique, and apparently the log houses of New Sweden were largely built by them. Many were of the simplest model – of round logs intersecting at the corners, 'saddle notched' (in American parlance). Others, however, were more sophisticated buildings of hewn logs, with dovetail joints and flush corners (**501** and cf. **1**, **2**, **6**, **35**, **41**).

Although the Swedish–Finnish settlement was seized by the Dutch in 1655, only to be taken from them by the English in 1664, the log house – or 'cabin' as it came to be called – had come to stay. In the second half of the seventeenth century the Swedes, encouraged by the Governor, Lord Baltimore, moved on into Maryland, naturally taking the log cabin with them. They also colonised the area later to become Pennsylvania, long before the arrival of William Penn's Quaker settlers for whom they smoothed the way, and by whom, later on, they were greatly appreciated. From now on every immigrant community adopted what was in fact the ideal type of house for pioneer conditions in all well forested areas. Its building required no specialised skills, no nails or bolts, no tool except the axe. Given accessible timber a one-roomed hut could be erected, with the help of neighbours, in a matter of days. The result was a solid, well insulated dwelling, cool in summer and warm in winter. It was not unduly inflammable. And it was reasonably proof against Indian or other marauders, even if they attacked with fire-arms.

Until now the distribution of the log cabin was still restricted: its great days were yet to come. New immigrants, attracted by the promise of religious and political freedom, were pouring in. In the last decades of the seventeenth century and onwards into the eighteenth the Pennsylvania Quakers were joined by great numbers of Lutherans, Calvinists, Methodists, Moravians and other sectarians from the Germanic States and from what is now Czechoslovakia.

501 'Log house in the forests of Georgia' after Captain Basil Hall, 1820s.

All were familiar with log building and gave a decisive impetus to the technique originally brought in by the Scandinavians, whom they now greatly outnumbered. Another important immigrant group, initially ignorant of log building, but soon to adopt it and take part in its dispersal, were Scottish Presbyterians. This community had been settled in Ulster since about 1600 and are commonly referred to by American writers as the 'Scotch-Irish'.

The smaller cabins, intended as a rule only as temporary dwellings, could measure as little as 3 × 4 m: these might have nothing but an earth floor and, if there was any chimney, an outside one of logs well daubed with mud or clay. A single unit could not exceed the normal maximum log length of 7 m; larger dwellings consisted therefore of two or more separate units joined up in various ways. The larger dwellings would have floors of split logs and more advanced chimneys, which could either be outside at one end of the cabin or in various internal positions, even in the centre. Corner-jointing naturally followed European models, hewn logs with flush, dovetailed corners being reserved for the more ambitious buildings. The logs, if not carefully squared and fitted together, would be caulked with moss or wet clay; or in rough buildings with badly fitting logs the spaces were filled with wood or stone fragments, smeared over with clay or adobe. Roofs were often raftered, the steeper pitch making space for a loft. But the drawing from Captain Basil Hall's book (**501**) shows the flatter purlin-roof exactly as once found among the primitive dwellings of the Finnish and Slavic tribes, and still to be seen in the field barns of northern Finland (**1**, **6**).

Besides ordinary dwellings with their outbuildings and bath-houses all other types of building needed for domestic or civic life were generally log-built. In early days many stockaded forts and garrison houses were required, some of these being constructed on the alternative principle known since prehistoric times – i.e. with the horizontal members not intersecting but slotted into stout vertical corner-posts (cf. **35** F). Courthouses and jails were also at times so built. Countless log-built farm buildings besprinkled the countryside, including barns with the timbers spaced for ventilation, exactly as in eastern Europe. There were log mansions (sometimes of several storeys), log schools, log churches and parsonages, log meeting houses and even log synagogues.

Once the daunting barrier of the Appalachians had been surmounted, about the middle of the eighteenth century, the great westward expansion from the old coastal colonies could begin in earnest. Now nationality and culture gradually lost their identity in 'the great American melting pot' and the new country soon declared its independence. The adventures of the pioneer families on the move with their covered wagons have, of course, been re-enacted in many a 'western' film. With the later stimulus of the Californian gold rush this mass migration continued unabated for a hundred years, until the mid nineteenth century, when its character began to change with the coming of the railways. Throughout this period and indeed until the end of the century the log cabin continued to play its vital part as every frontiersman's temporary if not permanent home. Thus in time it reached California and the Pacific.

On the Pacific coast we witness the re-uniting of two identical but long separated traditions of log building. There is no more curious episode in the great success story of this technique. It happened because the Russians, not content with an empire which already stretched across all northern Asia, had crossed the Bering Sea from north-eastern Siberia to Alaska and there set up a trading colony. Their forts, houses and churches – of which a few still stand – were naturally and inevitably of log construction. The port of Novo-Arkhangelsk (later Sitka) became, in the early nineteenth century, their base for hunting and trading forays down the Pacific coast which resulted in Russian fortified settlements springing up on the west coast (north of modern San Francisco) at Bodega Bay and Fort Ross (apparently a corruption of *Rus'*). This last-mentioned settlement, designed as a base for sea-otter hunting and for the supply of fresh food to Alaska, was manned by the Russians from 1812 to 1841. It comprised a well built log house for the Commandant and more than fifty other buildings, the surviving ones being preserved today in the Fort Ross Historic Park.

So log houses which had brought the Russians across Siberia, and those of the American adventurers which had seen them safely across the continent from Atlantic to Pacific (thus between them encircling the world), met here on the Californian coast. Both movements had taken something like two and a half centuries. Both owed much to the immemorial technique of log building, perfectly suited to the pioneers' needs on their great migrations, the *Völkerwanderungen* of the modern age.

Under the hard pioneering conditions of the New World in its infancy mere subsistence was a struggle and life possessed no frills. America, therefore, never saw the higher flights of the log-building technique which in any case was soon to be outstripped, in more prosperous times, by very different methods of construction. Nevertheless log building became the folk architecture, and played no small part in the folklore, of the United States (to some extent of Canada too). To have been born in a log cabin (as Abraham Lincoln was) became a mark of distinction. Today many original cabins are preserved in memorial parks and museums and many are still in use, if not for their original purposes. Some continue to be built, as in Scandinavia, to serve as mountain lodges, inns and restaurants, occasionally as private dwellings.

The American log cabin must be seen, however, as a bud whose potential remained unrealised, or as a larval creature – an axolotl – denied the prospect of full maturity. To see the flowers and fruits into which this bud was capable of bursting forth one must visit the settled communities of eastern Europe where the style is indigenous. As this book has sought to show, it was there that log building evolved along various divergent paths and there that it attained, in the eighteenth century, its apotheosis.

APPENDIX II

The vanished synagogues

No outline such as this could omit all reference to the east European wooden synagogues. Once numbering in all about one hundred and twenty, most of them were still standing in the 1920s and 1930s but every single one fell victim to the crazed anti-Semitism let loose in the Second World War. Their destruction is one more tragedy to add to the many tragedies that have beset the Jews from age to age, but it is also a grievous loss to the world's architectural heritage.

Central and east European synagogues as a whole, including those built in stone or brick, make a most interesting study. The earliest among those still surviving – the well known examples in Prague and Cracow – are beautiful Gothic buildings in which median columns divide the space into two aisles. They were, however, based on west European models, belonged wholly to the west European architectural tradition and, apart from their fittings, lacked any specifically Jewish characteristics.

It was long after – from the late 1500s onwards – that really distinctive synagogues began to be built in the area one may describe as Greater Poland, and this followed the major Jewish immigrations from the west earlier in that century. It was not surprising that Poland attracted persecuted Jewry from western Europe. The Jews already living there had enjoyed a relatively privileged existence for centuries. During the seventeenth and eighteenth centuries Jewish communities were still able to flourish and multiply, to pursue their commercial undertakings unhindered and to amass considerable wealth. Moreover, about the middle of the seventeenth century, the restrictions previously imposed on the building of synagogues in Poland were abrogated: thereafter they could be made as tall and conspicuous as the Jews wished, provided they were built in the ghetto area well away from Christian churches. This was a stimulating factor of which the Jews took full advantage. The seventeenth and eighteenth centuries saw indeed an unusual flowering of synagogue architecture in Poland: over a hundred were built in brick in the main centres and probably as many in timber, most of these latter in smaller towns and

502 Masonry synagogues. A. Lutsk, plan. B. Novogrudok, central pier incorporating Bima.

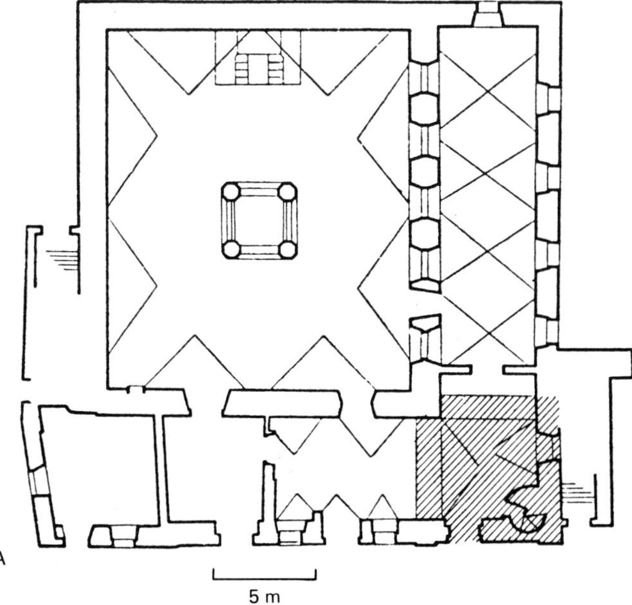

villages. These synagogues represented the nearest approach to a national architectural style that the Jews have ever produced. There is no doubt that many of the architects and builders were themselves Jews. It is also true that they absorbed current architectural fashions from gentile sources and did not hesitate to employ gentile craftsmen.

Synagogues consist of a hall which is the actual place of worship (*Ekhal*) and a vestibule (*Ulam*) (**502** A, **503**). In all post-medieval synagogues in eastern Europe the hall is approximately square so that all could hear the reading from the Bima in the centre, and to make further space available within earshot of the reader galleries were provided. It is interesting to note that, in both these respects, synagogues bear some resemblance to Protestant churches where similar arrangements ensure that the preacher can be seen and heard by the whole congregation. In synagogues the galleries also provided for the required segregation of women.

Synagogues in Europe are oriented like Christian churches since they likewise face towards Jerusalem. One or two doors lead into the western vestibule from which one enters the synagogue proper. Opposite this entry and built against the eastern wall is the richly adorned Ark of the Law (*Aron Hakodesh*) which enshrines the rolls of the Tora – i.e. the Pentateuch. In the midst of the open space, between door and shrine, is the Bima (or *Almemor*), a raised platform for the reading desk with encircling balustrade and (especially in wooden synagogues) an elaborately carved canopy (**504**). Besides the vestibule there might be other subsidiary rooms and offices since the synagogue was not only a place of worship but an all-purpose centre for the Jewish community. Nevertheless, with all its additions, the general plan of the complex approximated to a square and bore little resemblance, either inside or out, to a church.

While all of them are unlike churches it cannot be said that the seventeenth- and eighteenth-century synagogues of the Polish area showed any marked uniformity of style. Some of the brick-built ones much resembled fortresses: their massive walls, adorned with blind arcades and elaborate crenellations, were carried up high to conceal the roofs behind. A number of these – Lyuboml, Lutsk, Belz, Brody and Żółkiew (now Nesterov) – lie north of L'vov and in Volhynia, but they have no counterparts among wooden synagogues. Others, on the contrary, have (or had) rather plain outside walls, their effect depending on high roofs rising over the vaulting; examples are Kazimierz, Kurów, Włodawa and Szczebrzeszyn (Poland) and Pinsk (now Belorussia). It is these that were closely linked with the wooden synagogues, and no doubt there were mutual influences.

These two types of brick-built synagogue, dissimilar outside, share the internal arrangements already described and their most notable feature is the Bima which undergoes an extraordinary evolution. A synagogue at L'vov (1632) showed the origin of this new development. It had four pillars which helped to support the vaulted ceiling and divided it into nine practically equal squares. These pillars surrounded the Bima but did not touch it. Apparently the idea then arose that the four central pillars could be brought a little further inwards and joined up with the corners of the Bima: the ceiling space immediately above was thus much reduced. The last stage in this curious process of development was to amalgamate the four pillars to form one huge central pier supporting the ceiling vaults and swallowing up the Bima. The ceiling above was thus obliterated, or rather

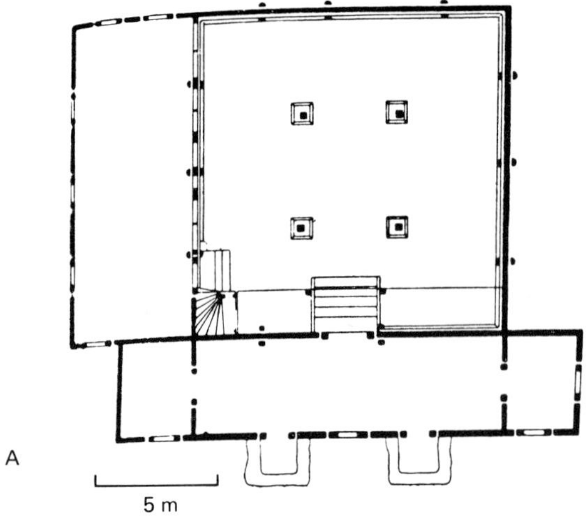

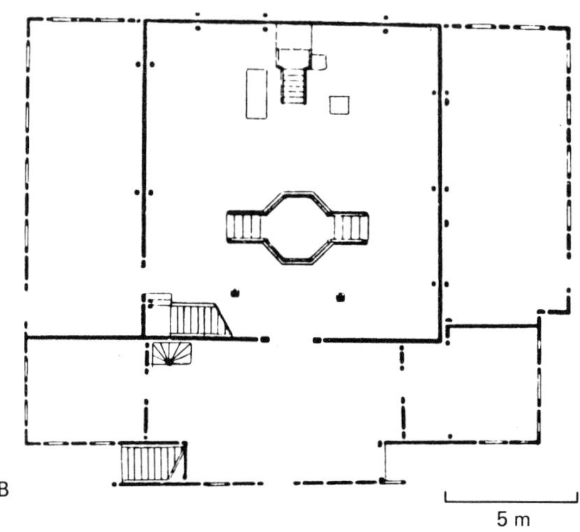

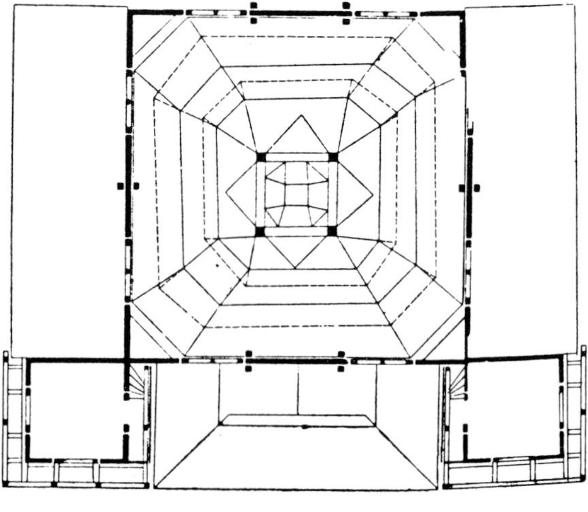

503 Plans of wooden synagogues. A. Olkienniki. B. Zabłudów with *Aron Hakodesh* and Bima. C. Volpa at upper-floor level with ceiling plan.

brought right down over the Bima. This now seemed to be carved out of the central pier, but still had stumpy pillars at the corners supporting arches on each side, and usually acoustic openings above the arches (**502** B).

Such was the unique and original feature of most brick-built synagogues in Greater Poland. Specimens illustrated in the literature include Żółkiew and Lutsk (now Ukraine); Slonim and Novogrudok (now Belorussia, Grodno region); Lublin, Przeworsk, Rzeszów, Zmigrod (Poland). A beautiful one was also built under Polish influence at Mikulov (Nikolsburg) in southern Moravia, a stone's throw from the Austrian border. But we must now turn to the wooden synagogues, which could not be understood without this brief preliminary account of those built in masonry.

I have said that well over one hundred wooden synagogues must originally have existed. Among these, detailed records survive of about thirty, which probably include all the more noteworthy examples. Some were built in the middle to late seventeenth century, the great majority in the eighteenth, while at the very end of that century, and at the beginning of the nineteenth, there was a recrudescence of building activity. The boundaries of Poland between the wars embraced most of the wooden synagogues, and we owe the valuable work in which they are definitively documented to a Polish couple, M. and K. Piechotkowie.

Their erstwhile distribution (roughly indicated on the general map) is now less easy to define in view of the drastic frontier changes following the Second World War. Broadly, they extended from near Poznań (Posen) in the west almost to Smolensk and Kiev in the east, from Lithuania in the north to the Carpathians in the south. Many sites remain in present-day Poland. The others are located in what is now Soviet territory: some in Lithuania, some in western Belorussia (especially the district of Grodno), some in eastern and southern Belorussia (but for some reason not in the middle) and many in Ukrainian Galicia. These are sites only; not one, as far as I know, survives.

Plans of the wooden synagogues, identical in principle to those of their brick-built antecedents, had a square core (the main hall of worship) with subsidiary rooms grouped around, sometimes including corner pavilions at the western angles (**503**). The two specimen sections show how high raftered roofs were raised upon walls of conventional east European blockwork (**504–505**). The sections also show that these tall roofs were designed mainly for external effect, since the elegant interior domes and vaulted ceilings, sometimes with additional supporting pillars as in **505**, were independent structures occupying only a fraction of the roof space. The splendour of these synagogues, as seen from outside, lay in their soaring roofs and, frequently, in the attractive woodwork of the external galleries (**506–511**). The great principal roof, whether gabled, hipped or pyramidal, was rarely constructed as a whole but divided horizontally into two or three sections by gaps or 'breaks' at which a change of gradient usually occurred. These roofs presented great variety but the most distinctive ones had only the topmost section gabled while those below sloped away in all directions. The synagogue's profile was further diversified by lesser roofs covering the various annexes, including the paired corner pavilions where these were present.

Loukomsky, following some earlier writers, has claimed that wooden synagogues preceded those built in brick and were even the direct descendants of the pagan wooden temples that must have existed in this area in prehistoric and early medieval times. These authors adduced the earliest Jews in Poland – the proselyte Khazars who came out of Asia in the eighth century A.D. – as intermediaries in handing on

504 Gvozdets, near Kolomya (seventeenth century). Axial section for comparison with **503** B.

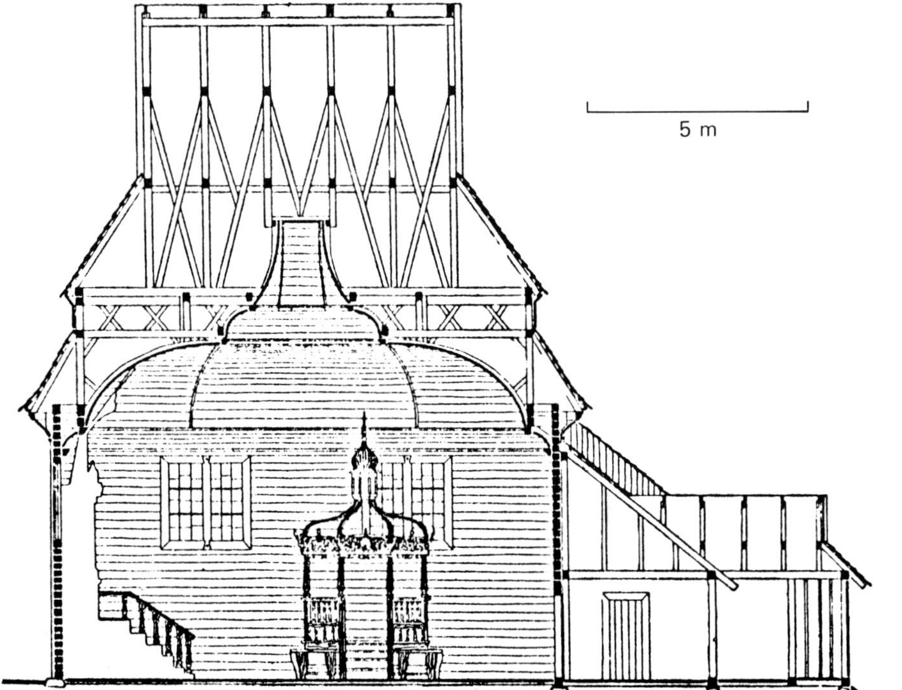

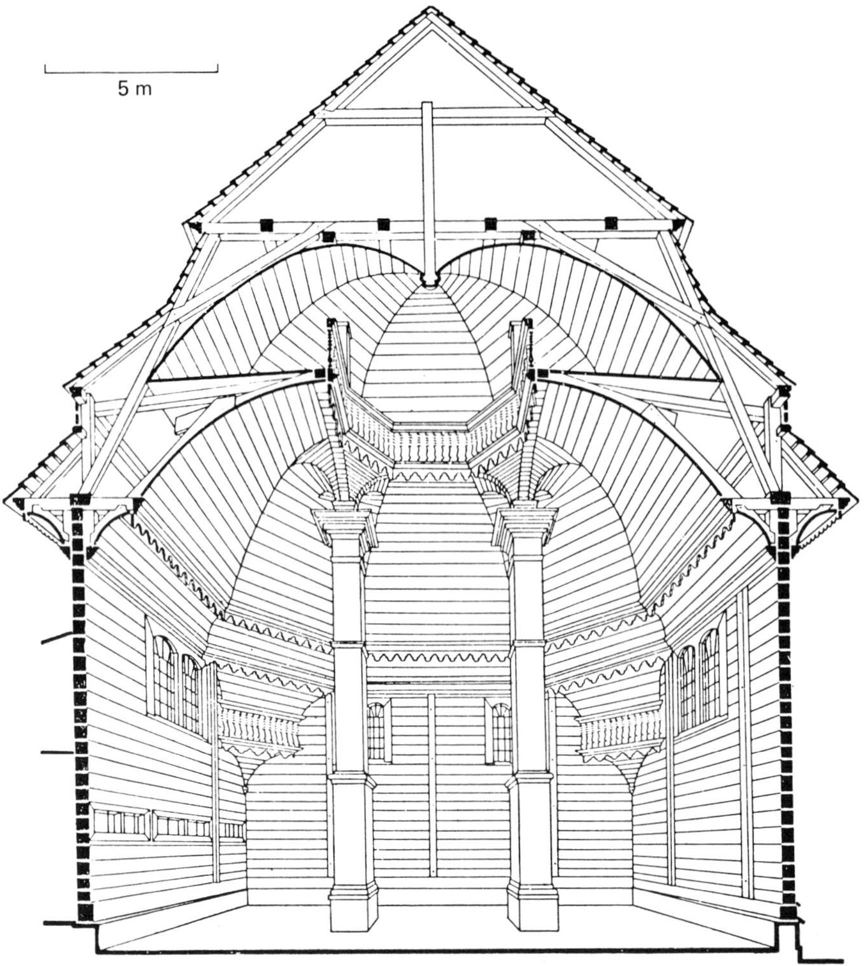

505 Olkienniki (late eighteenth century). Transverse section and eastward perspective for comparison with **503** A.

506 Jurborg (Yurbarkas), Lithuania (second half of the eighteenth century) after Andriolli's drawing, 1850.

507 Wysokie Mazowieckie, Poland (end of the seventeenth century) after a drawing of 1870. Pulled down, 1880.

508 Pohrebishche, Ukraine (mainly late seventeenth century).

these hypothetical pagan forms to subsequent generations. Such theories may be attractive but are untenable. What these complex timber structures do exhibit is all the sophistication and technical mastery of the seventeenth and eighteenth centuries, together with clear indications that their forms are derived from the international styles of their period. See for instance the sections of internal domes in **504–505**, both perfectly Baroque concepts.

Besides, though there were certainly reciprocal influences, these wooden synagogues are, broadly speaking, timber adaptations of the conventional masonry model. Their layout is identical, and the independent structure of ceiling vaults and outer roofs is common to the brick-built and wooden versions. One must add, however, that these latter, as a result of the adaptability of timber, displayed a variety of elaborate forms impossible in brick and a marvellous profusion of carved detail, especially in the canopied Bima in the middle and the *Aron Hakodesh* against the eastern wall.

A conclusive illustration of the dependence of the wooden synagogue on a masonry prototype is seen in the attempt made to reproduce in timber that most notable feature of local stone synagogues – the merging of the Bima with the central supports of the ceiling. Such supports were found, standing away from the Bima, in several wooden synagogues. Then at Volpa, which was one of the grandest of them all, these tall, slender wooden columns formed the corners of the Bima itself, whence they soared up into the recesses of the ceiling with its complex simulated vaulting (**511–512**).

There is no doubt, then, that the wooden synagogues owed much to their masonry counterparts, which embodied the age-old principles of synagogue planning, though a reciprocal influence is not to be denied. One must also consider the possibility that synagogues absorbed ideas from other local architectural traditions. A contributor to the 1914 edition of Grabar's *History of Russian Architecture* (though not identified, he was probably Professor Pavlutsky of Kiev) suggested that synagogue architecture had been influenced by the timber-built manor houses which even then had mostly disappeared from the Ukrainian countryside. The suggestion was sensible and some of the still existing manors in Poland, as well as inns and larger town houses, do throw light on the subject. These buildings generally have imposing mansard-type roofs with one or two 'breaks', and the wooden synagogues have them too. Moreover, a number of Polish manor houses, some brick-built and some wooden like Ożarów (**23**), possess the picturesque corner pavilions which were adopted in many of the finest wooden synagogues. Among the latter, once widely distributed, one may mention Nasielsk and Sniadowo in northern Poland; Olkienniki in Lithuania; Piaski, Sopochkinie and Volpa near Grodno in Belorussia; Zabłudów (a site of the same group remaining in Poland); Narovlia in south-east Belorussia. Of these Nasielsk, Volpa and Zabłudów are illustrated here (**509–511**). Both tall wooden roofs and corner pavilions re-appear in some masonry synagogues and are perhaps to be attributed to the counter-influence of the wooden upon the brick-built version, though the contrary could be argued.

It is well known that the Jews were always ready to fall in with current architectural trends for their synagogues, and it is also clear that they were attracted by civil rather than ecclesiastical models. Thus the transitional and Gothic synagogues of Worms, Prague and Cracow do not look like churches but seem rather to be influenced by Gothic halls (including monastic refectories). Again, the post-medieval synagogues of greater Poland have adopted Renaissance and Baroque features but bear little resemblance to the churches of those times, whether stone or wooden. I think it would be generally agreed that certain elements of local styles, coupled with the obligatory layout of the traditional synagogue and the inevitable interaction between wooden and stone versions, go some way towards explaining the character of these remarkable places of worship. But can they account for the fantasies of their roofs and domes or the ingenious and accomplished carpentry that went to their realisation? It is idle to suggest (as has been done) that the wealth and enthusiasm of the ghetto and its craftsmen could of themselves produce such impressive results. One gains the clear impression that an overall guiding inspiration was at work and that its sources – despite the basic blockwork of the walls – were west European.

509 Nasielsk, Poland (eighteenth century). Pulled down, 1880.

510 Zabłudów (seventeenth/eighteenth century). A model in the Museum of the Jewish Diaspora, Tel Aviv.

511 Volpa, Grodno district (early eighteenth century).

512 Volpa. Internal view showing roof supports amalgamated with the Bima.

Poland, of course, abounded in western influences, not least in architecture, as was seen in Chapter 6. On the domestic level a reminder of this fact is the mansard roof so widespread there (called after François Mansart, a leading early exponent of the French Baroque). On the monumental level a wide range of models was available locally in Poland – Dutch, French, Italian – and a wide range of domes could have inspired those which form the grand culminating feature of the more ambitious synagogue interiors. One might go further back and compare, for instance, a reduplicated dome as at Olkienniki (**505**) with the Dôme des Invalides in Paris, the work of Wren's contemporary, Mansart junior. But such research cannot now be based on the buildings themselves, all swept away in the holocaust of the 1940s.

BIBLIOGRAPHY

The selective bibliography printed here only includes books and papers I have used in the course of this study, or which will be found valuable for reference and further reading. As far as possible entries are arranged chronologically, according to dates of publication. A few works appear more than once under different chapter headings.

1. Introduction

Sirelius, U. T. 'Über die primitiven Wohnungen der finnischen und ob-ugrischen Völker', *Finnisch-Ugrische Forschungen*, 7 (1907)

Strzygowski, J. *Early Church Art in Northern Europe*. London, 1928

Strzygowski, J. *Altslavische Kunst*. Augsburg, 1929

Thompson, M. W. *Novgorod the Great*. London, 1967

Rajewski, Z. *Biskupin*. Polish. Warsaw, 1970

Lundberg, E. *Trä Gav Form*. Swedish with English captions. Stockholm, 1971

Hansen, H. J. (ed.) *Architecture in Wood*. Translated from German. London, 1971

Freudenreich, A. *Kako narod gradi na području hrvatske* (*Comment le peuple construit sur le territoire de la Croatie*). Croatian with French summaries. Zagreb, 1972

Pöttler, V. H. *Führer durch das österreichisches Freilichtmuseum*. Stübing bei Graz, 1972*

Swoboda, O. *Alte Holzbaukunst in Österreich*. Salzburg, 1975

Buxton, D. 'Wooden churches of eastern Europe', *Architectural Review*, 157 (January 1975); reprinted in *Architectural Conservation in Europe* (ed. S. Cantacuzino), London, 1975

Самойлович, В. П. *Народное архитектурное творчество по материалам украинской ССР*. (Samoylovich, V. P. *Popular architecture, based on material from the Ukrainian SSR*.) Russian. Kiev, 1977

Revista muzeelor şi monumentelor. Monumente istorice şi de artă (Bucharest), 1 (1979). Texts and summaries in several languages

2. Northern Russia

Грабарь, И. (ред.) *Исторія русскаго искусства*. (Grabar, I. (ed.) *History of Russian Art*.) Russian. Vols. I and II. Moscow, from 1910

Красовскій, М. *Курсъ исторіи русской архитектуры. Часть* I: *Деревянное зодчество*. (Krasovsky, M. *Course in the history of Russian architecture*. Part I: *Wooden architecture*.) Russian. Petrograd, 1916

Réau, L. *L'art russe, des origines à Pierre le Grand*. Paris, 1921

Alpatov, M. and Brunov, N. *Geschichte der altrussischen Kunst*. Augsburg, 1932

Ainalov, D. *Geschichte der russischen Monumentalkunst zur Zeit des Grossfürstentums Moskau*. Berlin and Leipzig, 1933

Соболев, Н. Н. *Русская народная резьба по дереву*. (Sobolev, N. N. *Russian popular wood carving*.) Russian. Moscow/Leningrad, 1934

Buxton, D. R. *Russian Mediaeval Architecture*. Cambridge, 1934

Забелло, С. Я. и др. *Русское деревянное зодчество*. (Zabello, S. Ya. and others. *Russian wooden architecture*.) Russian. Moscow, 1942

Pettersson, L. *Die kirchliche Holzbaukunst auf der Halbinsel Zaonež'e in Russisch-Karelien*. Finska Fornminnesföreningens Tidskrift 50 (Finnish with German captions) and 51 (German). Helsinki, 1950

Hamilton, G. H. *The Art and Architecture of Russia*. Pelican History of Art. Harmondsworth, 1954

Мехова, Г. И. и Балгин, В. И. *Русское деревянное зодчество*. (Mekhova, G. I. and Balgin, V. I. *Russian wooden architecture*.) Russian. Moscow, 1965

Смирнова, В. И. (ред.) *Кижи*. (Smirnova, V. I. (ed.) *Kizhi*.) Russian with separately printed Finnish, English and German texts. Petrozavodsk, 1971

Bartenev, I. and Fyodorov, B. *North Russian Architecture*. Translated from Russian. Moscow, 1972

Орфинский, В. *Деревянное зодчество Карелии*. (Orfinsky, V. *Wooden architecture of Karelia*.) Russian. Leningrad, 1972

* Among illustrated handbooks to the open-air museums this is the best I know. Others which I found useful in the course of travels included handbooks to the following:
The Village Museum, Bucharest; the open-air section of the Transylvanian Ethnographic Museum, Cluj; the Museum of Folk Architecture at Sanok (Poland); the Outdoor Museum at Seurasaari, Helsinki; Skansen, Stockholm (including many detailed booklets); the State Museum–Preserve of Architecture, History and Ethnography at Kizhi (N. Russia); the Museum of Folk Architecture and Life at L'vov (Ukraine).

Ополовников, А. В. *Реставрация памятников народного зодчества.* (Opolovnikov, A. V. *The restoration of monuments of folk architecture.*) Russian. Moscow, 1974

Faensen, H. and others. *Early Russian Architecture.* Translated from German. London, 1975

Fiodorov (Fyodorov), B. *Architecture of the Russian North.* Translated from Russian. Leningrad, 1976

Зайцев, Б. и Пинчуков, П. *Солнечные узоры: деревянное народное зодчество подмосковья.* (Zaitsev, B. and Pinchukov, P. *Sun patterns: wooden folk architecture of the Moscow neighbourhood.*) Russian. Moscow, 1978

3. *Ukrainian Galicia and Carpathia*

Sprawozdania Komisyi do badania historyi sztuki w Polsce. (*Reports of the Commission on art-historical research in Poland.*) Various articles (in Polish) especially those by K. and T. Mokłowski in 8 (1907), parts I and II, and by T. O. Obmiński in 9 (1914), parts III and IV

Zaloziecky, W. R. *Gotische und barocke Holzkirchen in den Karpathenländern.* Vienna, 1926

Konstantynowicz, J. B. *Ikonostasis: Studien und Forschungen.* Lwów (Lemberg), 1939

Łoziński, J. Z. and Miłobędzki, A. *Guide to Architecture in Poland.* Translated from Polish. Warsaw, 1967

Логвин, Г. Н. *По Україні: стародавні мистецькі пам'ятки.* (Logvin, G. N. *Around the Ukraine: ancient monuments of art.*) Ukrainian, with short Russian and English summaries. Kiev, 1968

Goberman, D. N. *Wooden Architectural Monuments in Trans-Carpathia.* Russian and English texts. Leningrad, 1970

Frický, A. *Ikony z východného Slovenska.* (*Icons from eastern Slovakia.*) Slovak, with short summaries and captions in English, etc. Košice, 1971

Lazišťan, E. and Michalov, J. *Drevené stavby na Slovensku.* (*Wooden buildings in Slovakia.*) Slovak. Martin, 1971

Skrobucha, H. *Icons in Czechoslovakia.* Translated from German. London/New York, 1971

Mapa kulturních památek ČSSR. (*Atlas of cultural monuments in Czechoslovakia.*) Czech. Prague, 1972

Логвин, Г. Н. *Украинские Карпаты.* (Logvin, G. N. *The Ukrainian Carpathians.*) Russian. Moscow, 1973

Макушенко, П. И. *Народная деревянная архитектура Закарпатья.* (Makushenko, P. I. *Wooden vernacular architecture of Trans-Carpathia.*) Russian. Moscow, 1976

Ochrona zabytków. (*The preservation of monuments of art.*) Many vols. Warsaw, since 1948

Katalog zabytków sztuki w Polsce. (*Catalogue of art monuments in Poland.*) Many vols. Warsaw, since 1959

4. *The Ukrainian plains*

Грабарь, И. (ред.) *Исторія русскаго искусства.* (Grabar, I. (ed.) *History of Russian Art.*) Russian. Vols. I and II. Moscow, c. 1910

Красовскій, М. *Курсъ исторіи русской архитектуры. Часть I: Деревянное зодчество.* (Krasovsky, M. *Course in the history of Russian architecture.* Part I: *Wooden architecture.*) Russian. Petrograd, 1916

Заболотний, В. Г. (ред.). *Нариси історії архітектури Української РСР.* (Zabolotny, V. G. (ed.) *Outline of the history of architecture in the Ukrainian SSR.*) Ukrainian. Kiev, 1957

Логвин, Г. Н. *По Україні: стародавні мистецькі пам'ятки.* (Logvin, G. N. *Around the Ukraine: ancient monuments of art.*) Ukrainian, with short Russian and English summaries. Kiev, 1968

Ukraine – A Concise Encyclopaedia. 2 vols. Toronto, 1963 and 1971

Таранушенко, С. А. *Монументальна дерев'яна архітектура лівобережної України.* (Taranushenko, S. A. *Monumental wooden architecture of the left-bank Ukraine.*) Ukrainian. Kiev, 1976

Чантурия, В. А. *История архитектуры Белоруссии.* (Chanturiya, V. A. *History of Belorussian architecture.*) Russian. Minsk, 1977

5. *Rumania, Hungary and Yugoslavia*

All titles in this section are Rumanian unless otherwise indicated.

Petranu, C. *Bisericile de lemn din județul Arad.* Sibiu, 1927

Petranu, C. *The Wooden Churches in the County of Bihor.* Rumanian and English texts. Sibiu, 1931

Vătăşianu, V. 'Contribuţie la cunoasterea bisericilor de lemn din Moldova' in *Inchinare lui Nicolae Iorga.* Cluj, 1931

Balogh, H. *Les édifices de bois dans l'architecture religieuse hongroise.* Budapest, 1940

Brătulescu, V. 'Biserici din Maramureş', *Buletinul Comisiunii Monumentelor Istorice,* 1941

Ionesco, G. *Arhitectura populară româneasca.* Bucharest, 1957

Vătăşianu, V. 'Contribuţie la studiul tipologiei bisericilor de lemn din ţările Române', *Anuarul Institutului de Istorie din Cluj,* 1960

Павловић, Д. Ст. *Цркве брвнаре у Србији.* (Pavlowitch, D. St. *Les vieilles églises serbes construites en bois.*) Serbian, with French captions and summary. Belgrade, 1962

Creţeanu, R. *Bisericile de lemn din Muntenia.* Bucharest, 1968

Greceanu, E. 'Tipologia bisericilor de lemn din zona centrală a Transilvaniei', *Monumentele Istorice. Studii şi lucrări de restaurare* (Bucharest), 3 (1969)

Fél, E. and others. *Hungarian Peasant Art.* Translated from Hungarian. London, 1971

Cristache-Panait, I. and Scheletti, I. 'Bisericile de lemn din Sălaj', *Buletinul Monumentelor Istorice,* 1 (1971)

Cristache-Panait, I. and Dimitriu, F. 'Bisericile de lemn ale Banatului', *Mitropolia Banatului,* 21 (1971)

Cristache-Panait, I. and Elian, T. 'Bisericile de lemn din Moldova', *Buletinul Monumentelor Istorice,* 2 (1972)

Godea, I. *Monumente de arhitectură populară din nord-vestul României.* Vol. I. Oradea, 1972

Cvitanović, D. 'Drvena sakralna arhitektura u sjevernoj hrvatskoj' ('Timber sacral architecture in northern Croatia'), *Arhitektura* (Zagreb), 146–7 (1973). Croatian with English summary

Schuster, D. T. 'Biserici de lemn din ţara Lăpuşului', *Buletinul Monumentelor Istorice,* 2 (1973)

Petrescu, P. *Holzbaukunst in den Dörfern Rumäniens.* Translated from Rumanian. Bucharest, 1974

Magyarország Autóatlasza [road atlas of Hungary with gazetteer]. Budapest, 1975

Pănoiu, A. *Din arhitectura lemnului în România.* Bucharest, 1977

Ionescu (Ionesco), G. 'Tipologii specifice ale clădirilor populare din lemn', *Revista muzeelor şi monumentelor. Monumente istorice şi de artă*, 2 (1977)

6. Catholic churches in Poland and Czechoslovakia

Kopera, F. *Kościoły drewniane Galicyi zachodniej*. (*Die Holzkirchen Westgaliziens*.) Polish with German summaries. Only part 1/1 published. Cracow, 1913

Mencl, V. *Dřevěné kostelní stavby v zemích českých*. (*Wooden churches in the Czech lands*.) Czech. Prague, 1927

Strzygowski, J. *Die Holzkirchen in der Umgebung von Bielitz-Biala*. Posen (Poznań), 1927

Krauze, A. (ed.) *The Sacral Art in Poland*. Translated from Polish. Warsaw, 1956

Krassowski, W. *Architektura drewniana w Polsce*. (*Wooden architecture in Poland*.) Polish. Warsaw, 1961

Łoziński, J. Z. and Miłobędzki, A. *Guide to Architecture in Poland*. Translated from Polish. Warsaw, 1967

Knox, B. *The Architecture of Poland*. London, 1971

Mapa kulturních památek ČSSR. (*Atlas of cultural monuments in Czechoslovakia*.) Czech. Prague, 1972

Smólski, J. and others. *Monuments of the Past in the Province of Cracow*. Translated from Polish. Cracow, 1975

Matuszczak, J. *Kościoły drewniane na Śląsku*. (*Wooden churches in Silesia*.) Polish with English and German summaries and captions. Wrocław, 1975

Ochrona zabytków. (*The preservation of monuments of art*.) Many vols. Warsaw, since 1948

Katalog zabytków sztuki w Polsce. (*Catalogue of art monuments in Poland*.) Many vols. Warsaw, since 1959

7. Protestant churches of the margins

Strzygowski, J. *Early Church Art in Northern Europe*. London, 1928

Strzygowski, J. *Altslavische Kunst*. Augsburg, 1929

Drummond, A. L. *The Church Architecture of Protestantism*. Edinburgh, 1934

Phleps, H. *Deutsche Fachwerkbauten*. Die Blauen Bücher. Königstein im Taunus, 1951

Crossley, F. H. *Timber Building in England*. London, 1951

Beskow, H. 'Bidrag till studiet av övre Norrlands kyrkor', *Kungl. Vitterhets Historie och Antikvitets Akademiens Handlingar* (Stockholm), 79:1 (1952). Swedish with English summary

Dehio, G. (revised by E. Gall). *Deutschordensland Preussen*. Handbücher der deutschen Kunstdenkmäler. Munich/Berlin, 1952

Pettersson, L. 'Die Problematik der Doppelkreuzkirchen von Hamina' in *Sitzungsberichte der Finnischen Akademie der Wissenschaften*. Translated from Finnish. 1959

Łoziński, J. Z. and Miłobędzki, A. *Guide to Architecture in Poland*. Translated from Polish. Warsaw, 1967

Jadwiszczok, K. *Kościół pokoju w Świdnicy*. (*The Church of Peace in Świdnica*). Polish. Warsaw, 1967

Knox, B. *The Architecture of Poland*. London, 1971

Pettersson, L. *Hailuodon palanut puukirkko ja sen maalaukset*. (*The burnt-down church of Hailuoto and its paintings*.) Finnish. Finska Fornminnesföreningens Tidskrift 73. Helsinki, 1971

Pettersson, L. 'Simon Silvénin suunnitelma haapaveden kirkoksi' ('Simon Silvéns Planung der Kirche in Haapavesi'), *Finska kyrkohistoriska samfundets handlingar*, 93 (1975). Finnish with German summary

Pettersson, L. *Kaksikymmentäneljäkulmaisen ristikirkon syntyongelmia*. (*On Finnish cruciformed timber-churches with twenty-four corners*.) Finnish with English summary. Finska Fornminnesföreningens Tidskrift 79. Helsinki, 1978

Bott, I. and others (Förderkreis Alte Kirchen e.V., Marburg). *Fachwerkkirchen in Hessen*. Die Blauen Bücher. Königstein im Taunus, 1978

Pettersson, L. *National and International Features of the Old Wooden Church Architecture in Finland*. Finnish and English texts. Yearbook of the Museum of Finnish Architecture. Helsinki, 1979

Appendix I

Weslager, C. A. *The Log Cabin in America*. New Brunswick, 1969

Appendix II

Loukomsky, G. 'Synagogues of Eastern Europe', *Architectural Review*, 97 (May 1945)

Loukomsky, G. *Jewish Art in European Synagogues*. London, 1947

Piechotkowie, M. and K. *Bóżnice drewniane*. (*Wooden synagogues*.) Polish. Warsaw, 1957

ACKNOWLEDGEMENTS

For sources not quoted in full see corresponding sections of the bibliography. All illustrations not listed here are reproduced from the author's own photographs.

1. *Introduction*

6–8. From Sirelius, 1907.
9. See 84.
11. From A. N. Demidoff. *Voyage pittoresque et archéologique en Russie exécuté en 1839*. (Drawings by A. Durand.)
21. Old Swiss photograph.
23. Redrawn by M. Rowe from author's photograph.
24. See 85.
25. From L. Réau. *L'art russe, des origines à Pierre le Grand*. Paris, 1921.
27, 29, 31. See 71.
28. See 65.
32, 58. From *The Russian North*. Moscow, 1972.
34. See 64.
35. A–C from Lundberg, 1971. D, F from Freudenreich, 1972. E see 186.
36, 52. Photographs by Raph Soto.
41. A, B see 186. C, D see 255. E, F from Freudenreich, 1972.
45–7. Redrawn by Elizabeth Waterfield from the author's photographs.
48. See 60.
50. See 81.
55. Photograph from Ukrainian sources.
57. Photograph from Russian sources.

2. *Northern Russia*

60. From Orfinsky, 1972.
61. Redrawn by M. Rowe after Sobolev, 1934.
62. Redrawn by M. Rowe after Dunaev (see 94).
63. From Yu. Shamurin. *Rostov Veliky*. Moscow, 1913.
64, 72, 91–2. Redrawn by M. Rowe after Grabar, 1910.
65, 74, 88. From Krasovsky, 1916.
66, 83, 93, 98, 102. From *The Russian North*. Moscow, 1972.
67, 77. Photographs by Dr Terence Armstrong.
69. From *Soviet Union*, 3 (1971).
70. Redrawn by M. Rowe after Ainalov, 1933.
71, 90, 104. From Opolovnikov, 1974.
75, 97, 112. From Pettersson, 1950.
76, 80, 116. Photographs from Russian sources.
78, 87, 105–6. From Fiodorov, 1976.
81, 89. Redrawn by M. Rowe after Krasovsky, 1916
84. From Adam Olearius. *The Voyages and Travells of the Ambassadors sent by Frederick Duke of Holstein to the Great Duke of Moscow, and the King of Persia, 1633–1639*.
85. From *Al'bom Meierberga*, St Petersburg, 1903. [The illustrated journal of Augustin Freiherr von Meyerberg, Ambassador from the Emperor Leopold I of Austria to Tsar Alexis Mikhailovich, 1661–2.] Drawings by R. Storng.
86. From the Mirovich version (c. 1700) of the Remezov Chronicle [a record of Yermak's exploits in Siberia in the late sixteenth century]. Original in the library of the Academy of Sciences, Leningrad.
94. From B. I. Dunaev. *Derevyannoe zodchestvo severo-vostoka kostromskoi gubernii*. Moscow, 1915.
95–6, 99–100, 113, 115. From *Kizhi*. Leningrad and Moscow, 1965.
103. From H. Seebohm. *The Birds of Siberia*. London, 1901.
108. From *Architectural monuments of Vladimir, Suzdal, Yuriev-Polskoy*. Leningrad, 1974
116. From *Moskau*, Berlin, 1928.

3. *Ukrainian Galicia and Carpathia*

118. A, C–F, H from Mokłowski, 1907. B, G from Obmiński, 1914.
119–20, 124–5, 128, 133–4, 153, 157–8, 163, 176, 183, 185. Photographs from Ukrainian sources.
135. Photograph by Raph Soto.
141, 170. From Logvin, 1968.
143, 162, 169, 177, 184. From Goberman, 1970.
150. From Obmiński, 1914.
160. A from Makushenko, 1976. B, C from Mokłowski, 1907.
161. Redrawn by M. Rowe after Mokłowski, 1907.
164. Old photograph.
165–6. See 81.
167. From R. Izbicki, *W Bieszczadach*, Warsaw, 1968.
171. A, E, F from Makushenko, 1976. B, C, D from Zaloziecky, 1926.
186. From Zaloziecky, 1926.
188. From O. Nehera. *Východné Slovensko*. Martin (Slovakia), 1973.

194. See 409.
198. From Zaloziecky, 1926.

4. *The Ukrainian plains*

203. From *Ukraina – obshchy obzor* in series 'Sovietsky Soyuz'. Moscow, 1969. Redrawn by M. Rowe.
204–6, 209–11, 216, 218, 220, 236, 246, 250. Photographs from Ukrainian sources.
215, 235, 244, 247. From Krasovsky, 1916.
221, 228. From Taranushenko, 1976.
222–3, 225–6, 229–34. Old photographs of churches no longer existing, from Ukrainian sources.
224. From Logvin, 1968.
227. From a wash painting by G. N. Logvin.
245, 253. From Zabolotny, 1957.
248–9. From Chanturiya, 1977.

5. *Rumania, Hungary and Yugoslavia*

254. A, B, D, G, H from Pănoiu, 1977. C, E, F from Ionesco, 1957.
255. From Ionesco, 1957.
272–3. From Pavlowitch, 1962
275. A. Redrawn by E. Waterfield from author's photograph. B. From Pavlowitch, 1962.
277. Photograph from Serbian sources.
278. From Cvitanović, 1973.
279. See 35 D.
291. A–C from Schuster, 1973. D from Cristache-Panait and Scheletti, 1971. E, H from Godea, 1972. F, J from Ionesco, 1957. G, I from Brătulescu, 1941.
292. From Godea, 1972.
293. From Petranu, 1931.
308. From Brătulescu, 1941.
309, 311. Drawings by Elizabeth Waterfield.
320. Photograph by Radu Creţeanu.
321, 323, 357–9. Photographs from Ukrainian sources.
322, 324. See 143.
344. From Cristache-Panait and Elian, 1972.
345. From G. Ionesco. *Histoire de l'architecture en Roumanie*. Bucharest, 1972.

6. *Catholic churches in Poland and Czechoslovakia*

360, 378. Photographs by Raph Soto.
366, 387. From Kopera, 1913.
369. See 478 A.
371. Old German photograph.
374, 385, 396. From Strzygowski, 1927.
375. Redrawn by M. Rowe after Kopera, 1913.
379, 408, 412. Photographs from Polish sources.
386. Anonymous etching.
409. From Krassowski, 1961.
413. A, B, D from Krassowski, 1961. C from Mencl, 1927.

7. *Protestant churches of the margins*

435. From Strzygowski, 1928.
445, 456. Original.
446. A from Jadwiszczok, 1967. B from Knox, 1971.
450. Redrawn by M. Rowe after Jadwiszczok, 1967.
454. From E. Lazišťan and J. Michalov. *Drevené stavby na Slovensku* (*Wooden buildings in Slovakia*.) Martin (Slovakia), 1971.
459. From O. Nehera. *Východné Slovensko*. Martin (Slovakia), 1973.
461. Old photograph.
462, 500. From Pettersson, 1971.
463. A, B from Pettersson, 1971. C, D from L. Pettersson. *Utajärven vaiheita*. Utajärvi, 1962.
478. A from Strzygowski, 1929. B–F from Pettersson, 1978.
488. From R. Mähönen. *Kirkkomaalari Mikael Toppelius*. Helsinki, 1975.
492. Photograph by P. O. Welin (also in Pettersson, 1978).
493. After an engraving by A. Perelle, 1669, anticipating the completion of the church.
494, 497. From Pettersson, 1959.

Appendix I

501. From Basil Hall. *Travels in North America in the years 1827 and 1828*. Edinburgh, 1829.

Appendix II

502. A from Piechotkowie, 1957. B from a drawing by G. Loukomsky in the *Architectural Review*, May 1945.
503–5, 509. From Piechotkowie, 1957.
506–8, 511–12. Redrawn by M. Rowe after Loukomsky, 1947.
510. Reproduced by permission of Beth Hatefutsoth (the Museum of the Jewish Diaspora), Tel Aviv.

INDEX

References in bold type are to illustration numbers.